Prisons in the Americas in the Twenty-First Century

Security in the Americas in the Twenty-First Century
Series Editor: Jonathan D. Rosen

Countries throughout the Americas face many challenges in the twenty-first century such as drug trafficking, organized crime, environmental degradation, guerrilla movements, and terrorism, among many other major threats. Security in the Americas in the Twenty-First Century will feature contributions on topics focusing on security issues in specific countries or regions within the Americas. We are interested in approaching this topic from a political science and international relations perspective. However, we invite manuscript submissions from other disciplines. The aim of this series is to highlight the major security challenges in the twenty-first century and contribute to the security studies literature. We invite both policy-oriented and theoretical submissions.

Titles in the Series

Prisons in the Americas in the Twenty-First Century

A Human Dumping Ground

Edited by Jonathan D. Rosen and Marten W. Brienen

LEXINGTON BOOKS
Lanham • Boulder • New York • London

Published by Lexington Books
An imprint of The Rowman & Littlefield Publishing Group, Inc.
4501 Forbes Boulevard, Suite 200, Lanham, Maryland 20706
www.rowman.com

Unit A, Whitacre Mews, 26-34 Stannary Street, London SE11 4AB

British Library Cataloguing in Publication Information Available

Library of Congress Cataloging-in-Publication Data

Prisons in the Americas in the twenty first century : human dumping ground / edited by Jonathan D.
Rosen and Marten W. Brienen.
pages cm. -- (Security in the Americas in the twenty-first century)
Includes bibliographical references and index.
ISBN 978-0-7391-9135-4 (cloth : alk. paper) -- ISBN 978-0-7391-9136-1 (electronic)
1. Prisons--America. 2. Imprisonment--America. 3. Corrections--America. I. Rosen, Jonathan D. II.
Brienen, Marten W.
HV8501.P75 2015
365'.97--dc23
2015001564

Printed in the United States of America

Content

Acknowledgments

Edited volumes require a tremendous amount of cooperation and collaboration. We would like to thank the authors for their hard work and dedication.

In addition, we want to thank our respective institutions and departments: the Universidad del Mar, Huatulco, Mexico, and Oklahoma State University. The book was part of a research project at the Universidad del Mar titled *La Guerra contra las drogas en América Latina y su impacto en la seguirdad* (CUP: 2IEI1402), which was approved by the Institute of International Studies on January 5, 2014.

A special thanks to the staff at Lexington Books for this opportunity and for helping improve the quality of the manuscript. We are forever grateful for their professionalism, dedication, and attention to detail.

Preface

Jonathan D. Rosen and Marten W. Brienen

In May 2011, approximately 200 inmates began to riot in Cancun prison in Mexico. The situation escalated into an episode of exceptional violence, leaving several inmates decapitated. According to Patrick Corcoran, this riot reflects various systemic problems in the criminal justice system in Mexico. He states, "Thanks in large part to the huge numbers of arrests produced by President Calderon's push against organized crime, Mexico's prisons are stuffed to bursting point. According to one recent report, the national system of prisons and jails is currently at 25 percent overcapacity. The Cancun prison, with some 1,200 residents, stands at 300 percent overcapacity, according to El Universal."[1] Mexico has witnessed a proliferation in the number of people in prison over time as the incarceration rate in the country has almost doubled since the mid-1990s, going from 103 inmates per 100,000 to 204 prisoners per 100,000 inhabitants in 2012.[2] A survey conducted by the Centro de Investigación y Docencia Económicas (CIDE) reveals that an astonishing 60 percent of the prisoners surveyed were incarcerated for drug-related crimes.[3]

Mexico has major problems with criminal activities behind prison walls: drug trafficking, prostitution, and extortion—among other illicit activities. Drug cartel leaders, or "shot callers," often control the drug trade on the outside from behind prison walls. It is estimated that 60 percent of Mexican prisons are self-governed.[4] Marc Lacy argues:

> Mexico's prisons, as described by inmates and insiders and viewed during several visits, are places where drug traffickers find a new base of operations for their criminal empires, recruit underlings, and bribe their way out for the right price. The system is so flawed, in fact, that the Mexican government is extraditing record numbers of drug traffickers to the United States, where they find it much harder to intimidate witnesses, run their drug operations or escape.[5]

In August 2009, fifty-three prisoners, many of whom had affiliations with one of Mexico's ruthless drug cartels, the Zetas, opened their prison cells and subsequently exited the prison and fled in vehicles that were waiting for them outside the prison walls. The prison guards made little effort to stop the escape, only pulling their weapons after it was too late.[6] Such events have occurred many times[7] since prison guards in Mexico are outnumbered and are susceptible to bribes as a result of low salaries and a lack of professionalism. Unfortunately, this escape is only one of many prison breaks (*fugas*) that have occurred in Mexico, the most infamous being the escape of Joaquín "El Chapo" Guzmán, the leader of the Sinaloa cartel, in 2001.[8]

Mexico, however, is not the only country suffering from overcrowding and facing a systemic crisis. Ecuadorian prisons, for instance, are designed to hold 12,338 people. In October 2013, the prison population in Ecuador increased to 24,203 inmates from 19,500 in 2007, demonstrating the severe overcrowding plaguing Ecuadorian prisons.[9] In Guatemala, prisons are at 280 percent capacity. Camilo Mejía states that "[o]verpopulated prisons are a serious problem in numerous Latin American countries. According to the CIEN report, Central America is one region with especially high levels of prison overcrowding, led by El Salvador (322 percent), and followed by Guatemala, Nicaragua, Costa Rica and Panama."[10] Brazil, like other countries in the region, is suffering from overcrowding. The country has 160 state prisons that are designed to house 126,000 inmates. As of October 2014, Brazil currently has 215,000 prisoners incarcerated in state prisons throughout the country. São Paulo alone has 218,983 prisoners, highlighting the excessive strain on the country's penitentiary system.[11] Andre Caramante argues that the government would have to build 105 new prisons to solve the overcrowding crisis in Brazilian prisons. Each prison would need 847 units to accommodate the 88,976 new inmates. However, the government would only be able to combat prison overcrowding if the 160 prisons that currently exist do not receive any new inmates. In other words, Brazil cannot build prisons fast enough to house its proliferating inmate population.[12]

In 2012, 300 inmates in a Honduran prison burned to death as they were unable to exit the prison during a fire. The prison was extremely overcrowded and the authorities lacked the proper training to respond to such crisis situations. Adriana Beltrán and Ashley David argue:

> Investigations later confirmed that not only had the prison been severely overcrowded and lacking sanitary and safe conditions, but the infrastructure of the facility was structurally unsound and the prison staff lacked sufficient training to respond to the crisis. Equally worrisome was the fact that over half of the inmates had not yet been convicted of any crime—they had been locked up, awaiting a trial. Issues such as these are not unique to Honduras, and are serious problems affecting many penitentiary systems throughout Latin America.[13]

One reason why the number of prisoners have proliferated is the desire to punish criminals, particularly individuals involved in drug-related crimes: consumption, possession, sales, and trafficking. In fact, in Ecuador, Bolivia, and Mexico, drug traffickers receive longer maximum and minimum sentences than individuals charged with murder. In Ecuador, for example, the maximum sentence for murder in 2013 was twelve years, while the maximum prison sentence for a drug trafficker was sixteen years. In Mexico, the maximum sentence for a prisoner convicted of drug trafficking was twenty-five years compared to twenty-four years for murder. On the other hand, in Bolivia, murderers receive a maximum sentence of twenty years, while drug traffickers can be sentenced to prison for twenty-five years.[14] The result of such disproportionate sentences is that the costs of incarcerating such a large number of inmates has increased throughout penitentiary systems across the region. The financial resources required to incarcerate prisoners could be invested in other more worthwhile endeavors such as education, prevention, treatment, and rehabilitation programs. Rodrigo Uprimny argues that "[t]he consequences of such disproportionate sentences include costly crises of mass incarceration throughout the region. Overloaded prison systems have drawn funds and focus away from legitimate regional concerns."[15]

One of the consequences of overcrowded prisons is the rapid spike in violence. In 2011, more than 400 inmates were killed in Venezuelan prisons.[16] In 2012, 591 prisoners died in Venezuela, reflecting a dramatic increase in the levels of violence resulting from overcrowding.[17] In January 2014, three prisoners in Brazil were decapitated and the gruesome event was recorded on video. In 2013, sixty inmates were killed in Brazil.[18] Overcrowding in Mexico also has resulted in extreme levels of violence as 269 clashes between prisoners occurred between 2010 and May 2013, which led to the death of 568 prisoners.[19]

While much has been written by journalists, human rights advocates, and lawyers, a major gap exists in the social science literature about prisons in the Americas. This volume is an effort to examine the relationship between drug trafficking, organized crime, and prisons and seeks to provide an analysis of prison systems at the outset of the twenty-first century, examining the major challenges posed by high incarceration rates as well as prevailing obstacles to reform.

VOLUME ORGANIZATION

We have compiled a group of leading experts in the field throughout the region. The volume begins with an introductory chapter by Astrid Arrarás and Emily D. Bello-Pardo on the general trends of prisons in the Americas. The book is then divided into case studies. We have asked the authors to consider some of the following questions: 1) what is the current state of prisons in this country? 2) What is the cost of housing prisoners? 3) What is the relationship between organized crime and prisons? 4) What is the recidivism rate? 5) Have any reforms been implemented? 6) What are some possible policy solutions to the problem at hand?

The first section of the book focuses on prisons in North America, examining the cases of the United States and Mexico. The case studies begin with a chapter by Susan A. Phillips and Jonathan D. Rosen on prisons in the United States. This chapter provides some general trends and focuses particularly on prisons in California. Roberto Zepeda Martínez examines the penitentiary system in Mexico, highlighting the major challenges as a result of organized crime and high levels of institutional corruption.

This section is followed by the Central American case of Guatemala. Tamara Rice Lave examines the major criminal organizations in Guatemala and highlights many of the underlying problems, such as institutional weakness and corruption.

The next section of the volume focuses on the Caribbean. Christa L. Remington and Jean-Claude Garcia-Zamor analyze the hellish Haitian penitentiary system. Haitian prisons are characterized by human rights abuses and horrific living conditions as research reveals that prisons in the country operate at over 400 percent of stated capacity. An astonishing 70 percent of the prison population is awaiting trial, which results in a major backlog of people waiting to have their day in court.[20] Dianne Williams and Randy Seepersad end the section with an examination of the prison system in Trinidad and Tobago.

The Caribbean cases are followed by analyses of four Andean countries: Venezuela, Ecuador, Bolivia, and Peru. Brian Fonseca and Pamela Pamelá analyze the Venezuelan prison system, which they define as organized chaos. Adrián Bonilla and Nashira Chávez examine the Ecuadorian penal system, focusing particularly on drug policies and their impact on the prison system. Marten W. Brienen continues this section with an analysis of the Bolivian penitentiary system. Lucía Dammert and Manuel Dammert G. conclude the section with an examination of the penitentiary system in Peru.

The case studies conclude with Marcelo Rocha e Silva Zorovich's chapter on the Brazilian penitentiary system and a chapter on the penitentiary system in Argentina by Khatchik DerGhougassian and Sebastián A. Cutrona. Finally, the volume concludes with a chapter by W. Andy Knight on prison reform, examining the role of international institutions, particularly the United Nations.

NOTES

1. Patrick Corcoran, "Riot, Decapitation Spell Chaos in Mexico's Prisons," *InSight Crime*, May 13, 2011, http://www.insightcrime.org/news-analysis/riot-decapitation-spell-chaos-in-mexicos-prisons, accessed October 2014. Adriana Varillas y Silvia Hernández, "Cancún: evacuan prisión por motín," *El Universal*, 12 de Mayo de 2011.

2. Steven Dudley, "Survey Shows Drug Trade Filling Mexico's Federal Prisons," *InSight Crime,* January 14, 2013, http://www.insightcrime.org/news-analysis/mexico-prison-survey-drug-trade, accessed October 2014.

3. Steven Dudley, "Survey Shows Drug Trade Filling Mexico's Federal Prisons;" *Resultados de la Primera Encuesta realizada a Población Interna en Centros Federales de Readaptación Social* (México City, México: Centro de Investigación y Docencia Económicas, 2012). Here is a link to the report: http://publiceconomics.files.wordpress.com/2013/01/encuesta_internos_cefereso_2012.pdf.

4. Luis Carlos Sáinz, *Rejas Rotas: Fugas, traición e impunidad en el sistema penitenciario mexicano,* (México, D.F: Gijalbo), 22.

5. Marc Lacey, "Mexico's Drug Traffickers Continue Trade in Prison," *The New York Times,* August 10, 2009.

6. Marc Lacey, "Mexico's Drug Traffickers Continue Trade in Prison," *The New York Times,* August 10, 2009.

7. For more, see Luis Carlos Sáinz, *Rejas Rotas: Fugas, traición e impunidad en el sistema penitenciario mexicano.*

8. Luis Brito, "'El Chapo' Guzmán: 13 años de la fuga del mayor narco mexicano," CNN México, 22 de febrero de 2014.

9. James Bargent, Ecuador Mass Prison Break Indicative of Overcrowding, Corruption," December 16, 2013, http://www.insightcrime.org/news-briefs/ecuador-mass-prison-break-indicative-of-overcrowding-corruption/, accessed October 2014.

10. Camilo Mejia, "Guatemala Prisons at 280% Capacity: Study," *InSight Crime,* August 8, 2014, http://www.insightcrime.org/news-briefs/guatemala-prisons-at-280-capacity-study, accessed October 2014; "Urge ampliar la infraestructura carcelaria, con planificación y control," *Cien,* 6 de Agosto de 2014.

11. Andre Caramante, "São Paulo's Overcrowed Prisons Stretched to the Breaking Point," *InSight Crime,* October 8, 2014, http://www.insightcrime.org/news-analysis/sao-paulo-overcrowded-prisons-stretched-to-the-breaking-point, accessed November 2014.

12. Ibid.

13. Adriana Beltrán and Ashley Davis, "Prison Reform in Latin America: The Costa Rican Experience," *Washington Office on Latin America,* August 15, 2014, http://www.wola.org/commentary/prison_reform_in_latin_america_a_costa_rican_perspective, accessed November 2014; Pien Metaal and Coletta Youngers, eds. *Systems Overload: Drug Laws and Prisons in Latin America* (Washington, D.C.: TNI/WOLA, 2010), http://www.wola.org/sites/default/files/downloadable/Drug%20Policy/2011/TNIWOLA-Systems_Overload-def.pdf, accessed November 2014.

14. Julie Turkewitz, "Is Drug Trafficking Worse Than Murder?" *Pacific Standard: The Science of Society,* May 13, 2013, http://www.psmag.com/navigation/politics-and-law/is-drug-trafficking-worse-than-murder-57445/, November 2014.

15. Rodrigo Uprimny, "Addicted to Punishment: Penalties in the War on Drugs More Severe than for Murder and Rape," April 9, 2013, *Open Society Foundation.* http://www.opensocietyfoundations.org/voices/addicted-punishment-penalties-war-drugs-more-severe-murder-and-rape, accessed November 2014.

16. Elyssa Pachico, "Bolivia Struggles to Resolve Its Prison Crisis," *InSight Crime,* September 24, 2014, http://www.insightcrime.org/news-briefs/bolivia-struggles-to-resolve-its-prison-crisis, accessed November 2014.

17. Marguerite Cawley, "Overcrowding Sows the Seeds of Violence in Mexico Prisons," *InSight Crime,* October 9, 2013, http://www.insightcrime.org/news-analysis/study-highlights-overcrowding-and-violence-in-mexicos-prisons, accessed November 2014.

18. Marguerite Cawley, "Brazil Prison Murders Highlight Rising Violence in Northern States," January 8, 2014. http://www.insightcrime.org/news-briefs/brazil-prison-murders-highlight-rising-violence-in-northern-states, November 2014; "Brazil: Ensure Justice in Prison Deaths," *Human Rights Watch,* January 8, 2014, http://www.hrw.org/news/2014/01/08/brazil-ensure-justice-prison-deaths, November 2014.

19. Marguerite Cawley, "Overcrowding Sows the Seeds of Violence in Mexico Prisons," *InSight Crime,* October 9, 2013, http://www.insightcrime.org/news-analysis/study-highlights-overcrowding-and-violence-in-mexicos-prisons, accessed November 2014.

20. Kyra Gurney, "Prison Break in Haiti Highlights Flailing Justice System," *InSight Crime,* August 13, 2014. http://www.insightcrime.org/news-briefs/prison-break-in-haiti-highlights-flailing-justice-system, November 2014; See also International Centre for Prison Studies, Haiti, http://www.prisonstudies.org/country/haiti, accessed November 2014.

ONE

General Trends of Prisons in the Americas

Astrid Arrarás and Emily D. Bello-Pardo

What has been the impact of the anti-drug and anti-gang policies on the prison system in the Americas? We will argue that these policies exacerbate poor and problematic preexisting prison conditions in the region. The organization of this chapter will consist of three sections. First, we will provide a historical background of prison systems in the Americas. Second, we will briefly discuss the anti-drug and anti-gang policies in the region. Third, we will identify current trends in the prison system such as overcrowding, ineffective state control over the facilities, prisons as schools and centers for the continuation of criminal activity, inhumane living conditions in the prisons, violence, and the demographic characteristics of the majority of inmates. Finally, we will provide a conclusion.

A BRIEF HISTORY OF PRISONS IN THE AMERICAS

A brief historical background of the prison system will allow the reader to understand the nuances and intricacies of the current state of prisons in the Americas and how the war on drugs has exacerbated these preexisting conditions. We provide a historical overview of the prison system in order to situate today's prison trends in its historical context. In this section, we will summarize the birth and adoption of the prison system in the Americas and describe some historical trends that continue to plague prisons in the twenty-first century.

In the region, the birth of the prison system occurred in the late eighteenth[1] and early nineteenth centuries.[2] At that time, prisons were not especially important in the punitive schemes developed and implemented by the elites in the region.[3] Prisons were neither institutionalized nor sought the reformation of the prisoner.[4] As a result of critiques of the inhumane conditions in the prisons of the nineteenth century, the penitentiary became the most widely adopted prison model in Europe and the United States. During this period, the states of Pennsylvania and New York—inspired by preexisting Quaker laws—led the charge in changing criminal codes and developed two distinct penitentiary systems, the Auburn and Pennsylvania models.[5] The reform of the codes, albeit different in both jurisdictions, broke with the colonial criminal justice systems by making imprisonment the most widespread method of controlling, deterring, and punishing crime.[6]

These innovative eighteenth-century reforms, combined with philosophical developments, such as Jeremy Bentham's Panopticon, comprised a paradigm shift in the question of how to control, deter, and punish crimes. This shift, moreover, assumed that prisoners had the ability to be reformed, given the right circumstances within the penitentiary model.[7] Therefore, the debate became whether punishment or rehabilitation should be the system's goal. After the wars of independence in Latin America, some of the local elites adopted the pioneering rehabilitative penitentiary models instead of the inefficient and outdated colonial prison systems.[8] During this period, modern penitentiaries were built in Latin America based on the competing American models and loosely following Bentham's Panopticon ideal. Some of these modern penitentiaries were the Casa de Correcao in Rio de Janeiro,[9] and the penitentiaries in Santiago, Chile and Lima, Peru.[10] In building these penitentiaries, these states sought to replace unhealthy, inefficient, and inhumane prisons with modern, rehabilitative institutions to transform criminals into law-abiding individuals.[11]

The construction of these prisons, however, did not lead to changes in the rest of the prison systems of these countries.[12] Some challenges to the penitentiary's success in the region comprised "scarce state resources, unsuitable legislation, prevailing patterns of social control, and the hegemony of discourses that justified traditional ways of interaction between classes, sexes and races."[13] However, despite these challenges, the penitentiary did not suffer a decline in favoritism as the best way to conduct penal reform in the region.[14] It should be highlighted that the mere building of some penitentiaries across the Americas in the nineteenth century impacted the region's overall system in a moderate manner due to the aforementioned incomplete reforms that were implemented in the region.

After these reforms in the early nineteenth century failed to produce the desired results of fostering the rehabilitation of criminals, the region once again adopted foreign penal and criminological doctrines after 1870, particularly the reformist and positivist models of criminology.[15] Although by 1930 there had been a paradigm shift toward positivism, prisons were not thoroughly reformed during this period. A noteworthy phenomenon that occurred during this time is that the rehabilitation of the criminal as the main objective of the penal reforms was displaced by an eagerness to transform the prison into well-administered institutions.[16] As a result, the state began to intervene into prisoners' everyday lives more than in previous periods[17] and prisons became the subject of study and generated knowledge about those who had been detained.[18]

Moreover, due to the positivist fascination with scientific knowledge, there were some limited reforms such as the building of more and larger prisons, the creation of offices for the constant monitoring of prisoners, and the centralization of prison administration within the state itself.[19] Certain techniques of identification and documentation of prisoners, such as photographs, fingerprinting, and identification cards, were widely implemented beginning in the 1880s.[20] The adoption of foreign models and some limited reforms in the early twentieth century, however, did not result in a substantive change of prison conditions across the region. Instead, even though the quality of life improved for some prisoners and some new prisons were built and old ones remodeled, around the 1940s the prison systems in the majority of the region showed symptoms of decay, inefficiency, and corruption and were places where detainees suffered and were overall abandoned.[21]

During the early twentieth century, certain trends were widespread in prisons across the Americas. Overpopulation, violence, lack of hygiene and basic health, insufficient food, corporal punishment, sexual abuse, and excessive work were prevalent during this era.[22] However, living conditions within the prisons depended upon power configurations, prestige and status—thus, some prisoners were able to secure relatively decent living conditions despite the generally terrible conditions within the prisons.[23] Racial and class differences were also influential with regard to the forms and administration of punishment, the assigning of physical space, and the distribution of privileges.[24] Therefore, unequal living conditions were something to be expected within the prison walls. Moreover, prisoners developed their own prison subcultures where slang, tattoos, and violence, were practices exercised inside the detention center and, sometimes, continued outside of it.[25]

All of these historical conditions can still be observed today, as subsequent chapters in this volume illustrate in detail. As a result of this historical overview, the reader can see that the majority of the contemporary challenges we will discuss in the third section of this chapter are nothing new. It should be noted that these historically precarious conditions did not improve over the twentieth century even when some reforms were implemented toward the end of it.[26] Indeed, prisons today remain overcrowded, underfunded, and plagued with human rights abuses throughout the region. And, although the causes for these inhumane conditions are varied, one of the contributing factors to the deterioration of these historical conditions has been the war on drugs.

THE WAR ON DRUGS AND ANTI-GANG POLICIES: EXACERBATING IMPRISONMENT IN THE AMERICAS

The U.S.-led war on drugs impacts the lives of individuals across the Americas in a variety of ways, one of which is the exacerbation of poor preexisting prison conditions in the region. However, the U.S. drug war is not the sole factor that has worsened these conditions over the past decades. Anti-gang policies also have contributed to the imprisonment of a larger number of individuals in the region, which contributes to over-crowding and worsens the precarious conditions that already existed in prisons across the Americas prior to the adoption of harsh anti-drug legislation.

The international drug control regime (IDCR) encompasses three international Conventions, signed under the auspices of the United Nations, which regulate psychoactive drugs. It is noteworthy that the U.S. has had a prominent and active role in promoting the IDCR since the early twentieth century.[27] The three treaties that comprise the IDCR are the 1961 Single Convention on Narcotic Drugs, the 1971 Convention on Psychotropic Substances, and the 1988 UN Convention against Illicit Traffic in Narcotic Drugs and Psychotropic Substances.[28]

Based on a prohibitionist approach to drugs, these Conventions—particularly the 1988 Convention—effectively criminalize and prohibit the use, production, and trafficking of psychoactive substances across the globe. It should be noted:

> States signatory to the 1988 Convention are obligated to "adopt such measures as may be necessary to establish as criminal offences under its domestic law" (art. 3, §1) production, sale, transport and distribu-tion for nonmedical purposes of the substances included in the sched-ules of the 1961 and 1971 Conventions. Penal sanctions should also apply to the "cultivation of opium poppy, coca bush or cannabis plants for the purpose of the production of narcotic drugs." The text estab-lishes a difference between the intent to traffic and personal consump-tion, stating that "the possession, purchase or cultivation of narcotic drugs or psychotropic substances for personal consumption" should also be classified as a criminal offence, but "subject to the constitutional principles and the basic concepts of its legal system" (art. 3, §2).[29]

Since the Conventions are legally binding on member states,[30] the inter-national framework has definitely influenced local drug laws, criminaliz-ing the aforementioned behavior. Currently, 184 countries are subject to the 1961 Convention,[31] 183 are parties to the 1971 Convention,[32] and 189 are parties to the 1988 Convention.[33] This means that the production, possession, and (oftentimes) consumption of controlled substances have become criminal activities in the eyes of the national governments in a majority of countries throughout the world.

Although the Americas did not have harsh drug laws before the adoption of the IDCR, in some cases the countries in the region promoted laws that are more punitive than required by the Conventions.[34] These laws also are generally disproportionate in the punishment of drug-related crimes vis-à-vis violent crimes, such as rape and murder, which tend to receive less severe penalties.[35] In other words, individuals imprisoned for drug-related crimes will receive longer and harsher criminal sentences than other crimes, which places stress on prison systems that are already weak.

Additionally, the United States has played a prominent role in the international control of narcotic substances, particularly after the war on drugs began in 1971. As a report from the Congressional Research Service explains:

> The United States has been involved in international drug control since at least the beginning of the 20th century. Contemporary U.S. counternarcotics efforts were brought to the forefront of U.S. policy debates in the late 1960s. In 1971, President Richard Nixon declared that illicit drugs were America's "public enemy number one." President Ronald Reagan followed with a directive in 1986 that identified narcotics trafficking a threat to U.S. national security. Successive administrations have continued to feature combating the international drug trade prominently among U.S. foreign policy priorities.[36]

As a result of the war on drugs, most of the U.S. counter-narcotics efforts are focused on the Western Hemisphere.[37] For the past three decades, combating the production and trafficking of drugs in the region has been a major focus of the United States' international drug control efforts.[38] One of the main tools in the U.S. strategy to combat drugs has been the provision of counter-narcotics assistance to foreign countries.[39] U.S.-led regional anti-drug policies[40] such as the Mérida Initiative,[41] Plan Colombia,[42] the Central America Regional Security Initiative, the Caribbean Basin Security Initiative,[43] and the Andean Strategy have had several unintended consequences in the region, including the increased incarceration rates for drug offenses. Moreover, as we have mentioned before:

> In Latin America—where the cocaine and some of the heroin and cannabis consumed in the United States originates—Washington has used its political influence and aid and trade policies to ensure collaboration with its so-called "war on drugs." By the late 1980s, the U.S. government was demanding implementation of harsh drug control legislation that included steep sentences and mandatory minimums—and much of the legislation that appeared in fact went beyond the requirements of the UN Conventions. In some cases, such as Law 1008 in Bolivia, the U.S. government was even drafting the proposed laws. By the 1990s,

the United States was routinely using arrest and seizure statistics to evaluate levels of Latin American drug-control cooperation. Washington has thus exported its model of harsh drug laws and mandatory minimum sentencing across the region. [44]

The requirement by the U.S. to achieve certification to have proactive counter-narcotic policies locally has created an incentive for local governments to be more stringent in their enforcement of the anti-drug laws. This enforcement, however, does not occur necessarily at the highest levels of drug-trafficking organizations. Instead, low-level traffickers and drug users are the ones who tend to be punished in this system. [45]

While some countries implemented anti-drug policies, others in Central America have been more focused on anti-gang policies since the early 2000s. These policies were driven by high levels of violence and the rise of citizen insecurity in El Salvador, Guatemala, and Honduras. Central American gangs were involved in many criminal activities, including drug trafficking. [46] In response to the rise of such gangs, these countries introduced a series of laws—some of them known as *Mano Dura* (Strong Hand) or *Super Mano Dura* (Super Strong Hand)—which enabled the governments to imprison people merely on suspicion of being a gang member. Due to these laws, thousands of young gang members were quickly removed from the streets and thrown into prison. [47] Given the earlier statement, the massive imprisonment of these suspected gang members contributed to the exacerbation of precarious and inhumane prison conditions in the Americas, as we will see in the next section.

CONTEMPORARY PRISON TRENDS IN THE AMERICAS

Although inhumane prison conditions in the region are to an extent rooted in historical trends, they have been exacerbated by the war on drugs and strong anti-gang policies. Some of the consequences of this phenomenon are overcrowding, ineffective state control over the prisons, deplorable and inhumane prison conditions, prison violence, characteristics of the majority of inmates, and prisons as schools and centers for the continuation of criminal activity.

The first major trend in the region today is overcrowding of the prisons. Following Carranza's definition, overcrowding becomes critical when a prison system's density is equal to 120 percent of capacity or higher. [48] This means, in layman's terms, that for a prison system to be considered critically overcrowded at least 120 prisoners are housed in spaces designed to house 100 people. To calculate this percentage, two numbers are needed: the total number of prisoners housed and the capacity of the prison(s) in question. Moreover, we refer to the incarceration rate as the number of prisoners per 100,000 of the general population. [49] This is an important distinction to make because an increased incarceration rate does not mean that there will necessarily be overcrowding in the prisons, and vice versa.[50] Prison density and incarceration rates are quantitatively useful to understand the critical situation of the prison system in the hemisphere.

In Table 1.1, we can see several quantitative trends across the region. First, the total number of detainees in the region is about 3.6 million. When we consider that there are more than 10.2 million prisoners in the world,[51] it is possible to see that about 35 percent of the world's prison population is held in the Americas. However, the United States' prison population—about 2.2 million, and considered the highest in the world—accounts for an overwhelming majority of the region's 3.6 million detainees. Without considering the United States, the Americas account for about 1.37 million imprisoned, or about 13 percent of the world's estimated prison population.

Second, the average percentage of pretrial detainees in the Americas is 43.22 percent. This means that about four in ten prisoners in the region are being held without having faced trial or even being charged. However, the percentage of those being held in pretrial detention also varies widely across the region. The range of this variation goes from a low of 14.8 percent of prisoners held in pretrial detention in Jamaica to 72.5 percent in Paraguay. Although the variation in the data is wide, the median percentage of prisoners held in pretrial detention is 43.1 percent, which is close to the average. This means that about four in ten prisoners in the region are being held without having faced trial or having been charged. It should be noted that the widespread use of pretrial detention, and the violation of its time limits, is one of the main contributing factors that has exacerbated overcrowding, and its attendant consequences, in the region.[52]

Finally, the average occupancy level in prisons across the region is a staggering 160.21 percent, which is higher than the 120 percent threshold for a country's prison system to be considered overcrowded. However, the median occupancy rate in the region is 140.9 percent—which is the average of the reported rates of Guyana and Honduras. Yet this third trend, overcrowding, is also subject to vast variation in the data. On one hand, there are eight countries that are not facing a situation of critical overcrowding because they do not have overpopulation rates of 120 percent or higher. These countries are Argentina, Bahamas, Belize, Chile, Jamaica, Puerto Rico, Trinidad and Tobago, and the United States. On the other hand, there are countries that face extremely high levels of overcrowding, with an occupancy rate over 200 percent, such as Bolivia, Ecuador, El Salvador, Guatemala, Peru, and Venezuela.

The second major trend in the region today is that prison authorities are unable to exercise effective control over the prisons. Different reasons can explain this lack of effectiveness. One reason is that, due to an unequal increase of the prison population and the prison staff, there is a

Table 1.1. Data on Prison Population, PreTrial Detainees, and Occupancy Rate

	Prison Population Total	Prisoners per 100,000	Pretrial detainees percent of prison population	Official capacity of Prison System	Prison occupancy rate (in percent)
Argentina	66484	161	50.3	60240	101.6
Bahamas	1433	379	42	1348	97.8
Belize	1650	495	40.8	1750	94.3
Bolivia	14771	138	83.3	5750	256.9
Brazil	548003	275	38	318739	171.9
Chile	44247	249	26.2	41034	110.9
Colombia	117037	238	35.4	76553	152.9
Costa Rica	17440	352	17.2	9803	151.3
Dominican Republic	26132	248	58.1	14656	174
Ecuador	24722	156	36	12089	204.5
El Salvador	27629	432	19.7	8328	320.3
Guatemala	16336	105	50.3	6492	251.6
Guyana	2032	269	34	1550	131.1
Haiti	10250	98	70.6	5958	172
Honduras	12969	160	50	8603	150.7
Jamaica	4201	152	14.8	4402	95.4
Mexico	254641	215	43.2	199828	127.4
Nicaragua	9168	153	12.3	4742	128
Panama	15208	386	62.5	8670	179.7
Paraguay	9413	137	72.5	7053	130.9
Peru	67891	222	54.2	31010	218.9
Puerto Rico	12244	335	15.7	15034	87.9
Trinidad and Tobago	4846	362	43.3	4090	118.5
United States	2228424	707	21.6	2265000	99
Uruguay	9599	281	64.9	7862	122.1
Venezuela	52933	174	66.8	16761	315.8
TOTAL or AVERAGE	3,599,703	264.58	43.22	3,137,345	160.21

Source: Authors' own elaboration using the World Prison Briefs from the International Centre for Prison Studies. International Centre for Prison Studies. "World Prison Brief." International, Centre for Prison Studies. October 1, 2014. Accessed November, 2014. http://www.prison studies.org/world-prison-brief.

power vacuum because the staff is insufficient to control higher numbers of detainees. As a result, the staff limits itself to control the perimeter of the prisons and does not exercise effective control over the facilities.

Therefore, the authorities allow the inmates to run the prisons. Inside, the prisoners have their own distinct organizations—in some places they are gangs or other criminal groups—and a leader or group of leaders exercise the authority over the rest of the detainees.[53] The leaders and groups make decisions over a vast array of issues ranging from food distribution, allocation of spaces and accommodations to discipline, rules, and justice.[54] The second reason is that guards are susceptible to bribes from prisoners.[55] Another reason is that detainees threaten the guards and their families, thereby coercing them into complying with what the prisoners want.

The third trend is that prisons have become a space for the continuation of criminal activities. Small-time offenders mixed with hardened criminals often join criminal networks within the prison.[56] As a result, the prisons become schools of crime for petty offenders.[57] Furthermore, inmates (especially members of drug trafficking cartels and members of gangs) continuously work with their counterparts outside of the prison.[58] For example, imprisoned gang members are in constant communication with their cliques (groups) outside of prison. They use cell phones or computers that have been smuggled inside the prisons or send messages via their visitors. Through these means of communication, they order cliques (groups) outside the prison to carry out extortions, abductions, murder, robberies, and drug trafficking. Visitors give inmates a portion of the revenues from these criminal activities. Inmates use this "income" to pay leader(s) of their group for space, accommodations, and services inside the prison.

A fourth trend is the existence of deplorable and inhumane conditions within the prisons. States are using buildings and facilities that were not originally designed to imprison citizens or to house so many inmates. This situation has created a plethora of problems that impact the inmates' well-being, such as lack of sanitation and adequate nutrition, inadequate provision of health services, decreased access to water and prison activities, and other violations of basic human rights.[59] One important impact of these deplorable conditions centers on the inmates' mental health, which is affected by the inhumane circumstances that they face in these detention facilities and the lack of access to quality healthcare.[60]

A fifth trend is prison violence. Prison violence refers to violence between prisoners, state agents against prisoners, or prisoners against state agents. Some examples of violence are riots, murders, and attacks against prison authorities. Violence has become more common as a result of overcrowding and inhumane prison conditions. Riots have recently occurred in countries such as Brazil (August and October 2014),[61] Honduras (March 2012 and August 2013),[62] and Venezuela (January 2013.)[63]

A final trend is related to the characteristics of the prison population arrested due to the anti-drug and anti-gang laws. In the Americas, the drug laws are extremely punitive and "(. . .) in general the legislation does not distinguish between levels of involvement in the business—treating street sellers and transporters on par with large-scale drug traffickers, and failing to distinguish between violent and non-violent offenses."[64] Most of the persons imprisoned for drug-related offenses are from the lower-levels of the drug-trafficking chain. For example, in Colombia only about 2 percent of those imprisoned for drug-related offenses are mid-to-high-level drug traffickers. [65]

Another characteristic of the prison population is that the majority of the individuals imprisoned for drug charges come from vulnerable and marginalized social sectors. Many studies have indicated that most of these inmates are poor, have little formal education, have limited sources of employment, and belong to minority groups.[66] Moreover, if the prisoner is an income-generating member, the sudden loss of income could have a dramatic economic impact on the rest of the family.[67]

CONCLUSION

Anti-drug and anti-gang policies have worsened preexisting precarious historical conditions in the prisons of the Americas. Before these laws were even introduced, the prison system in the region already confronted several problems. Before the 1950s, some of these challenges were overpopulation, violence, lack of hygiene and basic health. Moreover, the living conditions within the prisons depended upon specific power configurations, prestige, and status. Finally, prisoners were known to develop their own subcultures within the prison walls and continued outside of them.

Within the context of the precarious conditions in the prison systems, several countries in the Americas implemented anti-drug and anti-gang laws. During the second half of the twentieth century, the United States, along with other countries of the region, confronted rising levels of drug production and trafficking. In response, they adopted several laws as part of the so-called war on drugs. These laws were implemented as part of the international drug control regime, which aims to stop the flow of drugs into societies. Moreover, Central American countries had severe problems with gangs, which were responsible for the increasing rates of violence and criminal activities in the region. In response, many Central American governments adopted iron-fist anti-gang laws to control the growing levels of violence.

The implementation of anti-drug and anti-gang laws has exacerbated the historical prison problems throughout the Americas. Among the various trends of the conditions of the prison systems in the region, we have identified overcrowding, ineffective state control over the facilities, prisons serving as schools of violence and centers for the continuation of criminal activities, and deplorable living conditions. These issues have been historical challenges that the region has faced, but today they have reached a critical point.

NOTES

1. Harry Elmer Barnes "Historical Origin of the Prison System in America." *Journal of Criminal Law and Criminology* 12, no. 1 (1921): 36. Accessed October 25, 2014. http://scholarlycommons.law.northwestern.edu/cgi/viewcontent.cgi?article=1772&context=jclc.

2. Carlos Aguirre. "Cárcel y sociedad en América Latina: 1800-1940." *Historia social urbana. Espacios y fujos.* Quito: FLACSO, 2009, 210.

3. Aguirre, "Cárcel y sociedad," 212.

4. Aguirre, "Cárcel y sociedad," 212.

5. Barnes, "Origin of the Prison System," 40–48.

6. Barnes, "Origin of the Prison System," 48.

7. Aguirre, "Cárcel y sociedad," 217.

8. Aguirre, "Cárcel y sociedad," 214.

9. Ricardo D. Salvatore and Carlos Aguirre, eds. *The Birth of the Penitentiary in Latin America: Essays on Criminology, Prison Reform, and Social Control, 1830-1940.* (Austin, TX: University of Texas Press, 2010).

10. Aguirre, "Cárcel y sociedad," 215.

11. Salvatore and Aguirre, *The Birth of the Penitentiary in Latin America*, ix.

12. Aguirre, "Cárcel y sociedad," 216.

13. Salvatore and Aguirre, *The Birth of the Penitentiary in Latin America*, x.

14. Salvatore and Aguirre, *The Birth of the Penitentiary in Latin America*, x.

15. Aguirre, "Cárcel y sociedad," 220.

16. Aguirre, "Carcel y Sociedad," 231–232.

17. Aguirre, "Carcel y Sociedad," 232.

18. Aguirre, "Cárcel y sociedad," 230.

19. Aguirre, "Cárcel y sociedad," 232.

20. Aguirre, "Cárcel y sociedad," 232, citing Carlos Aguirre. *The Criminals of Lima and Their Worlds. The Prison Experience, 1850-1935.* Durham: Duke University Press, 2005, 73.

21. Aguirre, "Carcel y sociedad," 234.

22. Aguirre, "Cárcel y sociedad," 234.

23. Aguirre, "Carcel y sociedad," 235.

24. Aguirre, "Carcel y Sociedad," 235, citing Aguirre, *The Criminals of Lima and Their Worlds*, 228.

25. Aguirre, "Cárcel y sociedad," 237–238.

26. Mark Ungar. "Prisons and Politics in Contemporary Latin America." *Human Rights Quarterly* 25, no. 4 (2003): 909–934.

27. Francisco E. Thoumi "Marijuana in the United States and the international drug control regime: Why what is promoted abroad is not applied at home." *Crime, Law and Social Change* 61, no. 3 (2014): 274.

28. For more information on these Conventions, see Letizia Paoli, Victoria A. Greenfield, and Peter Reuter. "Change is possible: The history of the international drug control regime and implications for future policymaking." *Substance use & misuse* 47, no. 8–9 (2012): 923–935, and Bewley-Taylor, David, Tom Blickman, and Martin Jelsma. *The rise and decline of cannabis prohibition: The history of Cannabis in the UN drug control system and options for reform* . (Amsterdam: Transnational Institute, 2014).

29. Martin Jelsma. "The development of international drug control: lessons learned and strategic challenges for the future," (working paper, Global Commission on Drug Policies, January 2011:8) http://www.globalcommissionondrugs.org/wp-content/themes/gcdp_v1/pdf/Global_Com_Martin_Jelsma.pdf.

30. Harm Reduction Coalition. "International Law Overview: The UN Drug Conventions." The Harm Reduction Coalition. January 1, 2011. Accessed November 12, 2014. http://harmreduction.org/wp-content/uploads/2011/10/InternationalLawOverview.pdf.

31. United Nations Treaty Collection, "Chapter VI. Narcotic and Psychotropic Substances. Single Convention on Narcotic Drugs, 1961, amended by Protocol." Accessed August 1, 2014. https:// treaties.un.org/Pages/ViewDetails.aspx?src=TREATY&mtdsg_no=VI-18&chapter=6&lang=en.

32. United Nations Treaty Collection, "Chapter VI. Narcotic and Psychotropic Substances. Convention on Psychotropic Substances." Accessed August 1, 2014. https:// treaties.un.org/Pages/ViewDetails.aspx? src=TREATY&mtdsg_no=VI-16&chapter=6& lang=en.

33. United Nations Treaty Collection, "Chapter VI. Narcotic and Psychotropic Substances. Convention against Illicit Traffic in Narcotic Drugs and Psychotropic Substances." Accessed August 1, 2014. https:// treaties.un.org/Pages/ViewDetails.aspx? src=TREATY&mtdsg_no=VI-19&chapter=6&lang=en .

34. Pien Metaal and Coletta Youngers, eds. *Systems Overload: Drug Laws and Prisons in Latin America.* Amsterdam / Washington: Transnational Institute and the Washington Office on Latin America, 2011, 5.

35. Rodrigo Uprimny Yepes, Diana Esther Guzman, and Jorge Parra Norato. "Addicted to Punishment: the disproportionality of drug laws in Latin America," (working paper 1, Centro de Estudios de Derecho, Justicia y Sociedad, Dejusticia. January 2013.)   http://www.opensocietyfoundations.org/sites/default/files/addicted-punishment-20130530.pdf

36. Liana Sun Wyler, *International drug control policy: Background and US Reponses* (CRS Report No. RL34543) (Washington, DC: Congressional Research Service, 2013.) 11–12, http://fas.org/sgp/crs/row/RL34543.pdf.

37. Wyler, *International drug control policy,* 14.

38. Clare Ribando Seelke, Liana Sun Wyler, June S. Beittel, Mark P. Sullivan, *Latin America and the Caribbean: Illicit Drug Trafficking and US Counterdrug Programs* (CRS Report No. R41215) (Washington, DC: Congressional Research Service, 2011.) 9 http:// fas.org/sgp/crs/row/R41215.pdf.

39. Seelke, Wyler, Beittel, Sullivan, *Latin America and the Caribbean,* 9.

40. For a thorough breakdown and background of these policies, see Seelke, Wyler, Beittel, Sullivan, *Latin America and the Caribbean.*

41. Seelke, Wyler, Beittel, Sullivan, *Latin America and the Caribbean,* 14–15.

42. For more information about Plan Colombia and the Andean Counterdrug Program, see Seelke, Wyler, Beittel, Sullivan, *Latin America and the Caribbean,* 12–14.

43. For background information about the CBSI, see Seelke, Wyler, Beittel, Sullivan, *Latin America and the Caribbean,* 18.

44. Metaal and Youngers, eds. *Systems Overload,* 9.

45. Metaal and Youngers, eds. *Systems Overload,* 6.

46. Jose Miguel Cruz. "Central American Maras: From Youth Street Gangs to Transnational Protection Rackets." *Global Crim* 11, no. 4 (2010): 389–390, and "How the Street Gangs Took Central America." Foreign Affairs. November 13, 2014. Accessed November 13, 2014. http://www.foreignaffairs.com/articles/60803/ana-arana/how-the-street-gangs-took-central-america.

47. Cruz, "Central American Maras," 390.

48. Elias Carranza. "Situación penitenciaria en América Latina y el Caribe¿ Qué hacer?." *Anuario de Derechos Humanos* 8 (2012), 33.

49. United Nations. *Handbook on Strategies to Reduce Overcrowding in Prisons.* New York: United Nations, 2013, 8.

50. United Nations. *Handbook on Strategies to Reduce Overcrowding,* 9.

51. Roy Walmsley. "World Prison Population List (Tenth Edition)." International Centre for Prison Studies. November 21, 2013. http://www.prisonstudies.org/sites/ prisonstudies.org/files/resources/downloads/wppl_10.pdf

52. Open Society Foundations. *Presumption of Guilt: The Global Overuse of Pretrial Detention.* New York: Open Society Foundations, 2014, 30.

53. For an example of this situation see Jose Luis Sanz. "El Rey Justo De La Cárcel Del Infierno—El Faro." Elfaro.net. January 13, 2014. Accessed November 13, 2014. http://salanegra.elfaro.net/es/201401/cronicas. The English version of this article can be found in Insight Crime, via Sanz, Jose Luis. "The Just King of Honduras' Prison from Hell." Insight Crime: Organized Crime in the Americas. January 15, 2014. Accessed November 13, 2014. http://www.insightcrime.org/news-analysis/the-just-king-of-honduras-prison-from-hell?highlight=WyJqdXN0IiwiJ2p1c3QiLCJraW5nIiwia2

54. Hannah Stone, Inmates Run Honduras Prison as Micro-State. In SightCrime, July 19, 2012. http://www.insightcrime.org/news-analysis/inmates-run-honduras-prison-as-micro-state

55. Elyssa Pachico. "Pre-Trial Detention Brews Crisis in LatAm Prisons." Pre-Trial Detention Brews Crisis in LatAm Prisons. February 20, 2012. Accessed November 13, 2014. http://www.insightcrime.org/news-analysis/pre-trial-detention-brews-crisis-in-latam-prisons?highlight=WyJwcmUtdHJpYWwiLCJkZXRlbnRpb24

56. Pachico, "Pre-Trial Detention."

57. Metaal and Youngers, eds. *Systems Overload,* 95.

58. Cruz, "Central American Maras," 392.

59. United Nations. *Handbook on Strategies to Reduce Overcrowding.*

60. United Nations. *Handbook on Strategies to Reduce Overcrowding.*

61. Jonathan Watts, "Brazilian prisoners behead two inmates during riot." The Guardian August 25, 2014. "Brazil prisoners end hostage drama at Guarapuava jail." BBC News October 15, 2014. http://www.bbc.com/news/world-latin-america-29627625

62. Geoffrey Ramsey, "At Least 13 killed in Honduran prison Riot, Fire." Insight Crime, March 30, 2012. http://www.insightcrime.org/news-briefs/at-least-13-killed-in-honduran-prison-riot-fire and Honduras troops sent to take control of jail after riot BBC News August 3, 2013. http://www.bbc.com/news/world-latin-america-23565124

63. Catherine Soichet, "Report: Prison riots kills dozens in Venezuela." January 26, 2003 http://www.cnn.com/2013/01/26/world/americas/venezuela-prison-riot/.

64. Metaal and Youngers, eds. *Systems Overload,* 5.

65. See Metaal and Youngers, eds. *Systems Overload.*

66. United Nations. *Handbook on Strategies to Reduce Overcrowding.*

67. United Nations. *Handbook on Strategies to Reduce Overcrowding,* 15.

TWO

Broken Systems

Prisons and Prison Gangs in California and the United States

Susan A. Phillips and Jonathan D. Rosen

Two generations of prison scholars and activists have critiqued the consequences of the war on drugs and excessive incarceration in the United States.[1] Turnarounds of this massive system have been slow to counter policies that continue to disproportionately penalize minority communities,[2] that are ineffective at decreasing crime, and that remain in violation of national and international human rights standards.[3]

For African Americans and other communities of color, incarceration provides a contemporary replay of historic sequestering practices such as slavery, convict leasing, Jim Crow laws, and ghettoization.[4] Growing awareness of racial disparities at every level of criminal justice—from arrest and conviction to sentencing—has begun to create a partial shift in public opinion. Activists, lawmakers, community groups, and sometimes prisoners themselves have helped to push through policy changes that attempt to rectify such disparities. Recent notable reforms have included the repeal of the crack laws (described below) (2010), the closure of several juvenile prisons in California (2010–present), outlawing the death penalty for juvenile offenders (2005), halting mandatory application of juvenile life without the possibility of parole (2013), and the elimination of the death penalty in six states over a six-year period (2007–2013). These victories have been hard-won, coming after years of protracted struggle.

But with 2.4 million people currently behind bars, the U.S. prison system shows no signs of diminishing in scope.[5] Many problematic parts of the system remain common practice domestically and are continuing to spread globally. These include both routine and exceptional human rights abuses such as long-term solitary confinement; poor treatment of mentally ill persons, immigrants, and aging individuals; chronic over-crowding, violence and disease; the trying of juveniles as adults; and continued sentencing (no longer mandatory) of juveniles to life without the possibility of parole. These practices have been underscored by broader socioeconomic shifts attendant on neoliberal trajectories, the pri-vatization of the prison market, the involvement of union lobbies and corporate interests in pro-penal legislation, the exponential growth of the immigrant detention system, and the global spread of U.S. penal pedago-gies.[6] U.S. state and corporate interests actively inform penal trajectories for many if not all of the countries outlined in this volume.

This chapter uses one Californian example to analyze some of the problems with the current U.S. prison system and to challenge the notion of the prison as a closed system. We rely on both the vast literature surrounding mass incarceration and on firsthand fieldwork with drug dealers, gangs, and traffickers both inside and outside of incarcerated settings. The chapter is divided into three parts. The first discusses the growth of the prison population via the war on drugs. The second exam-ines the rise of prison gangs and their ability to tax street drug sales through dependable incarceration streams. The third analyzes a Califor-nia case study of prison gang leaders who mounted a statewide hunger strike against long-term solitary confinement. We conclude with policy recommendations.

BUILDING A RACIALIZED PRISON POPULATION

The now more than forty-year-old U.S.-led global war on drugs has fo-cused on combating the trafficking, sales, and consumption of drugs.[7] Under the auspices of the war on drugs, the United States has imple-mented harsh penalties not only for drug dealers but also for drug users. Law enforcement officials have worked tirelessly to incarcerate users and traffickers, and, as a result, the U.S. has witnessed the proliferation of the number of people behind bars. The logic remains that "bad guys" need to be removed from the streets in order to improve neighborhoods. In other words, drug traffickers, drug dealers, and drug users belong behind bars and should be punished for their crimes. The war on drugs has resulted in the U.S. incarcerating people at a rate higher—750 per 100,000 peo-ple—than any other country in the world. The U.S. incarcerates its citi-zens at a higher rate than authoritarian or repressive regimes such as China and Russia.[8] In sum, the war on drugs and the desire to incarcerate people for drug-related offenses has been a major factor in the drastic increases in the number of people behind bars.

President Richard Nixon launched the war on drugs in 1971. Nixon recognized that the drug trade was an economic problem and drug dealers would continue to sell drugs as long as a market existed.[9] As a result, Nixon had a more balanced approach as opposed to focusing solely on stopping the supply of drugs from coming into the country. President Ronald Reagan focused on combatting the supply of drugs from entering the U.S. from other countries and incarcerating drug users as opposed to reducing demand through education, prevention, treatment, and rehabilitation. Reagan viewed halting the drug supply as an imperative, particularly because he witnessed the devastation that drugs had on communities, particularly in inner cities of large urban areas such as Chicago, Los Angeles, and New York. For Reagan, drugs were noxious substances that needed to be combatted because they had the ability to erode the moral values of the U.S. Ted Galen Carpenter describes the philosophy of the Reagan administration regarding drugs, stating:

> For conservatives of Reagan's stamp, widespread drug use was not merely a public health problem, it offended a wide range of deeply held social views. They blamed drugs for the massive increase in street crimes, noting that compulsive drug users committed a high percentage of robberies, burglaries, and other offenses to support their habits . . .[10] In addition to assuming links between drug use and crime, many conservatives were alarmed that drugs were corrupting America's youth. The drug culture, in their view, both reflected and contributed to the decline of "traditional morality" and "family values."[11]

In sum, Reagan viewed drugs as a major national security issue as opposed to a health issue that required treatment and rehabilitation and sought to increase the security in the U.S. by combatting drug trafficking and usage.[12] He believed that drug traffickers and users should be incarcerated to prevent crime and improve safety in communities throughout the U.S.

The war on drugs and the desire to incarcerate drug traffickers and users continued beyond the Reagan years. Washington forgot Richard Nixon's warnings about the need to reduce demand, focusing solely on treating drugs as a security issue and incarcerating violators of the drug laws. The consequence of such strategies has been the proliferation of the number of people in prison over the years. As of 2011, 1 in every 99.1 adults in the United States was either in a local, state, or federal prison.[13] As of 2013, 219,087 people are currently held in federal prisons, according to the Bureau of Prisons.[14] The Drug Policy Alliance states:

> The United States is home to less than 5 percent of the world's population but nearly 25 percent of its prisoners, in part because of the overly harsh consequences of a drug conviction. Many of the 2.3 million people behind bars (and 5 million under criminal justice supervision) in this country are being punished for a drug offense. If every American

who has ever possessed illicit drugs were punished for it, nearly half of the U.S. population would have drug violations on their records. [15]

The statement by the Drug Policy Alliance highlights the fact that the U.S. continues to incarcerate millions of people, many of whom have been charged with drug-related offenses, as opposed to focusing on treatment, rehabilitation, and education.

African Americans and Hispanics have faced discrimination, and as a result, these groups comprise the vast majority of prisoners in the U.S., making much of the war on drugs and the laws racist in nature. One of the best examples can be found in the crack-cocaine mandatory sentencing laws. Crack-cocaine is a cheaper derivative of powdered cocaine, but it is much easier to make and can be smoked. Powdered cocaine, however, tends to be used more as a party drug because of the high cost. In 1986, the Reagan administration developed new mandatory sentencing laws, which resulted in the incarceration of large numbers of African Americans suffering from crack addiction. David Musto describes the crack laws, stating:

> The clamor for a crackdown on drugs and drug users as agents of disease and crime was irresistible to most authorities. At congressional hearings the effects of crack cocaine were dramatically described as far more powerful and damaging than powdered cocaine, with the result that Congress mandated a severe penalty for possession of 5 grams of crack cocaine, equal to the penalty for possession of 500 grams (about one pound) of powdered cocaine, a ratio of 1:100. The penalty is 5 to 40 years imprisonment for an uncomplicated violation; the sentence cannot be suspended, nor can the convict be paroled or placed on probation. [16]

Fortunately, the Obama administration repealed the mandatory sentencing laws, but this does nothing for the plethora of people who suffered as a result of this racist law. [17]

African Americans continue to be victims of the war on drugs. The sentencing of African Americans and Hispanics compared to Caucasians is highly disproportional with 67 percent of people incarcerated in state prisons for drug-related violations being either Hispanic or African American. This, however, is despite the fact that more Caucasians in the U.S. statistically use drugs than African Americans. [18] Michelle Alexander describes the role of race in U.S. prisons, declaring that:

> The racial dimension of mass incarceration is its most striking feature. No other country in the world imprisons so many of its racial or ethnic minorities. The United States imprisons a larger percentage of its black population than South Africa did at the height of apartheid. In Washington, D.C., our nation's capital, it is estimated that three out of four young black men (and nearly all those in the poor neighborhoods) can

expect to serve time in prison. Similar rates of incarceration can be found in black communities across America. [19]

The results of such draconian policies and the disproportionate rates of incarceration of African Americans can be compared with the other systems of control and exclusion, such as the Jim Crow laws. [20] Even after serving their sentences, prisoners are discriminated against when they apply for jobs, and in essence, they have a permanent red flag next to their names. [21] Felons also are denied access to student loans and cannot improve themselves through education, [22] which only makes finding a well-paying job a more daunting task. Alexander echoes such sentiments, stating:

> What is completely missed in the rare public debates today about the plight of African Americans is that a huge percentage of them are not free to move up at all. It is not just that they lack opportunity, attend poor schools, or are plagued by poverty. They are barred by law from doing so. And the major institutions with which they come into contact are designed to prevent their mobility. . . . The current system of control permanently locks a huge percentage of African American communities out of the mainstream society and economy. [23]

In essence, the prison system has the complete opposite effect as it fails to rehabilitate prisoners and merely facilitates the permanent exclusion of convicted offenders from society.

THE RISE OF PRISON GANGS IN CALIFORNIA

Shifting from the national context to that of California, this section explores the rise of prison gangs to demonstrate overlapping failures in the U.S. system of incarceration. California prison gangs began as race and place-based protective groups in the 1960s. Four main historic gangs emerged in competition and cooperation with one another. These included the Aryan Brotherhood (White), La Eme (Southern California Latino), Nuestra Familia (Northern California Latino), and Black Guerilla Family (African American). [24] Today, white prison gangs also include Nazi Lowriders. African American prison gangs have formed newer affiliations around Blood and Crip designations, including the Consolidated Crip Organization, Blood Line, and United Blood Nation. Despite the proliferation of these groups, patterns of alliance have remained stable. White and Southern California Latino prisoners share a loose alliance, as do Northern California Latino prisoners and African Americans. Racial animosity is pervasive and culminates in race-based riots, although most murders occur within as opposed to outside of these groups for political reasons.

The growth of prison gangs is linked to both the drug trade and the drug war. Prison gangs maintain a base of power through street and prison-based drug sales as well as other illicit economic activities. Both African American and Latino prison gangs levy taxes on street gangs' neighborhood drug sales. Their main coercive mechanism for enforcing taxation is a dependable stream of inmates, and the certainty that members of every street gang will eventually be incarcerated. If street gangs refuse to cooperate with taxation, prison gangs will violently target individuals associated with uncooperative gangs. This coercive power has been highly effective, and as a result prison gangs have a high degree of integration into street gang political economies. As prison gang members use the prison infrastructure to cement leadership, they maximize the control they have over others by taking advantage of a system designed in part to destroy them. Through the prison system, prison gangs have developed a solid foundation of exploitative ideological power that is dependent upon rather than eroded by mass incarceration.

In California prisons, representatives from disparate street gangs form groups that harness existing neighborhood affiliations. As people from neighborhoods across California share space within the confines of prisons, broader elements of gang affiliation and regional identity come into play. Frequent movement from street to prison has connected local street gangs into networked systems that span large geographic regions.

Gang members make use of prison sentences to negotiate new alliances and to extend and strengthen their social networks. Few street gang members become core members of the prison gangs listed above, as actual prison gang membership comprises a kind of elite class. Most prisoners are street gang members who remain under the control of prison gangs and who affiliate with other members of their race. The process of affiliation becomes conflated with prison gang allegiances and responsibilities. Prison-based gang leadership has emerged to create organized networks based in part upon the rhetoric of racial empowerment and financial gain.

Nationalist sentiment and empowerment movements periodically surge through prison-based and street-based gang culture. Gangs sometimes make efforts to extend alliances and increase racial unity in the face of conflicts with the larger society. Patterns of unity gain and lose momentum with current events and shifts in consciousness.

The excessive cost of a prison system like California's has been unable to deter drug use and gang activity despite the fact that prisoners are behind bars in securely confined areas. In fact, the opposite has been true. "Shot callers" for gangs and other drug dealing organizations have numerous connections to the outside as well as to correctional officers who are employed to monitor the prisoners twenty-four hours a day, supposedly to prevent such activities from occurring. In states like California, corruption among prison guards is rampant in a system that costs up-ward of seven billion dollars per year.[25]

A framework of coercive power, periodic unity in the face of the larg-er system, and ongoing political struggle informed by contexts inside and outside of prison leads into the next section, which describes the way that prison gang leaders mobilized over 30,000 people to protest the inhu-mane use of solitary confinement in California prisons.

THE SHORT CORRIDOR COLLECTIVE

Because gangs have developed significant power behind bars, one tactic used to deal with them has been the sequestration of prison gang leaders into permanent solitary confinement.[26] In general, inmates may be kept in continuous solitary confinement for disciplinary or administrative purposes. Disciplinary segregation, referred to as "the hole," is short-term solitary confinement and is usually used as punishment for break-ing rules. Administrative segregation, also referred to as "ad. seg." or the SHU (Secure Housing Unit), is long-term solitary confinement. Some prisons, such as Pelican Bay, where many prison gang leaders are housed, were constructed as "supermax" prisons where all units are de-signed for long-term solitary confinement. In solitary confinement, pris-oners are in near-total isolation and experience an extreme loss of privi-leges. Doors are opened by computer, and there is limited or no access to phones, showers, the outdoors, jobs, and rehabilitative programs.[27]

With some exceptions, inmates are held for twenty-three hours a day in small cells devoid of daylight. For one hour per day, SHU prisoners are given access to an exercise pen, which is another small room, often with a skylight ceiling. This regime prohibits contact with other prisoners and minimizes contact with guards or the outside world. The deprivation of human contact, natural light and air, and free bodily movement has been shown to create mental instability, mental illness, and violent behavior. Additional problems include insomnia, anxiety, memory loss, physical deterioration, depression, anger, cognitive disturbances, perceptual dis-tortions, paranoia, and psychosis.[28] Lorna Rhodes, who writes about soli-tary confinement in Washington State prisons, asserts that:

> . . . a mechanized, almost seamless, containment of prisoners' bodies exacerbates or produces extreme states of mind. Raging, depressed, or hallucinating men "knot up" within the tiny confines of their cells. A second, paradoxical, effect is that tight control over the body precipi-tates extreme uses of the body itself. These resist containment despite the multiple steel doors and scripted practices designed to manage them.[29]

Prisoners in long-term solitary confinement include people deemed a serious risk to other inmates, people who have violated informal or formal codes of conduct, prison gang members, and prisoners who have been attacked by other inmates and need to be separated for their own protection. While a common sentence to the SHU is five years, any prison gang member may be placed in the SHU without restriction regarding the length of that stay. The only way to be removed from the SHU is to debrief, which means to inform on the gang. This places people wishing to leave the gang or the SHU behind at extreme risk of violence if they are thought to have provided information to authorities. Lengths of long-term solitary confinement vary by individual, but some have been in the SHU for more than two decades. Approximately 25,000 people in the U.S. live in permanent isolation.[30]

In the case of Pelican Bay, prison gang leaders from each of the four historic prison gangs (La Eme, Nuestra Familia, the Aryan Brotherhood, and the Black Guerilla Family) happened to be housed in the same area of the prison—on what they called the "short corridor." Though isolated from direct contact, these individuals were within communicative distance of one another. From that vantage point, historic enemies began to find common ground in protesting their conditions. They asserted that the treatment they received in the SHU was a violation of their eighth amendment constitutional protections against cruel and unusual punishment. Long-term solitary confinement fits the definition of torture by international human rights standards, and the United States is alone in its use among developed countries.[31] Studies have shown that, beyond approximately ten days, essentially no benefits to isolation can be found.[32] The harmful effects of long-term solitary confinement on prisoners, on the other hand, are clear. In addition to the above, 69 percent of suicides that occurred in a one-year time span in Californian prisons were committed by prisoners in SHUs.[33] Furthermore, high rates of recidivism and crime post-release demonstrate a continued threat to public safety by those held in solitary confinement.[34] Even if the only rationale for isolating prison gang members in SHUs is to prevent communication with other gang members, the events of the 2013 hunger strike disprove that notion entirely.

On July 8, 2013, the four leaders—calling themselves the "Short Corridor Collective"—began a hunger strike to protest the conditions of their solitary confinement as cruel and unusual punishment.[35] They had spread the word slowly throughout the entire prison system over a period of months. In order to do so, they partially reconfigured communicative strategies used to organize the underground economies of their respective groups. This involved writing to individuals on the outside, who then wrote or spoke to individuals on the inside and helped to post demands on line. The hunger strike was not a secret. Demands were made known months before the strike to the California Department of Corrections and Rehabilitation (CDCR) and were posted on several websites to help spread the word:

The principal prisoner representatives from the PBSP [Pelican Bay State Prison] SHU Short Corridor Collective Human Rights Movement does hereby present public notice that our nonviolent peaceful protest of our subjection to decades of indefinite state-sanctioned torture, via long term solitary confinement will resume on July 8, 2013, consisting of a hunger strike/work stoppage of indefinite duration until CDCR signs a legally binding agreement meeting our demands, the heart of which mandates an end to long-term solitary confinement (as well as additional major reforms). Our decision does not come lightly. For the past (2) years we've patiently kept an open dialogue with state officials, attempting to hold them to their promise to implement meaningful reforms, responsive to our demands. For the past seven months we have repeatedly pointed out CDCR's failure to honor their word—and we have explained in detail the ways in which they've acted in bad faith and what they need to do to avoid the resumption of our protest action.[36]

Inmates throughout California knew the date and the demands. On July 8, along with the four at Pelican Bay, over 30,000 prisoners across the State of California refused their food. Most of the prisoners would fast only two or three days. But a core group of 136 held out for over two months. The state issued a force-feeding order in August 2013 for individuals who had signed do not resuscitate orders.[37] Inmates were strapped to restraining chairs and fed with nasogastric tubes—standard fare at Guantanamo Bay. The argument the state used to justify force feeding was that they could not tell which individuals prison gangs had coerced into participating in the hunger strike, and which individuals were participating of their own free will. This argument eroded the capacity of the four inmates at Pelican Bay, or other participants, to lead this movement by being willing to sacrifice their own lives. In this case, authorities used the coercion associated with prison gangs to suppress nonviolent action. Journalists also were prevented from contacting or visiting the strike leaders or other participants. The California Department of Corrections and Rehabilitation closed the entire prison system to reporters for the duration of the hunger strike. This functionally suppressed the ability of news coverage and knowledge of prisoner conditions to impact the voting public.[38] The hunger strikers called an end to the strike on September 5, a full nine weeks after its inception.

As of March 2014, dialogue continues regarding the demands of the collective, particularly around solitary confinement. The four prison gang leaders have now been dispersed into different locations and are still in SHU housing.

In the example of the Short Corridor Collective, prison gang leaders comprised a new set of protagonists. They became human rights activists, they rewrote networks of gang communication around human rights issues, they confronted challenges to eighth amendment rights, and they defied the notion of prisons as closed institutions. Theorists have long remarked on the prison as a total social institution.[39] But as institutions, prisons are decidedly porous. Communicable diseases spread between inside and outside, the suppression of communication only engenders increased prisoner ingenuity regarding communicative strategies, gangs shift easily from outside to inside and back again, and relationships between guards and prisoners vary from favors to outright corruption. According to Peter Wagner and Leah Sakala of the Prison Policy Initiative, "[T]he enormous churn in and out of our confinement facilities underscores how naive it is to conceive of prisons as separate from the rest of our society."[40] As the number of people with direct prison experience increases, so has public awareness of the harm, costs, and ineffectiveness of incarceration in the United States.

CONCLUSION

This chapter supports the notion that prisons do not function anywhere in the Americas. The United States is the richest country in the world with the highest per capita incarceration rate. The incarceration of 2.4 million people has created countless problems in communities as well as institutions. This massive system has shifted the allocation of resources away from education and economic development models that might have created greater inclusivity and overall prosperity.[41] Prisons fail to rehabilitate inmates and have high recidivism rates across the board.[42] Instead of rehabilitating people, prisons have systematically destroyed the lives of individuals and communities and have continued cycles of poverty and addiction. Prisons continue to be dominated by drug dealers and gangs, and lack of oversight contributes to cultures of violence on the part of guards and inmates alike. The prison system in the U.S. is unworkable and unsustainable.

In this chapter, we have examined the linkages between the war on drugs, race, and incarceration; the rise of prison gangs; and a prison-based human rights movement against solitary confinement. In conclusion, we set forth several broad-based policy recommendations.

These are as follows:

- Align the U.S. prison system with national and international human rights standards. This would mean, among other things, halting practices of long-term solitary confinement, ceasing to sentence juveniles as adults, and ceasing to sentence juveniles to life without the possibility of parole. We need to minimize practices of non-criminal immigration detention, and create special protections for minors, mentally ill persons, and elderly individuals. After much organizing and community struggle, the State of Illinois in 2012 closed its supermax prison at Tamms because politicians agreed its operation was ineffective, costly, and problematic from a human rights perspective.[43] Other states need to follow suit.

- Create systems of oversight for federal, immigration, state, county, and city jails and improve media access to houses of detention. Prisons should no longer be treated as closed institutions but as integrated parts of our broader society.

- Decrease the prison population. Overcrowding is a key cause of violence and disease, and the number of prisoners has no correlation to rates of crime.[44] Decreasing the prison population is critical both within individual institutions and as a whole. There should be a moratorium on the construction of new prisons.[45] Private prisons should be phased out at every level of incarceration. The United States has too many prisoners and prisons given the size of its population and needs to find other solutions to social problems besides incarceration.

- Allocate money for treatment, education, and rehabilitation. Instead of treating drug users as criminals, we should view them as people battling major addictions and attempt to re-route them to treatment and rehabilitation centers. Drug use should be treated as a public health issue as opposed to a security or law enforcement issue. We also need to restore access to public benefits, such as low-income housing and food stamps, for drug-related felons.

- Continue to debate the legalization of drugs.[46] Major political obstacles exist in terms of legalization of all drugs, although some politicians[47] favor an end to the war on drugs and the legalization of all drugs. The decriminalization of milder drugs such as marijuana would prove to be a major cost-saving mechanism as the U.S. has continued to arrest and jail marijuana users.[48] The complete legalization of marijuana would drastically cut costs and stop the destruction of the lives of many people who consume this drug recreationally and have been labeled as criminals. It would also undercut the power of prison gangs to capitalize on the political economy of drugs and to rely on the steady stream of drug-based inmates entering institutions.[49]

- Decouple prison policy from corporate and union interests. Prison guards unions in some states lobby for stronger sentences. Private prison corporations seek to create or continue poor policies, attempt to spread them to other countries, and cut corners because they benefit the owners.[50] Privately owned prisons have more incentives to continue high levels of incarceration in order to maximize profit. In addition, private prison corporations employ lobbyists that lobby on behalf of the prisons.

- Halt the use of the death penalty and all practices in which the state takes the lives of individuals, either through life sentences or through death sentences. Public support for the death penalty has eroded in recent years, partly because of multiple exonerations of innocent individuals.

Finally, we argue for the use of restorative rather than retributive justice methods, among youth and all individuals impacted by the criminal justice system. The foundational narrative of retributive punishment supports the outcomes described above despite multi-generational coalition building around mass incarceration. Only by finding alternative pathways that emphasize restorative techniques as opposed to continued exclusion, that prioritize educational reform both inside and outside communities, and that carve out pathways for individuals returning from prison can we begin to heal communities harmed by the pervasive damage of incarceration.

NOTES

1. See, for example, Eric Schlosser, "The Prison-Industrial Complex," *The Atlantic Monthly*, December 1,1998; Angela Y. Davis, "Masked Racism: Reflections on the Prison Industrial Complex," *Colorlines Magazine*, September 10, 1998; Marc Mauer, *Race to Incarcerate* (New York, N.Y.: The New Press, 1999).

2. See Bruce Western, *Punishment and Inequality* (New York: Russell Sage Foundation, 2006); Katherine Beckett and Theodore Sassoon, *The Politics of Injustice: Crime and Punishment in America* (Thousand Oaks, CA: Sage Publications, 2004).

3. Tom Dart, "Texas prisons violate international human rights standards, report says," *The Guardian*, April 23, 2014.

4. Although Michelle Alexander's recent book, *The New Jim Crow* (New York, N.Y., The New Press, 2010), gave widespread publicity to this argument, both Angela Davis and Loic Wacquant made similar arguments previously. See Angela Y. Davis, "From the Convict Lease System to the Super-Max Prison," *States of Confinement: Policing, Detention, and Prison* (New York: Palgrave Macmillan, 2002), and Loïc Wacquant "Deadly Symbiosis: When Ghetto and Prison Meet and Mesh," *Punishment and Society*, 3/1 (2001): 95–134.

5. Peter Wagner and Leah Sakala, "Mass Incarceration: The Whole Pie," Prison Policy Initiative, March 12, 2014, http://www.prisonpolicy.org/reports/pie.html

6. See, for example, Julia Sudbury, "A World Without Prisons: Resisting Militarism, Globalized Punishment, and Empire," *Social Justice*, 31, 1/2 (2004).

7. For more on the U.S.-led war on drugs, see Brian Loveman, ed. *Addicted to Failure: U.S. Security Policy in Latin America and the Andean Region* (Lanham, Maryland: Rowman & Littlefield Publishers, Inc, 2006); Bruce M. Bagley and William O. Walker III, eds. *Drug-Trafficking in the Americas* (Coral Gables, Fla: University of Miami, North-South Center, 1994); Russell Crandall, *Driven By Drugs* (Boulder, Colo.: Lynne Rienner, 2002).

8. Michelle Alexander, *The New Jim Crow: Mass Incarceration in the Age of Colorblindness* (New York, N.Y.: The New Press, 2010), 6; PEW Center on the States, *One in 100: Behind Bars in America 2008* (Washington, D.C.: Pew Center, Feb. 2008), 5; Marc Mauer, *Race to Incarcerate*, rev. ed. (New York. The New Press, 2006).

9. Bruce Bagley, "Drug Control Policies in the United States: What Works and What? Patterns, Prevalence, and Problems of Drug Use in the United States," in *Drug Trafficking, Organized Crime, and Violence in the Americas Today*, eds, Bruce M. Bagley and Jonathan D. Rosen (forthcoming, Gainesville: University Press of Florida, Bagley, 2015), 16; Alfonso Cuellar, "America's Forgotten War." *The Washington Post*. October 29, 2008.

10. Ted Galen Carpenter, *Bad Neighbor Policy: Washington's Futile War on Drugs in Latin America* (New York, N.Y.: Palgrave Macmillan, 2003), 20; see also Jeremiah Denton (R-AL) and his statements during the Senate Committee on the Judiciary, Subcommittee on Security and Terrorism, *DEA Oversight and Budget Authorization, Hearing,* 95 Cong, 2nd session, March 9, 1984, 6.

11. Ted Galen Carpenter, *Bad Neighbor Policy*, 20.

12. For more on the war on drugs and society, see Marc Mauer and Ryan King, *A 25-Year Quagmire: The "War on Drugs" and Its Impact on American Society* (Washington, D.C.: Sentencing Project, 2007);

13. See "Drug War Statistics," Drug Policy Alliance, http://www.drugpolicy.org/drug-war-statistics , accessed September 2014.

14. See Federal Bureau of Prisons, http://www.bop.gov/news/quick.jsp.

15. See "Mass Criminalization," Drug Policy Alliance, http://www.drugpolicy.org/mass-criminalization , accessed September 2014.

16. See David F. Musto, *American Disease: Origins of Narcotic Control,* 3rd edition (Oxford, Oxford University Press, 1999). The first edition was published in 1973; PL 98-473 (1984); see also *Public Law No. 255,* 82nd Congress, approved 2 No. 1951.

17. See *Cocaine and Crack Facts* (New York, N.Y.) Drug Policy Alliance. See http://www.drugpolicy.org/drug-facts/cocaine-and-crack-facts; "President Obama Signs Bill Reducing Cocaine Sentencing Disparity," ACLU, August 3, 2010. https://www.aclu.org/drug-law-reform/president-obama-signs-bill-reducing-cocaine-sentencing-disparity , accessed September 2014.

18. For more, see NAACP Criminal Justice Fact Sheet, at http://www.naacp.org/pages/criminal-justice-fact-sheet

19. Michelle Alexander, *The New Jim Crow: Mass Incarceration in the Age of Colorblindness,* 7, see footnote 9.

20. Ibid., 4; for more on this topic, see also Donald Braman, *Doing Time on the Outside: Incarceration and Family Life in Urban America* (Ann Arbor: University of Michigan Press, 2004), 3; Katherine Beckett and Theodore Sassoon, *The Politics of Injustice: Crime and Punishment in America* (Thousand Oaks, CA: Sage Publication, 2004).

21. For more on this, see Michelle Alexander, *The New Jim Crow;* see also, Marc Mauer, "The Hidden Problem of Time Served in Prison," *Social Research* 74, no. 2 (Summer 2007); Marc Mauer and Meda Chesney-Lind, eds. *Invisible Punishment: The Collateral Consequences of Mass Imprisonment* (New York: The New Press, 2002).

22. Bruce Bagley, *Tráfico de drogas y crimen organizado en América Latina y el Caribe en el Siglo XXI: retos de la democracia,* Ecuentro International Drogas, Usos, y Prevenciones, 16 al 18 de Mayo 2012. Quito, Ecuador. http://www.youtube.com/watch?v=sLbYHUs7F5c.

23. Michelle Alexander, *The New Jim Crow: Mass Incarceration in the Age of Colorblindness,* 13.

24. David Skarbek, "Putting the 'Con' into Constitutions: The Economics of Prison Gangs," *Journal of Law, Economics, and Organization,* 26/2 (2010):183–211; Susan A. Phillips, *Wallbangin: Graffiti and Gangs in L.A.* (Chicago: University of Chicago Press, 1999); and Tony Rafael, *The Mexican Mafia* (New York: Encounter Books, 2007).

25. See Michael Santos, a former prisoner, accounts many instances of abuse throughout his book. See Michael Santos, *Inside: Life Behind Bars in America* (New York, N.Y.: St. Martin's Press, 2007). The Vera Institute reports that in 2010 California prisons incurred 7 billion dollars in prison expenditures. See http://www.vera.org/files/price-of-prisons-california-fact-sheet.pdf.

26. Benjamin Wallace-Wells, "Is Solitary Confinement an Impossible Idea?" *New York Magazine,* Feb. 24, 2014. Retrieved from http://nymag.com/news/features/solitary-secure-housing-units-2014-2/. For more information on solitary confinement, see also "Buried Alive: Solitary Confinement in the U.S. Detention System," Physicians for Human Rights, 2014, https://s3.amazonaws.com/PHR_Reports/Solitary-Confinement-April-2013-full.pdf.

27. James Ridgeway and Jean Casella,"America's 10 Worst Prisons: Pelican Bay," *Mother Jones*, May 10, 2013. http://www.motherjones.com/politics/2013/05/10-worst-prisons-america-pelican-bay.

28. See, for example, Caroline Isaacs and Matthew Lowen, *Buried Alive: Solitary Confinement in Arizona's Prisons and Jails* (Tucson, AZ: American Friends Service Committee, 2007). Retrieved October 28, 2009 (http://www.nicic.org/Library/023058), or Sharon Shalev, *Supermax: Controlling Risk Through Solitary Confinement* (New York: Routledge, 2013).

29. Lorna Rhodes, *Total Confinement: Madness and Reason in the Maximum Security Prison* (Berkeley: University of California Press, 2004), 29.

30. Angela Browne, Alissa Cambier and Suzanne Agha, "Prisons Within Prisons: The Use of Segregation in the United States," *Federal Sentencing Reporter*, 24, No. 1, "Sentencing Within Sentencing" (October 2011).

31. Tracy Hresko, "In the Cellars of the Hollow Men: Use of Solitary Confinement in U.S. Prisons and Its Implications Under International Laws against Torture," Pace International Law Review 18 (2006). Available at http://digitalcommons.pace.edu/pilr/vol18/iis1/1.

32. John J. Gibbons, Nicholas de B. Katzenbach, "Confronting Confinement," A Report of the Commission on Safety and Abuse in America's Prisons, June 2006. Retrieved from http://www.vera.org/sites/default/files/resources/downloads/Confronting_Confinement.pdf.

33. "USA: The Edge of Endurance. Prison Conditions in California's Security Housing Units." *Amnesty International.* 2012. http://www.amnestyusa.org/sites/default/files/edgeofendurancecaliforniareport.pdf.

34. See again "Confronting Confinement."

35. Benjamin Wallace-Wells, "The Plot from Solitary," *New York Magazine*, February 26, 2014, http://nymag.com/news/features/solitary-secure-housing-units-2014-2/

36. Todd Ashker, Arturo Castellanos, Ronald Dewberry, aka SitawaAntonio Guillen, "June 20 Statement from Pelican Bay Short Corridor Collective!" Prisoner Hunger Strike Solidarity Website, June 21, 2013. http://prisonerhungerstrikesolidarity.wordpress.com/2013/06/21/june-20-statement-from-pelican-bay-short-corridor-collective/.

37. Don Thompson, "California Prisons Can Force-Feed Hunger Strikers," *Huffington Post*, August 20, 2013. http://www.huffingtonpost.com/2013/08/20/california-force-feeding_n_3784899.html.

38. Nancy Mullane, "Silenced: No Prison Access, No Prison Story," *The Life of the Law*, Website, October 4, 2013. Retrieved from http://www.lifeofthelaw.org/pelican-bay-prison-cell/.

39. See, for example, Erving Goffman, *Asylums: Essays on the Social Situation of Mental Patients and Other Inmates* (Garden City, NY: Anchor Books, 1961); or Michel Foucault, *Madness and Civilization: A History of Insanity in the Age of Reason* (New York: Pantheon, 1965).

40. Peter Wagner and Leah Sakala, "Mass Incarceration: The Whole Pie," Prison Policy Initiative, March 12, 2014, http://www.prisonpolicy.org/reports/pie.html

41. See, for example, Van Jones, *The Green Collar Economy: How One Solution Can Fix Our Two Biggest Problems* (New York: Harper One, 2008).

42. For more on this, see Jeremy Travis, *But They All Come Back: Facing the Challenges of Prisoner Reentry* (Washington, D.C.: Urban Institute, 2002). See also Bruce Western, *Punishment and Inequality in America* (New York: Russell Sage Foundation, 2006).

43. See ACLU, Tamms Prison Closing, at https://www.aclu.org/blog/tag/tamms-prison-closing

44. See, for example, Michelle Alexander, *The New Jim Crow: Mass Incarceration in the Age of Colorblindness* (New York, N.Y.: The New Press, 2010); Paul Butler, *Let's Get Free: A Hip Hop Theory of Justice* (New York, N.Y.: The New Press, 2010).

45. Angela Davis, Are Prisons Obsolete? (New York, N.Y.: Seven Stories Press, 2003).

46. It is important to note that various experts have been arguing for the legalization and end to the war on drugs for many years. For example, see Milton Friedman, "There's No Justice in the War on Drugs," in *The Drug Legalization Debate*, ed. James Inciardi (London: Sage, 1999), 77.

47. For more on Ron Paul and drug legalization, see https://www.youtube.com/watch?v=c4Eca-INIOw.1

48. The Drug Policy Alliance notes that in 2011 alone, 757,969 people were arrested for breaking the marijuana laws. In addition, the vast majority of people arrested—87 percent—were also charged and now have criminal records, continuing the cycle of delinquent behavior.

49. For more on legalization, see Ethan Nadelmann, "Addicted to Failure," *Foreign Policy*, no. 137 (Jul/Aug 2003), 94–94., Ethan Nadelmann/ *Uso y Prohibicion De Drogas*, 13-13; Andreas, Dead-End Drug Wars, 106–128; Andreas, *Free Market Reform and Drug Market Prohibition: US Policies at Cross-Purposes in Latin America*, 75–88.

50. For more on private prisons, see Byron E. Price, and Charles Morris. "Prison Privatization: The Many Facets of a Controversial Industry." Google Books. Accessed July 5, 2013.http://books.google.com/books?id=Diiv47MGmVMC&pg=RA1PA259&lpg=RA1PA259&dq=importing+and+exporting+inmates+prisns&source=bl&ots=ZoPjg0JYuD&sig=7L

THREE

The Penitentiary System in Mexico

An Institution Permeated by Corruption and Controlled by Organized Crime[1]

Roberto Zepeda Martínez

This chapter examines the penitentiary system in Mexico, focusing on its characteristics as well as the evolution of the prison population in Mexico. Plagued by corruption, Mexico's penitentiaries have become "schools" of crime which promote illegal activities. Most prisons are run by inmates who control illegal endeavors from behind bars, including extortion, kidnapping, and drug trafficking. Mexican prisons also face severe levels of overcrowding, and, as a result, inmates live in inhumane conditions. Escapes involving members of drug cartels have taken place in recent years, revealing the failures of the Mexican penitentiary system. A number of factors help to explain the aforementioned problems and challenges. In particular, the failed democratization process, the high levels of corruption in official institutions, and the lack of accountability and transparency explains the situation of Mexican prisons.

In the first section of this chapter, I conduct a brief analysis of the political and institutional context in Mexico in order to more effectively assess the characteristics and operation of the penitentiary system. Then, I analyze recent trends in terms of prison population in the world with a special emphasis on Latin America, concentrating on the case of Mexico. In this section, the main questions are as follows: what is the state of prisons in Mexico? What have been the prison population trends in Mexico over the last twenty years? What are the main characteristics of Mexi-

31

can prisons and the living conditions of inmates? What types of criminal activities occur in Mexican prisons?

MEXICO'S POLITICAL SYSTEM AND THE PENITENTIARY SYSTEM

Mexico is a country that has experienced an authoritarian political system for more than seventy years. From 1929 to 2000, Mexico was ruled by a party-state system with a strong presidency, which exerted authoritarian control over social sectors. Mexico's political system emerged after the Mexican revolution (1910–1920) but more clearly since the 1930s and continued to dominate during the past century. Since the late 1980s, political pressure intensified and resulted in the democratization of the country in 2000[2] when the PRI (*Partido Revolucionario Institucional*, Institutional Revolutionary Party) was defeated in the presidential elections and was removed from the highest political position in the country. It should be noted, however, that some studies suggest that Mexico had effectively become democratic with the election of Ernesto Zedillo in 1994.[3]

In the first decade of the twenty-first century, Mexico had a political regime with three dominant political parties: the PRI, PAN (*Partido Acción Nacional*, The National Action Party), and PRD (*Partido de la Revolución Democrática*, The Party of the Democratic Revolution), a significant departure from the PRI-dominated single-party regime that prevailed between 1929 and 2000. The PAN, a conservative right-wing party, represented the opposition since the late 1930s. In the 2000 elections, the PAN candidate Vicente Fox won the presidency of the republic, ending seventy-one years of the PRI's dominance of Mexican politics.

During the 2000s, many analysts observed that significant components of the former PRI authoritarian regime still prevailed in the country. Although Mexico became democratic in 2000, authoritarian features of the political regime still persisted at the regional level.[4] Moreover, the levels of insecurity increased significantly in the democratic period of 2000–2012, a period in which the PAN governed Mexico with the Vicente Fox (2000–2006) and Felipe Calderón administrations (2006–2012). Luis Astorga defines this paradox, stating that despite being governed by the PRI for so many years, Mexico was more secure. In reality, the election of the PAN in 2000 can best be described as a "bumpy" democratic transition path and, as a result, insecurity increased.[5]

Mexico in the twenty-first century remains a country with severe problems in the public realm and many authoritarian elements continue to exist even within the democratic political system. Democracy in Mexico is limited to the electoral system but it must expand to the rest of the public institutions such as the Congress, the Judiciary, and various security-related institutions, mainly the police, the Office of the Mexican Attorney General (PGR in its Spanish initials) and the military. In order to do so, key institutions have to be reformed to increase transparency and promote accountability in order to combat the high levels of corruption and impunity. The penitentiary system is among the institutions that must be reformed, since, as I will demonstrate below, prisons are among the most corrupt institutions in the country.

Paradoxically, Mexico has become more corrupt during the democratic era, from 2000 to 2012 and drug cartels have increased their leverage. According to Transparency International (TI),[6] in 2013 Mexico was ranked 105 out of 175 countries in terms of corruption, where the higher the position, the more corrupt. If we compare this data with ten years ago, we find that Mexico has become more corrupt over the years; in 2002, for example, Mexico occupied the 57th position in this ranking, which means that the levels of corruption have drastically increased from 2002 to 2013. The TI index reveals that the most corrupt institutions in Mexico were political parties, the police, public officials, public servants, the legislative power, and the judiciary. Mexico, therefore, is among the most corrupt countries in the world. Corruption helps strengthen organized crime and weakens democratic governance. Public institutions in charge of providing security to Mexican citizens are corrupted by criminal organizations.

Bruce Bagley[7] points out that during the democratic era, Mexico has not been able to implement a reform of the penitentiary system, the police institutions, and the judiciary. He explains that many drug traffickers who have been captured and imprisoned continue leading drug trafficking operations from prisons.[8] Bagley summarizes the problem, stating that "democratization presents opportunities for organized crime, as criminal groups take advantage of the weakness of public institutions in Mexico and the absence of new institutions."[9] In other words, organized crime benefits from the weakness of public institutions in Mexico, among them the penitentiary system, to continue their criminal activities and enhance their power.

Corruption is one of the pernicious characteristics of public institutions in Mexico. Since 2006, the Mexican government has launched a "war on drugs" but it has failed so far since crucial institutions, such as the police and security-related official institutions, are plagued by corruption. Felipe Calderón (2006–2012) "stepped up the offensive against organized crime when he took office in late 2006, with military and police crackdowns that resulted in thousands of arrests but no new prisons;" as a result, "many of Mexico's facilities became overcrowded, and inmates accused of drug crimes were mixed with locals accused of petty crimes."[10]

Despite the fact that numerous criminals have been captured, they continue their criminal operations from prisons as a result of tolerance and complicity on the part of authorities operating the institutions. In this way, many criminals operate with impunity from prisons and control

penitentiaries charging fees and taxing inmates for certain basic necessities, such as food, shelter, and water. The drug war in Mexico has
spread to prisons, where convicts from drug cartels are fighting for control of penitentiary centers. In addition, other characteristics of the prisons such as overcrowding and corruption among public officials make
Mexican prisons hotbeds of organized crime and violence in the country. [11]

MEXICAN PRISON POPULATIONS IN THE INTERNATIONAL CONTEXT

Before analyzing the conditions and features of prisons in Mexico, it is
important to explore the state of prisons in the world, considering the
countries with large prison populations (both in absolute numbers and
per capita), as well as the major trends in the last decades, to see where
Mexico ranks in terms of these various indicators. The United Nations
Office on Drugs and Crime defines prisons, penal institutions or correctional institutions as all public and privately financed institutions where
persons are deprived of their liberty. These institutions comprise penal,
correctional, and psychiatric facilities under the prison administration. [12]

Prison populations grew in 78 percent in countries worldwide between 2008 and 2011, and in 71 percent in countries in the previous two
years. [13] The number of people in prisons has increased during the last ten
years in most countries in the world, with a rise of 60 to 75 percent
worldwide. There are a significant number of countries with very high
proportions of people detained pending trial, which is a major cause of
overcrowding in prisons. More than half of the prison population is in
pretrial detention in one-third of countries in Africa and the Americas
(for which data is available) and the greatest levels of overcrowding also
are observed in countries in these regions. [14]

According to recent data provided by the International Centre for
Prison Studies, more than 10.1 million people are imprisoned in the entire
world. [15] Around half of the penitentiary populations are located within
four countries: the United States, China, Russia, and Brazil. The United
States has 2,239,751 prisoners, by far the highest number in this regard;
China occupies the second position with 1,640,000 prisoners, while Russia has 682,900. Finally, Brazil incarcerates 548,003 people. Together,
these four countries have around 50 percent of the world's prison population but only 28 percent of the world's population. Other countries with
large populations, however, do not incarcerate such large percentages of
their societies. India, for instance, has one of the largest populations in
the world, but it is not among the countries with the most number of
prisoners. In terms of population, Mexico is the eleventh biggest country
in the world, and it has 246,226 prisoners (see Table 3.1).

On the other hand, the average prison population rate in the world is 146 per each 100,000 inhabitants. The United States has the highest rate in this regard with 716 prisoners per 100,000 inhabitants. Other countries with small populations have very high prison population rates: St. Kitts and Nevis (714), Seychelles (709), Virgin Islands (709), Cuba (510), Rwanda (492), Anguilla (United Kingdom) (487), Russia (477), and others (see Table 1). Mexico ranks 67 as it has 210 prisoners per 100,000 inhabitants, according to data from 2013.[16]

Overcrowded prisons (prisons which exceed their capacity limits) are a defining characteristic of most penitentiary systems worldwide. Only 88 out of 194 countries experience less than 100 percent overcrowding in the prison system; 106 countries are experiencing overcrowding between 100 and 200 percent. Haiti tops the list at 417 percent of its occupancy capacity. Other countries with the highest occupancy rates in the world are El Salvador (325 percent), Benin (307 percent), Philippines (300 percent), Venezuela (270 percent), Bolivia (270 percent), Sudan (255 percent), and Guatemala (252 percent). Most of these countries are in Latin America, which means that prison overcrowding is one of the main characteristics of the region (Table 1). In this category, Mexico occupies the 72th position in the world with an occupancy rate of 123.1 percent of its intended capacity. Thus, penitentiary centers in Mexico have a capacity for

Table 3.1. Total Prison Population, Population per 100,000 Inhabitants; Selected Countries, 2013

Position world ranking	Country	Prison population: total numbers	Prison population per each 100,000 inhabitants
1	United States	2,239,751	716
2	China	1,640,000	121
3	Russia	682,900	477
4	Brazil	548,003	274
5	India	372,296	30
6	Thailand	279,854	398
7	Mexico	246,226	210
8	Iran	217,000	284
9	South Africa	156,370	294
10	Indonesia	144,332	59

Source: Prepared by the author with data from International Centre for Prison Studies, http://www.prisonstudies.org, accessed on September 4, 2013.

196,742 people but their prison population is actually 244,960, which means that prisons are overpopulated by 48,218 inmates.[17]

Over the last fifteen years, most OECD countries have experienced a continuous rise in prison population rates. On average, across the thirty OECD countries, this rate has increased from a level of 100 persons per 100,000 of the total population in the early 1990s to 140 persons per 100,000 in the late 2000s. This rate is three to four times higher than the second highest OECD country (Poland) and has increased rapidly. The increase in the prison population extends to most other OECD countries. Since 1992, the prison population rate has more than doubled in the Netherlands, Mexico, and Turkey, while it declined in Canada, Denmark, Hungary, Korea, and Switzerland.[18] In several countries, the rapid rise in the prison population has stretched beyond the receptive capacity of existing institutions; occupancy levels are above 100 percent in more than half of OECD countries, and above 125 percent in Greece, Mexico, and Spain.[19]

In Latin America, the countries with the largest prison populations per 100,000 inhabitants were Belize, El Salvador, Panama, Costa Rica, Uruguay, and Brazil. The countries with the fewest number of people in prison as a percentage of the total population in Latin America are Guatemala, Paraguay, Bolivia, and Argentina. In contrast, considering the population confined in penitentiary centers, the countries with more prisoners are Brazil (548,003), Mexico (246,226), Colombia (118,201), Peru (61,390), Argentina (60,789), Cuba (57,337), Venezuela (48,262), and Chile (46,718).[20]

THE PENITENTIARY SYSTEM IN MEXICO

The penitentiary system in Mexico is a crucial part of the states' public policies designed to combat crime. The configuration of this system is defined in article 18 of the Mexican constitution, which states: "Prisons shall be organized on the basis of the respect for human rights, as well as access to work, training programs, education, health and sports, in order to rehabilitate inmates, advising him/her not to transgress again and explaining to him/her the benefits of complying with the law. Women and men shall be imprisoned in separate places."[21]

This article, which was reformed in 2011, emphasizes that human rights should be the key concept of the penitentiary system.[22] Nevertheless, the reality is quite the contrary, as Mexican prisons have never fulfilled these objectives, which are clearly defined in the constitution.

According to many experts, penitentiaries in Mexico are permeated by corruption as similar to many other public institutions in Mexico, including the police forces. The war on drugs in Mexico has resulted in the arrest and incarceration of many criminals, but the government has failed

Table 3.2.   Prison Population Rates, per 100,000 Inhabitants in Latin America, 2013

Country	Prison population per 100,000 inhabitants	Total prison population
Belize	476	1,562
El Salvador	422	26,568
Panamá	404	15,126
Costa Rica	314	14,963
Uruguay	282	9,524
Brazil	274	548,003
French Guyana	267	694
Chile	267	46,718
Guyana	260	1,962
Colombia	245	118,201
Mexico	210	246,226
Peru	202	61,390
Suriname	191	994
Venezuela	161	48,262
Honduras	151	12,263
Ecuador	149	21,080
Nicaragua	148	9,168
Argentina	147	60,789
Bolivia	130	14,770
Paraguay	115	7,901
Guatemala	105	16,336

Source: Prepared by the author with data from the International Centre for Prison Studies, September 2013.

to build more penitentiary centers in order to keep up with rising rates of incarceration. Roth argues: "Mexico's prison system has not been able to shake its well-earned reputation for corruption, with most accounts indicating guards and wardens are susceptible to bribery."[23] Furthermore, most prisons are overpopulated and the living conditions for inmates are unhealthy. Rather than a place for reforming criminals, these centers are environments where criminal culture is reproduced.

Consequently, the central objective of imprisonment as a public policy is hardly ever achieved as convicts are enclosed within an environment where they continue to participate in criminal activities, often in order to survive. In fact, prisons have become "schools of crime" in Mexico according to experts such as Luis Astorga.[24] Furthermore, organized crime controls the majority of the prisons in the country. Around 60 percent of prisons in the country are controlled by inmates, according to a recent report of the National Commission of Human Rights in Mexico.[25] Criminals, mainly kidnappers, extortionists, drug dealers, among others, operate from their prisons with wide impunity and tolerance from the official authorities. A recent article by *The Economist* describes the situation in Mexican prisons as follows:

> In Mexico prisoners do what they please in some jails run by local governments. Last year police raided a prison in Acapulco to find 100 fighting roosters, nineteen prostitutes and two peacocks on the premises. A few months earlier prisoners in a Sonora jail were found to be running a raffle for a luxury cell that they had equipped with air conditioning and a DVD player. In 2010 it emerged that guards at a jail in Durango had allowed prisoners out at night to commit contract killings.[26]

The ability for inmates' relatives to visit penitentiary centers and to access basic needs such as food, furniture, clothes, and so on, are strictly controlled by prison authorities and depends on the amount of money paid to them. The average Mexican prisoner lives in hellish conditions because as many as twenty people often live in a cell designed for eight people. Very few prisoners, such as powerful criminals like drug lords, live in single well-equipped cells with electronic devices, mobile phones, and access to restaurant services.

To say the least, prisons fail to rehabilitate criminals, instead fostering such criminal activities and promoting corruption. Mexico simply does not have the necessary resources to continue building prisons. Convicted criminals enter the prisons and are housed in terrible conditions with some of the most dangerous and violent people in Mexico. The prison system in Mexico helps embolden criminals and has been an utter failure in terms of rehabilitation.[27]

In February 2012, a riot in a northern Mexican prison located in Apodaca, Nuevo León, left forty-four people dead, "providing yet another sign of the violence and crowding overwhelming Latin American prisons."[28] Unfortunately, deadly rioting is commonplace in Mexican and Central American prisons as a drug war rages among criminal groups and government forces, and the number of Mexican prisons have continued to proliferate filling prisons and jails well beyond their capacities.[29]

Moreover, diverse criminal activities are conducted from prisons, especially by telephone and computer communication. An increasingly common crime committed by prisoners is extortion by mobile telephones. According to INEGI, an official institution, around 4.4 million extortions occurred in 2011 alone, but independent organizations claim that citizens report only 3 out of 100 cases of extortion.[30] Mexico City is where most of the extortion via telephone calls occurs. The official Security Council of Mexico City registers around 10,000 phone extortions per month. In the last four years, approximately 56,000 telephone numbers of extortionists have been detected, most of them from stolen devices; approximately 80 percent of these extortion telephone calls come from prisons, according to civil organizations such as the Citizens Council of Mexico City (in Spanish the *Consejo Ciudadano del DF*) and Common Cause (*Causa en Común*).[31] The use of mobile phones can be prevented in prisons by the installation of signal blockers.[32] However, there has not been any program to install this kind of equipment in Mexican prisons by the relevant authorities.

Another major limitation of the penitentiary system has been the lack of sufficient resources necessary to reform the system. The overcrowding in prisons is the result of the relatively small number of penitentiary centers in the country, especially at the local and state levels. The federal prisons have received more official resources and training in the last years, but state prisons face multiple challenges. According to a recent report,[33] in the states of Mexico, the average cost of housing prisoners is around 11 U.S. dollars per inmate (137 Mexican pesos) per day.

In Mexico, the penitentiary system consists of different kinds of correctional institutions. Like the police and other security-related institutions, federal, state, and municipal governments manage Mexican prisons. The governmental institution in charge of the federal penitentiary system in Mexico is the Ministry of the Interior (*Secretaría de Gobernación*), which controls the administration, training, and maintenance of prisons and prison staff. The governments of the states run the local prisons, which constitute the bulk of such institutions in the country. The state governments control 72 percent of the prisons in Mexico; the municipal governments run 22 percent; the Mexican City government controls 3 percent of prisons; while the federal government only controls 4 percent of all prisons in the country.

By mid-2013, there were 416 penitentiary centers in Mexico, which are administered by regional authorities. The federal government managed fifteen prisons centers located in different states, which housed 24,811 prisoners charged with federal crimes. State governments in Mexico also administer their own prisons; by 2013, there were a total of 299 prisons. The largest penitentiary centers are located in Mexico City, which has eleven prisons. Municipal governments administer ninety-one prisons. Seven Mexican states are home to 52 percent of the prison population in the country: Federal District, State of Mexico, Baja California, Jalisco, Sonora, Nuevo León, and Puebla.[34]

Overall, the prison population in Mexico is 95 percent male and only 5 percent female. Most of the prison population, around 80 percent, is in prison for committing local crimes, while 20 percent are incarcerated for federal crimes. Not all the prisoners have received a sentence. In fact, around 42 percent of them are still awaiting sentencing, while 58 percent have been found guilty and are currently serving their sentence.

The federal government created 800 prison spaces in the penitentiary system during the first half of the 1990s. In 1991, Mexico opened its first maximum-security prison at *Almoloya de Juárez*. Other prisons sent major drug traffickers to this modern facility, where the prison's 408 cells were always under surveillance thanks to closed-circuit television and other security devices.[35] In March 2005, an attempt was made to control Mexican prison gangs in a sweep through the Nuevo Laredo Penitentiary. Soldiers found cell phones, a pool table, a disco sound system, and firearms including an AK-47. A number of former drug kingpins lived in luxury at this institution.[36]

THE EVOLUTION OF THE PRISON POPULATION IN MEXICO

From 1995 to 2013, a notable 162 percent increase in the prison population occurred in Mexico from 93,574 in 1995 to 244,960 in 2013. The number of arrested criminals has more than doubled, which had never occurred before over similar time periods. Furthermore, in 2006, Mexico had a rate of 245 prisoners per each 100,000 inhabitants, which was one of the highest in Latin America. Compare such statistics to 1996, when Mexico experienced 102 prisoners per 100,000 inhabitants. Said differently, each night around a quarter of a million people sleep crowded in the prisons.[37] Indeed, if we consider the conditions of some prisons located in Mexico City, we find they are the most crowded in all of Latin America.[38]

The number of people residing in prison who have not been sentenced more than doubled in the last decade from 47,874 prisoners in 1996 to approximately 87,500 in 2007. In December 2011, the prison population without a sentence increased to 99,730.[39] By May 2013, the number of prisoners awaiting sentencing in Mexico was around 103,000 prisoners, which is approximately 42 percent of the total imprisoned population in the country.[40]

As previously mentioned, over the 1980s and 1990s, Mexico experienced a dual transition toward a political democratic system and a neoliberal economic model. These transitions, especially the political transition, have failed to create a consolidated democracy with strong institutions. In contrast, public security institutions, such as the penitentiary system, continue to be plagued by major problems and have not been reformed. Recently, President Peña Nieto (2012-2018) vowed to reform the prison system in order to improve the conditions of the prisoners. In August 2013, Peña Nieto outlined his strategy on security and one of the main goals was the transformation of the penitentiary system. He argued that the prison system must be improved in order to effectively rehabilitate prisoners and help them become productive members of society after serving their sentences. He supported the implementation of policies to control penitentiary centers to fulfill these objectives and avoid the vicious cycle or revolving doors from prison to the streets and back to prison. However, after one year of his administration, Peña Nieto has relegated the reforms of the penitentiary system, as other priorities such as energy and education reforms have been more important.

CRIMES OF SENTENCED PRISONERS

Regarding criminal offenses, it is pertinent to highlight the number of offenses in the federal realm. In 2004, there were a reported 81,539 criminal offenses, while in 2008, the number increased to 136,091. By 2009, the number of criminal offenses recorded was 131,582. In Mexico, individuals cannot be charged with drug trafficking, but they are charged with what is referred to as "criminal offenses against health."[41] In addition, people who consume drugs also can be charged with criminal offenses against health. From 2004 to 2008, these offenses increased by 120 percent (to 34,689).[42]

In 2004, criminal offenses against health represented 35 percent of the total number of offenses. By 2008, this percentage increased to 55 percent of the total number of transgressions registered. In 2009, criminal offenses against health represented nearly 50 percent of the total number of federal criminal transgressions. Therefore, these criminal offenses increased almost three times more than the rest of the federal offenses in the period. The figures are significant if we consider that there are hun-

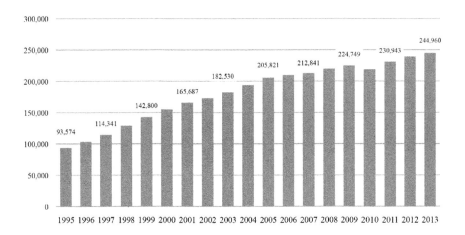

Figure 3.1. Prison Population in Mexico (1995–2013). Source: prepared by the author with data from Peña Nieto, 2013.

Table 3.3.   Table 3.3. Prison Capacity and Population in Mexico, 1995-2013.

Year	Capacity	Population	Overcrowding		Local Jurisdiction	Federal Jurisdiction
1995	91,422	93,574	2,152	2%	70,288	23,286
1996	97,565	103,262	5,697	6%	76,921	26,341
1997	99,858	114,341	14,483	15%	85,900	28,441
1998	103,916	128,902	24,986	24%	97,050	31,852
1999	108,808	142,800	33,992	31%	105,681	37,119
2000	121,135	154,765	33,630	28%	113,118	41,647
2001	134,567	165,687	31,120	23%	121,093	44,594
2002	140,415	172,888	32,473	23%	125,112	47,776
2003	147,809	182,530	34,721	23%	133,370	49,160
2004	154,825	193,889	39,064	25%	144,271	49,618
2005	159,628	205,821	46,193	29%	154,350	51,471
2006	164,929	210,140	45,211	27%	160,923	49,217
2007	165,970	212,841	46,871	28%	164,275	48,566
2008	171,437	219,754	48,317	28%	169,836	49,918
2009	173,060	224,749	51,689	30%	173,380	51,369
2010	181,876	219,027	37,151	20%	175,405	43,622
2011	187,752	230,943	43,191	23%	183,127	47,427
2012	194,062	239,089	45,027	23%	189,662	49,427
2013	200,100	244,960	44,860	22%	195,457	49,503

Source: prepared by the author with data from Peña Nieto, 2013.

dreds of different federal offenses. In addition, more than 60 percent of the offenses against health were related to drug possession. [43]

On the other hand, according to a 2012 Survey conducted by the *Centro de Investigación y Docencia Económicas* (CIDE), the most frequent type of crime committed by prisoners in the federal penitentiary system are those related to "criminal offenses against health." Following CIDE's survey, after the criminal offenses against health, the crimes for which most inmates were sentenced were in order of relevance: crimes related to weapons, organized crime, and robbery. In the case of male prisoners, 57.6 percent were sentenced and subsequently incarcerated for crimes against health whereas in the case of female prisoners, the number was 80 percent. The other crimes were as follows: crimes related to weapons, 27 percent of male and 5.3 percent of female prisoners; organized crime, 16 percent of male and 4.2 percent of female prisoners; robbery, 13.4 percent of male and 4.2 percent of female prisoners; homicide, 13.5 percent of

Table 3.4. Total Number of Prisoners in Mexico: On-Trial and Sentenced; Total, Local and Federal Jurisdictions, 2013

	Sentenced	On-trial	Total	Percent
Total Prison Population	141,663	103,297	244,960	100
Local Prison Population	117,778	77,679	195,457	80
Federal Prison Population	23,885	25,618	49,503	20

Source: prepared by the author with data from the *Comisión Nacional de Seguridad* (May 2013).

male and 2.1 percent of female prisoners; kidnapping, 6.5 percent of male and 4.2 percent of female prisoners (see Table 3.6).

CHARACTERISTICS OF MEXICAN PRISONS

In 2011, the National Commission of Human Rights (*Comisión Nacional de los Derechos Humanos, CNDH*) conducted field research in 100 penitentiary centers and applied 29,000 surveys among the prison populations. The outcomes revealed the major structural inadequacies and terrible living conditions of prisoners in Mexico. Around 60 percent of all the prisons visited in Mexico are self-governed and controlled by organized criminal networks as opposed to being governed by prison guards and authorities.[44] In these cases, organized crime members control the internal security of prisons, as well as the activities and services performed within prisons. This report highlights, among others, the following concluding points:

- Overcrowding in a large number of prisons visited.
- The conditions of penitentiary centers and the hygiene in dorms, kitchen, and dining rooms are deficient.
- Low control by the official authorities of some prison centers, regarding security in diverse activities performed within these centers (sports, culture, etc), as well as services (light, water, food, among others), which generates self-government or co-government.
- The presence of tools and illegal drugs.
- There is not any scheme for preventing addiction and voluntary rehabilitation.

A recent 2013 field study of the penitentiary system report reveals that the increase of prisoners in recent years can be explained by various factors, among them: campaigns to combat organized crime during the Calderón administration; the rise in the number of crimes punishable by

Table 3.5.   Assessment of Prisoners and Penitentiary Centers for Criminal Offenses of Local Jurisdiction in Mexico, 2011. Sorted according to type of offense

Robbery (Theft)	70,623
Lesions	12,125
Homicides	8,744
Domestic Violence	4,668
Violation	4,636
Property Damages	4,290
Fraud	3,552
Sexual Abuse	2,522
Kidnapping	2,079
Plunder	1,825
House Invasions	1,478
Extortion	1,112
Drug Dealing	926
Threats	805
Human trafficking	293
Total	115,817

Source: prepared by the autor with data from INEGI (2012) *Centro Nacional de Gobierno, Seguridad Pública y Sistema Penitenciario Estatales 2012.*

prison sentences; the excessive use of preventive detainment, and the inability of inmates to afford the bail required for release.[45]

As a result of prison overcrowding, levels of insecurity are very high and many prison staff members work in extremely dangerous and volatile conditions. Fights, homicides, escapes, suicides, hunger strikes, self-mutilation, attempted escapes, and rape are some of the problems in Mexican prisons. At the national level, there is an average of one prison guard per seventy-three inmates, revealing that prison guards are extremely outnumbered by dangerous, angry, and volatile inmates. From 2009 to 2012, 365 staff members, such as custodians, security managers, and directors have been put on trial as a result of investigations of prison escapes during their tenure. "In Mexico prison deaths have risen in tandem with the expansion of organized crime, from 15 in 2007 to 71 in 2011 and more than 80 in the first three months of 2013," according to Eduardo Guerrero.[46]

In 2011, the Calderón administration requested that the American Correctional Association (ACA), which oversees the penitentiary system in the United States, certify both the state and federal penitentiary centers

Table 3.6.   Main Criminal Offenses of Prisoners of Federal Jurisdiction, Classified by offense (2012)

Criminal offenses	Total (percent)	Males	Females
Criminal offenses against health	60.2	57.6	80.0
Criminal offenses related with guns	24.5	27.0	5.3
Robbery, scam and peculation	14.6	15.2	10.5
Organized delinquency	14.6	16.0	4.20
Intentional homicide, manslaughter	12.2	13.5	2.1
Kidnapping, illegal deprivation of liberty	6.2	6.5	4.2

Source: CIDE (2012), *Primera Encuesta en Centros Penitenciarios Federales.*

in Mexico, as part of the Mérida Initiative;[47] after the evaluation, only 13 out of the 431 regional and federal prisons in the country met international standards. In 2012, the ACA certified to four federal prisons, which successfully met all the established requirements. Such centers were *El Altiplano*, in the state of Mexico, *El Noroeste* in Tamaulipas, and *El Rincon* in Nayarit. By September 2013, nine penal centers have been certified. Four of them are federal prisons (*Huimanguillo*, Tabasco; *Noroeste*, Durango; *Norponiente*, Sinaloa, and *Oriente*, Veracruz) and five of them are state prisons (four in Chihuahua and on in Baja California). Similarly, the National Academy of Penitentiary Administration (*Academia Nacional de Administración Penitenciaria*), an agency of the Ministry of the Interior, where staff of penitentiary centers are trained, was also certified.

As a result of the Mérida Initiative, "secure Federal prisons have increased from 5 to 14, and their quality has increased even more."[48] However, the majority of prisons in Mexico, which are administered by the state governments, do not fulfill the minimum requirements for their operation. The resources from the Mérida Initiative must combat corruption and inefficiency in local prisons. Seelke and Finklea observe that "while U.S. assistance has helped federal prisons expand and improve, thousands of federal prisoners are still being housed in state prisons that are overcrowded and often extremely insecure."[49]

A 2013 report by the U.S. embassy in Mexico pointed out that the government of the United States has provided special equipment to Mexico to identify inmates from the federal and state prisons. The objective is the integration of a modern database of the prison population, which include data such as fingerprints and genetic information. Since 2009, the U.S. government has sought to improve Mexican prisons by allocating resources from the Mérida Initiative which have included the training for more than 1,500 public servants of the penitentiary system in Mexico. [50]

PRISON BREAKS AND RIOTS

Violence and prison escapes have increased in Mexico's prisons. In 2013, The National Human Rights Commission found that the number of riots, fights, escapes, and homicides has increased from 2011 to 2012. Over this period, 73 acts of violence occurred that left 154 inmates dead and 103 wounded. In addition, 261 inmates escaped. This commission's report detected that in "49 prisons, inmates have 'privileged areas' that house banned substances and objects as well as prostitution" and "at least 52 prisons are overpopulated." [51]

Prison breaks have become increasingly common practice in Mexico in the last years. The first major prison escape occurred in the 1970s when Alberto Sicilia, the major drug trafficker in Mexico and the United States, escaped from the Lecumberri prison in Mexico City through a 492 ft. tunnel which connected to a house next to the prison. However, this tendency has continued with the escape of Joaquín "El Chapo" Guzmán, the notorious leader of the Sinaloa Cartel, who was considered the most important drug lord in the world at that time. On January 19, 2001, "El Chapo" Guzmán exited through the main door of the federal penitentiary center "Puente Grande" located in Jalisco, paradoxically considered as a prison of maximum security in the country with closed-circuit television devices. About El Chapo's escaping from prison, Watt and Zepeda (2012) observe:

> His 'escape,' one month after the PAN took power, was facilitated (. . .) by a twenty million dollar bribe offered to Vicente Fox when he was governor of the state of Guanajuato. For narcotraffickers, (. . .), the transition to "democracy" and the supposed political disagreements between the two parties made little difference, other than the evident opportunities to increase and expand their activities which the *cambio* presented. It allowed *El Chapo* Guzmán to become the world's most powerful trafficker and a number of cartels to control the trade in narcotics, which has become one of the economy's principal sources of revenue. Perhaps the most significant change in narcotrafficking as the new millennium began was that the cartels now started to treat members of the army, police forces, bankers and political officials as their employees, a reversal of the relationship under the previous PRI rule and a turnaround which spelt the end of the cozy arrangements of the *plaza* system. [52]

Other relevant cases include important drug traffickers and murderers who have escaped from Mexican prisons. From 2000 to 2012, many escapes from prisons in Mexico occurred, most of which were prisoners arrested and incarcerated for drug trafficking-related offenses. Between 2006 and 2012, all prison breaks occurred at the state and local level as opposed to the federal level.[53] The total number of prison breaks in this period was 451, of which 1,512 prisoners escaped from different federal, state and municipal penitentiary centers in the country; in the same way, a significant number of riots, fights, homicides, and suicides occurred in the same period.[54]

The provincial states with more prison escapes between 2000 and 2011 also were regions with high levels of organized criminal activity. For instance, Tamaulipas in the northeast of the country registered sixty-three escapes; Sinaloa, fifty-two; Chihuahua and Sonora recorded thirty-three each; as well as Michoacán with twenty-two and Zacatecas with twenty-one. Regarding the number of prisoners that have escaped from prison, Tamaulipas is the state with the most fugitives (325) from 2000 to 2012, followed by 109 in Tabasco, 134 in Sinaloa, 111 in Zacatecas, 101 in Quintana Roo, 89 in Chihuahua, and 73 in Michoacán.[55] In recent years, important prison breaks occurred in various Mexican prisons: the biggest escape occurred in December 2010, when 141 prisoners escaped from a penitentiary center in Nuevo Laredo, a city in the northern border of Mexico in the state of Tamaulipas. In July 2011, a fight among inmates and prison guards took place in the prison of Nuevo Laredo in which 59 prisoners escaped. On September 17, 2012, around 130 inmates exited through a tunnel in a prison at Piedras Negras, Coahuila, close to the border with the United States.[56]

In this manner, prison breaks have become routine in Mexican prisons, demonstrating the weakness of this crucial institution and the inability of the prisons to control inmates even while behind bars. If the Mexican government does not provide more resources and improve security within the prisons, then illegal activities such as drug trafficking and other forms of organized crime will continue and prisons will remain extremely corrupt institutions that fail to achieve their basic goals: punishing and rehabilitating offenders.

CONCLUSIONS

Despite the fact that Mexico has advanced toward a democratic system, it has failed to create robust institutions. Public security institutions in Mexico are weak as a result of chronic problems like corruption and impunity inherited from an authoritarian political system. Accordingly, official institutions need to be reformed introducing schemes of accountability and transparency to reduce corruption and impunity. The penitentiary system needs to fulfill its function to effectively rehabilitate convicts and prepare them for their reinsertion into society.

With respect to overcrowding, most of the problems with this issue occurred in the prisons administered by the state governments. It is evident that these types of prisons need more resources to build new facilities. Otherwise, overcrowding will continue in local prisons as many criminals committing federal crimes are housed in local prisons. On the other hand, most of the funds of the Mérida Initiative since 2008 have been allocated to help federal penitentiary centers, which as we have seen, represent only 4 percent of the total penitentiary centers in Mexico as opposed to state prisons, which account for 72 percent of total prisons. Federal prisons account for 20 percent of the prison population in Mexico while local prisons house 80 percent of the total number of prisoners.

Regarding the control and security of prisons, there has been a consolidation of criminal organizations and the expansion of their influence; for example, more than 60 percent of the penitentiary centers in Mexico are controlled by organized crime, meaning prisoners continue their criminal activities from prisons, such as drug trafficking, extortion, and kidnapping. The drug war in Mexico has extended to prisons, where convicts from drug cartels are fighting for the control of penitentiary centers. Furthermore, other characteristics of the prisons such as corruption among public officials, make the Mexican prisons the breeding ground of the criminal world in the country.

NOTES

1. I appreciate the help and contribution of Jonathan D. Rosen in the composition of this chapter.
2. Frances Hagopian and Scott Mainwaring (eds.), *The Third Wave of Democratization in Latin America: Advances and Setbacks* (Cambridge University Press, 2005).
3. United Nations Development Programme (UNDP). *Democracy in Latin America. Towards a Citizens' Democracy*, Volume 2, Alfaguara, 2004.
4. Kevin J. Middlebrook, (ed.), *Dilemmas of Political Change in Mexico* (London: University of London, 2004).
5. Luis Astorga, "Drogas = Violencia / no igual a Fortalecimiento de las Instituciones", *Foro Internacional: Drogas. Un balance a un siglo de su prohibición*, México: México Unido contra la Delincuencia, February 14, 2012. Available on line: http://www.mucd.org.mx/forodrogas/luis-astorga-en-el-foro-internacional/ [accessed September 2013].
6. Deborah Hardoon, and Finn Heinrich, *Global Corruption Barometer 2013*, Transparency International, 2013.
7. Bruce Bagley, Sergio Aguayo, and Luis Aguilar, L. "Nuevos enfoques y políticas para el estudio de la relación México-Estados Unidos," Seminario de Seguridad, El Colegio de La Frontera Norte, July 8, 2010.
8. Osiel Cardenas and El Chapo Guzmán are some significant cases.
9. Ibid.
10. Eduardo Castillo, "Violence among Inmates on the Rise in Mexico, Report Says," *The Huffington Post*, 2013 available on line: http://www.huffingtonpost.com/2013/11/20/violence-inmates-mexico_n_4310199.html , consulted in November 29 2013.

11. For more about the main characteristics of prisons in Mexico, see "NarcoMexico: alfombra roja para los muertos," *Cuatro*, Spain. Available on line: http://www. youtube.com/watch?v=VByCVpl27aY [accessed November 2013].

12. United Nations. Statistical Division. *Manual for the Development of a System of Criminal Justice Statistics* (Vol. 89). United Nations Publications, 2003, 109.

13. UNODC, *Handbook on strategies to reduce overcrowding in prisons*. (United Nations Office on Drugs and Crime, 2010.

14. Ibid.

15. For more, see http://www.prisonstudies.org, accessed on September 4, 2013

16. International Centre for Prison Studies, available at: http://www.prisonstudies.org, accessed in September 4, 2013.

17. This is official data is May 2013.

18. OECD, "Prison population," in OECD, OECD Factbook 2010: Economic, Environmental and Social Statistics , OECD Publishing.

19. Ibid.

20. International Centre for Prison Studies, available at: http://www.prisonstudies.org, accessed in September 4, 2013.

21. Constitución Política de los Estados Unidos Mexicanos, art. 18. Translated by author and Jonathan D. Rosen.

22. For more about the reform of the penitentiary system, see: Guillermo Zepeda L. (2012), "Diagnóstico del Sistema Penitenciario Mexicano," en Antonio Sánchez (edit.), La transformación del Sistema Penitenciario Federal: una visión de Estado , México: Secretaria de Seguridad Pública / Centro de Investigación y Estudios en Seguridad.

23. Mitchel P. Roth, *Prisons and Prison Systems: a Global Encyclopedia* (Westport, CT: Greenwood Publishing Group, 2006), 176.

24. BBC MUNDO, "Cárceles en México: escuelas del crimen," BBC MUNDO.com, November 4, 2005, available on line: http://news.bbc.co.uk/hi/spanish/specials/2005/carceles/newsid_4377000/4377278.stm [Accessed October 2013].

25. Comisión Nacional de Derechos Humanos (CNDH), "Diagnóstico nacional de supervisión penitenciaria 2011, México: CNDH.

26. "Prisons in Latin America: A journey into hell," *The Economist*, printed edition, September 22, 2013.

27. Despite the fact that official statistics do not show high recidivism rates (around 15 percent at the national level), this figure is underestimated due to the low levels of punishment in the country. See Leslie Solís, Néstor de Buen, Sandra Ley, "Prisons in Mexico: What For?" (México Evalúa: Centro de Análisis de Políticas Públicas, 2013).

28. Randal C. Archibald, "In Mexico, Prison Riot Kills at Least 44 People," *The New York Times*, February 19, 2012.

29. Ibid.

30. Raquel Seco, "Las prisiones mexicanas se especializan en extorsión telefónica," *El País*, July 6, 2013.

31. Ibid.

32. Ibid.

33. Leslie Solís, Néstor de Buen, and Sandra Ley, "Prisons in Mexico: What For?" (México Evalúa: Centro de Análisis de Políticas Públicas, 2013).

34. Comisión Nacional de Seguridad, "Cuaderno mensual de información estadística penitenciaria nacional," Secretaria de Gobernación, Mayo 2013.

35. Mitchel P. Roth, *Prisons and Prison Systems: a Global Encyclopedia*, (Westport, CT: Greenwood Publishing Group, 2006), 176.

36. Ibid.

37. Official data obtained from the *Secretaría de Seguridad Pública* (Ministry of Public Security), 2012.

38. Elena Azaola, and Marcelo Bergman. "De mal en peor: las condiciones de vida en las cárceles mexicanas." *Nueva sociedad*, 208 (2007): 118–127.

39. Guillermo Zepeda Lecuona, "Diagnostico del Sistema Penitenciario Mexicano," in Antonio Sánchez Galindo (Ed.), *La transformación del Sistema Penitenciario Federal: Una visión de Estado* (México: CIES, 2012).

40. Comisión Nacional de Seguridad, "Cuaderno mensual de información estadística penitenciaria nacional", Secretaria de Gobernación. May, 2013.

41. This is the legal term used by the Mexican government to refer criminal offenses related to drug trafficking.

42. INEGI, Seguridad Pública y Justicia, 2010, 14.

43. Ibid.

44. Comisión Nacional de Derechos Humanos (CNDH), "Diagnóstico nacional de supervisión penitenciaria 2011, México: CNDH.

45. Asilegal, Documenta, Instituto de Derechos Humanos Ignacio Ellacuría *Informe EPU Sobre Sistema Penitenciario en México 2013*, México, Universidad Iberoamericana Puebla, 2013.

46. "Prisons in Latin America: A journey into hell," *The Economist*, printed edition, September 22, 2013.

47. The Mérida Initiative is a 1.9 billion dollars U.S.-financed program designed to strengthen cooperation between Mexico and the U.S. in order to combat organized crime and drug trafficking. For more, see: Clare Ribando Seelke and Kristin M. Finklea, *US-Mexican Security Cooperation: The Mérida Initiative and Beyond.* (Washington DC: Congressional Research Service, 2013).

48. United States Government (2013). "U.S.-Mexico security cooperation: an overview of the Merida Initiative 2008-present," hearing before the Subcommittee on the Western Hemisphere of the Committee on Foreign Affairs, House of Representatives, One Hundred Thirteenth Congress, first session, May 23, 2013.

49. Clare Ribando Seelke and Kristin M. Finklea, *US-Mexican Security Cooperation: The Mérida Initiative and Beyond* (Washington DC: Congressional Research Service, 2013).

50. Silvia Otero, "Preparan registro biométrico de presos," *El Universal*, November 23, 2013).

51. Agence France Presse (AFP), "The Majority of Mexico's Prisons are Controlled by Inmates," *Business Insider*, November 19, 2013 available on line: http://www.businessinsider.com/mexico-prison-inmate-control-2013-11#ixzz2n6Q8wH6F

52. Peter Watt and Roberto Zepeda, *Drug War Mexico: Politics, Neoliberalism and Violence in the New Narcoeconomy* (London: Zed Books, 2012).

53. Sergio Ramos, "México: Gobierno construye ocho cárceles de máxima seguridad," April 12, 2012 InfosurHoy, available at: http://infosurhoy.com/es/articles/saii/features/main/2012/12/04/feature-02 , accessed on November 29, 2013.

54. Luis Carlos Sainz, *Rejas Rotas, Fugas, Traición e Impunidad en el Sistema Penitenciario Mexicano*, (México, Grijalbo, 2013).

55. Ibid.

56. El Universal, "Cronología: fugas masivas de reos en México," *El Universal*, September 18, 2012.

FOUR

Drugs, Crime, and Prisons in Guatemala

Tamara Rice Lave

Drug traffickers have been able to penetrate the institutions in this country by employing the resources and money they have. We are talking about the security forces, public prosecutors, judges. Drug money has penetrated these institutions and it is an activity that directly threatens the institutions and the democracy of countries.
—Guatemalan president Otto Pérez Molina, 2013[1]

When it comes to Central American cocaine trafficking, all roads lead to Guatemala.
—United Nations Office on Drugs and Crime, 2012[2]

On July 18, 2012, four gunmen in the city of Esquintla, Guatemala, murdered Amilcar Corado Gonzalez.[3] Just fifteen days before, Corado had become director of the notorious maximum security "El Infiernito" prison, which houses gang leaders and powerful members of organized crime. Although ostensibly locked up, these individuals have used their time behind bars to plan murders, run extortion and drug rings, and recruit new members. Corado angered gang members by ordering disciplinary reforms aimed at halting this criminal activity, and the killing was reportedly payback.

Sadly, Corado's murder was not an isolated event.[4] In 2009, four prison officials were killed in three attacks that occurred within a span of several hours.[5] Once again, the killings were blamed on gang members angry at efforts to increase security and order in the prisons. "What happened is a reaction from gangs who want control of the prisons," Fernando Carrera Castro, director of the Central American Institute for Fiscal

51

Studies in Guatemala City, explained to CNN. "They're trying to show strength through force."

Incarcerating dangerous criminals is supposed to have the benefit of protecting society; how then have inmates been able to repeatedly orchestrate serious crimes from behind bars? This chapter will attempt to answer that question. It will begin by briefly describing Guatemala's strategic geographic importance, its history of state-inflicted violence and impunity, and its institutional weaknesses. After laying out this necessary context, the chapter will go on to describe the major criminal groups in Guatemala, how they operate, and the deadly consequences of their behavior. Finally, the chapter will discuss possible ways of combating these organizations and thereby making Guatemala safer.

GEOGRAPHY

In a very real sense, many of Guatemala's problems have to do with its geography. Located on a breathtaking piece of land abutting Mexico, Guatemala has rugged mountains, luscious rain forests, and picturesque beaches. Its proximity to Mexico (and thus the United States) makes it an appealing place for organized crime.[6] Guatemala's unique position allows it to be used as a transit point or storage ground for contraband including drugs, armaments, stolen cars, illegal migrants, and trafficking of human beings.

To the north lies Mexico, which means that for those attempting to transport contraband into the United States by land, almost all will pass through Guatemala instead of Belize, which shares a much smaller border. To the west lies the Pacific Ocean providing a clear passage for those wanting to smuggle drugs or other contraband by sea. To the east shines the Caribbean and more ports for smuggling. The heavily forested mountains provide cover for airstrips, storage facilities, poppy and marijuana cultivation, and methamphetamine labs.

HISTORY

Guatemala's location also makes it of strategic importance to the United States. In 1954, the United States helped engineer the overthrow of democratically elected Guatemalan president Jacobo Arbenz because of his socialist leanings and to protect the property interests of some powerful Americans.[7] This coup ended ten years of calm and ushered in a thirty-six-year period of civil war with U.S.-supported right-wing military governments using force to maintain the unequal distribution of land and other resources.[8] In the early 1980s, the Guatemalan government entered a new era of repression. During the tenure of elected president General Fernando Romeo Lucas Garcia (7/1/78-3/23/82) and his successor through a coup d'état, evangelist General José Efraín Ríos Montt (3/23/82-8/8/83), hundreds of villages were razed, women were systematically raped, and thousands of people were either murdered or "disappeared."[9]

The United States supported these regimes as part of its cold war policy and because it was concerned with the aspirations of Marxist rebels throughout the region. In 1979, the Sandinistas overthrew the Somoza regime in Nicaragua and instituted socialist policies. For twelve years in El Salvador, communist insurgents battled to topple the military dictatorship that had ruled since 1930. The U.S. government responded by helping to organize, train, and arm the Contras in Nicaragua despite known human rights violations, and it provided military aid and logistical support to the right-wing Junta in El Salvador, even though it had tortured and killed tens of thousands.[10] In Guatemala, according to the Commission for Historical Clarification (Comisión para el Esclarecimiento Histórico—CEH) which was created in 1994 under the auspices of the United Nations as part of the Oslo Peace Accord, the United States provided "military assistance (which) was directed towards reinforcing the national intelligence apparatus and for training the officer corps in counterinsurgency techniques, key factors which had significant bearing on human rights violations during the armed confrontation."[11]

In 1994, the Human Rights Office of the Archdiocese of Guatemala embarked on the Recovery of Historical Memory (Proyecto Interdiocesano de Recuperación de la Memoria Histórica or REMHI) project to document how Guatemalans had suffered during the civil war.[12] In the process, over six thousand interviews were conducted, and in 1998, *Guatemala: Never Again!* was presented to the world. The report concluded that 150,000 people had been killed and an additional fifty thousand had disappeared during thirty years of fighting.[13] This included student leaders, journalists, activists, and union organizers. Government forces were responsible for 80 percent of the casualties, and the report named specific officers. One year later, the Commission for Historical Clarification (Comisión para el Esclarecimiento Histórico or CEH) released its report: *Guatemala: Memory of Silence* in which they concluded that more than 200,000 individuals had died during the civil war and that the military was responsible for 93 percent of them.[14]

Two days after the Archdiocese's report was released, the person who spearheaded the investigation and formally presented it to the world, Bishop Juan Jose Gerardi, was brutally murdered. It took three years to bring the case to trial, due in part to death threats against witnesses, investigating magistrates, and judges.[15] Although there was evidence implicating then President Alberto Arzu, those arrested, charged and convicted were Colonel Disrael Limon Estrada (the former Chief of Military Intelligence), two other officers who were former members of the Presidential Guard, and a Priest.[16] The chief public prosecutor who oversaw these convictions fled the country with his family in response to death threats. After serving just ten years in prison, Colonel Limon was released from custody.[17]

And what about the individuals responsible for the massacres that Bishop Gerardi sacrificed his life uncovering? General Lucas died at the age of eighty-five without ever being held accountable for his actions,[18] and Retired General Ríos Montt remained for many years a popular figure, even serving fifteen years as a Congressman.[19] With support from the United Nations, however, Attorney General Claudia Paz y Paz did the unthinkable—she mounted a serious prosecution of General Ríos Montt in which dozens of survivors testified. Human Rights advocates were amazed when Paz y Paz was able to convict Montt of crimes against humanity and genocide in November 2013. It seemed that Guatemala's history of impunity might be coming to an end, but these hopes were short-lived. Just ten days after Montt's conviction, the Guatemalan Constitutional Court overturned it.[20] Many believe that the genocide conviction was annulled because of testimonies implicating President and former Army commander Otto Pérez Molina in the atrocities.[21] Eighty-seven-year-old Montt remains free, and with his retrial delayed until at least January 2015, it's unlikely that he will ever have to answer for his crimes.[22]

INSTITUTIONAL FAILURES

As is evident from the account above, the Guatemalan criminal justice system is deeply flawed. More than 98 percent of crimes in Guatemala are never prosecuted.[23] Part of the problem is that there are simply not enough police officers, and those that exist are underpaid and inadequately trained.[24] In October 2012, the Guatemalan Interior Minister announced that over the preceding four years the government had withdrawn the National Civilian Police (PNC) from thirty-two municipalities—twenty-four of which border Mexico and are "areas of high risk for organized crime."[25] The Minister explained that the government must develop a larger and better-trained police force to effectively handle the Mexican drug cartels operating in Guatemala. Helen Mack, Human Rights activist and former head of Guatemala's Police Reform Commission, stated that Guatemala needed at least 80,000 police officers to provide security to its citizens.[26] Esquintla exemplifies the problem: this province, with its strategic port on the Pacific Ocean and the highest murder rate in Guatemala, has just 17 investigators and 1,027 police officers for a population that exceeds 731,300.[27]

The low pay and inadequate training make the PNC vulnerable to bribes. These are not just low-level police officers; corruption exists at the highest levels. In 2005, Adan Castillo, Chief of the Guatemalan Anti-Narcotics Police (*Servicio de Analisis e Informacion Antinarcoticos,* or SAIA), and his deputy, Jorge Aguilar, pleaded guilty to cocaine smuggling.[28] More recently, in 2010, National Police Chief and former anti-Drug Czar Baltazar Gomez and anti-drug czar Nelly Bonilla were arrested for stealing 1,540 pounds of cocaine from a drug trafficker's warehouse.[29] Those brave enough to stand up against drug traffickers risk being killed, especially because they are often seriously outgunned. This is what allegedly happened in June 2013 when eight officers were executed and the deputy inspector kidnapped in retaliation for seizing a ton of cocaine.[30]

President Pérez Molina has promised to add thousands of officers and reform the national police.[31] In the meanwhile, he is trying to make good on his promise to rule with a *mano dura* (iron fist) by using the military to battle crime. He has placed the army in high crime areas and assigned extra military to the border regions in an effort to combat drug trafficking. President Pérez has been criticized for using the military to perform tasks usually reserved for the police because doing so undermines the legitimacy of the police and weakens the morale of individual officers.[32]

Regardless of whether it is the police or the army, however, they are unlikely to receive much help from locals.[33] After years of human rights abuses perpetrated by the state, many Guatemalans are extremely distrustful of both the military and the police. This suspicion further hinders the ability of the state to investigate crime and prosecute those responsible.

Should someone actually get arrested, the prosecutorial system is stymied by corruption, inadequate pay, and even death threats and murder. If a person is convicted of a crime, he is sent to prisons that are overcrowded, with inadequate sanitation and food, and insufficient guards. Better conditions hinge on a prisoner's ability to pay, not the seriousness of his crime or his behavior in prison.[34] For the most powerful criminals, prison is just a different venue from which they can plan and commit crimes.

There have been some recent attempts to improve Guatemala's criminal justice system. Although Attorney General Claudia Paz y Paz has attempted to aggressively prosecute drug traffickers and corrupt officials, the Guatemalan constitutional court recently ruled that she must be removed from office seven months early. Paz y Paz was appointed to replace Attorney General Conrado Reyes who was removed after just seventeen days because of ties to organized crime. Although the constitutional court's decision was allegedly based on a technical issue regarding when Paz y Paz's four-year term began, many believe that it was improperly influenced by outside forces who did not like her aggressiveness as a prosecutor.[35] Whatever the reason for the decision, it sends a clear message that there will not be consequences for violating the law in Guatemala.

A FOCUS ON PRISONS

In an ideal world, prisons would provide those convicted of crimes with the opportunity to reflect on what they have done and garner new skills so that they can lead a law-abiding life upon release. Prisons would also benefit society by removing dangerous people from the streets. If that is the measure for penal success, Guatemala fails miserably.

To begin with, many of those imprisoned have never actually been convicted of a crime. According to the International Centre for Prison Studies, in 2013, 8,209 people or 50.3 percent of the prison population were waiting to face trial,[36] a process that takes an average of three to four years to complete.[37] Such a denial of due process is detrimental to the rule of law in Guatemala. The innocent lose faith in the state because they are being deprived of their liberty even though they have done nothing wrong. Those who have actually committed a crime feel justified in doing so because they see that the state does not abide by the law. Force alone cannot maintain respect for the law; people must also believe in its legitimacy.

Making matters worse is the fact that conditions in Guatemala's prisons are horrendous. Prison capacity is at 251 percent.[38] With 17,000 inmates held in prisons that are supposed to have a maximum capacity of 6,500, Guatemala's prisons are ranked tenth in the world in terms of overcrowding. This tinderbox situation is exacerbated by Guatemala's inadequate system for classifying and housing prisoners. The only separation is based on gender and gang membership.[39] Other factors like the age and the type of criminal record an inmate has are not considered, which means that violent, hardened criminals are housed with those who are more vulnerable and less able to defend themselves. In addition, Guatemala has just one guard for every twelve inmates, which is only 25 percent of the level recommended by the United Nations.[40] With insufficient and easily bribable guards, inmates are able to smuggle in cell phones, drugs, and weapons.[41]

Contraband and lax control are a deadly combination. In 2005, gangs flexed their power by organizing attacks and riots that occurred almost simultaneously in seven prisons and left thirty-one inmates dead.[42] The next year, the authorities fought to retake control of Pavón Prison.[43] Some ten years before, guards had stopped going into the overcrowded and dangerous prison, leaving inmates to run it instead. Seven prisoners were killed in the battle, but the authorities eventually prevailed.

In a recent study, the Center for National Economics Research in Guatemala (*Centro de Investigaciones Económicas Nacionales* or CIEN) concluded that Guatemala has lost control of its prisons.[44] Gangs use deadly force to dominate other inmates and commit new crimes, and guards do little to stop it. If an inmate is placed in solitary confinement as punishment for misconduct, he can simply buy his way out. This corruption exists at the highest levels of the prison system as evidenced by inmates' ability to pay for a transfer to a different prison.[45]

The Guatemalan government may have succeeded in locking up high-level gang leaders and members of organized crime under its *"mano dura"* policies, but these individuals are using their time behind bars to recruit new members and commit additional crimes.[46] According to the Guatemalan National Civil Police, between January 2008 and October 2013, 9,957 crimes were planned from prisons in Guatemala.[47] Of these, 9,547 were extortions, 407 were murders, and three were kidnappings. CIEN estimates that inmates order 75 percent of the extortions in the country.[48] With overcrowding, violence, and a lack of drug treatment or other rehabilitation, it's no wonder that recidivism stands at about 90 percent.[49]

CRIMINAL GROUPS IN GUATEMALA

According to Antonio Maria Costa, Executive Director of the United Nations Office on Drugs and Crime (UNODC), "Corruption, poverty and poor criminal justice capacity make Guatemala extremely vulnerable to organized crime."[50] The UNODC describes some of these groups as transnational, meaning that they traffic contraband across more than one country. Others are territory-bound, meaning that their goal is to control where they are and to demand payments from those in their territory whether they are engaging in legal activity (like operating a bus company) or illegal activity (like drug dealing).[51]

In 2013, the Guatemalan Interior Ministry identified over fifty-four drug trafficking groups in Guatemala.[52] Some are considered "branches" of larger organizations, whereas others are independent. Below is a snapshot of some of the more powerful criminal groups as of March 2014. Arrests and assassinations, however, can lead to the loss of power and control.[53]

Sinaloa Cartel

The Sinaloa Cartel is reputed to be the most powerful transnational drug cartel in the Western Hemisphere. It is based in Mexico and operates from Buenos Aires to New York City.[54] It has been called different names depending on alliances with other drug cartels. For instance, it was called the Federation after several trafficking groups joined together, and it is now called the Pacific Cartel because of an alliance with the Gulf Cartel against the Zetas.[55]

In April 2009, President Obama identified the Sinaloa Cartel as a significant foreign narcotics trafficker pursuant to the Foreign Narcotics Kingpin Designation Act.[56] As a result, U.S. persons are barred from conducting financial or commercial transactions with the Sinaloa Cartel. It also freezes any assets the Sinaloa Cartel may have under U.S. jurisdiction. In addition, on a number of occasions the Treasury Department has named specific individuals associated with the Sinaloa Cartel under the Kingpin Act in an effort to undermine the Cartel's power.[57]

Although the Sinaloa Cartel is willing to kill to get its way, it prefers to use bribes over brute force.[58] It has cultivated strong connections with political and business elites, including members of the Mexican National Action Party (PAN). The Sinaloa Cartel has business relations with almost every drug transporter in Guatemala, and some of these relations stretch back over many years.

In addition to trafficking in cocaine, the Sinaloa Cartel produces and sells marijuana, heroin, and methamphetamine.[59] In the last few years, the Sinaloa Cartel has started using Guatemala as a place for storing the precursor chemicals used to make methamphetamine as well as for cooking it.[60] In 2011, 1600 tons of precursor chemicals were seized in Guatemala as compared with 400 tons the year before.

Observers believe that the Sinaloa Cartel is a more stable organization and poses a more long-term threat to Guatemala than other criminal groups.[61] Even though it is more expensive to pay bribes, in the long run, it is worth the investment. Because the Sinaloa Cartel has cultivated relations with politicians, police officials, landowners, and drug transporters, it will be difficult to destroy.

The Zetas

The Zetas were formed in 1997 by thirty-one members of an elite unit within the Mexican army who defected and started working as assassins, bodyguards, and drug runners for the Gulf Cartel.[62] They have also recruited from a controversial Special Forces operation in Guatemala called the Kaibiles.[63] In 2002, the Zetas split from the Gulf Cartel and created their own independent cartel that specializes in the trafficking of drugs, arms, and humans. They are a transnational group that stretches from Mexico through Central America and they have recently gained control of a trafficking route from Venezuela to Africa and Europe.[64] The Zetas are renowned for their extreme and unpredictable violence as well as their ability to corrupt local law enforcement and security forces.

In July 2011, President Obama declared in Executive Order 13581 that the Zetas were a "significant transnational criminal organization" meaning that they "have reached such scope and gravity that they threaten the stability of international political and economic systems [and they] are becoming increasingly sophisticated and dangerous to the United States."[65] As a result of this designation, all property and property interests of the Zetas that are in the United States or later come into the United States or come into the possession or control of any United States person, including any overseas branch "are blocked and may not be transferred, paid, exported, withdrawn, or otherwise dealt."[66]

In 2008, the Zetas made a concerted effort to gain control of Guatemala's lucrative drug market and trafficking routes. Their methods were merciless, including threats against politicians, the killing of powerful Guatemalan-based drug traffickers and the assassination of a prosecutor. In 2011, the Zetas massacred twenty-seven farmworkers in the Petén region of Guatemala, decapitating twenty-six and leaving threats to the ranch owner written in human blood.[67] Instead of solidifying their power, this massacre had the opposite effect.[68] It united other criminal groups against the Zetas, and both competitors and allies began providing information to the government. On its own, that would not have been enough, but Attorney General Paz y Paz began rounding up Zetas. Over 100 were arrested, including some of the most powerful members in Guatemala, and this weakened the group.[69] Although the Zetas still traffic large quantities of cocaine, they are less dominant in Guatemala than they were before.

Lorenzana Family

According to the Guatemalan Public Ministry, the Lorenzanas began smuggling cocaine in the 1970s.[70] They operate in the northeast of the country, in the border regions of Honduras and El Salvador. The Lorenzanas own several legitimate businesses (including construction companies, transportation fleets, and fruit and vegetable exporters), which have allowed them to launder drug money. The patriarch of the family, Waldemar Lorenzana, was able to conduct his illegal business because he was popular with the locals. He offered them employment, and he also provided goods that should have been provided by the government—building sports fields and medical clinics and installing public lighting. Only after these measures were exhausted did he use force to achieve what he wanted.

The United States has tried to weaken the group. In 2010, the U.S. Treasury Department designated three members of the Lorenzana family "Specially Designated Narcotics Traffickers," meaning that U.S. citizens could not conduct business with them. In 2012, it named two more members of the family.[71] After four failed attempts, Waldemar Lorenzana was arrested with the help of the DEA and is being extradited to the United States.[72] Later that same year, his son was also arrested.[73]

Jairo Orellano Morales

Jairo Orellano Morales is believed to be a major drug trafficker who works closely with the Zetas.[74] He allegedly ordered the 2011 massacre in Petén described above.[75] Orellano is also a "tumbe" meaning that he steals drugs from other groups. In 2013, the Sinaloa Cartel tried to assassinate him for stealing 1.5 tons of cocaine. On a personal note, Orellano has a child with one of the Lorenzanas.,

Ironically, Orellano's importance is a direct result of the U.S. success in helping to dramatically curtail the transport of cocaine by air.[76] Because Orellano controlled land on the border of Honduras, he gained power by controlling a major transport point overland from South America to the United States.[77] In 2013, the U.S. Treasury Department added Orellano to its drug Kingpin list.[78]

The Mendoza Family

The Mendoza Family operates in the northeast of Guatemala, in the province of Izabal.[79] Izabal is a strategically important province because it borders Honduras, and it contains the Caribbean port of Porto Barrios. Like the Lorenzanas, the Mendozas have both legal and illegal businesses. They own land that is used for ranching and farming, and in the 1990s they started trafficking in drugs.[80] Traditionally, the Mendozas have been allied with the Gulf Cartel, but when the Gulf Cartel started to lose their influence, the Mendozas allied with the Sinaloa Cartel.[81] They are enemies of the Zetas. According to the UNODC, the Mendozas have hundreds of members and are one of the most powerful drug trafficking groups in Guatemala.[82]

GANGS

The upheaval during the 1980s drove many Central Americans to flee the countryside for cities, neighboring countries, and the United States.[83] In Guatemala, over one million people were internally displaced, and over a million more left the country.[84] Many went to Guatemala City where they experienced profound poverty—often squatting on vacant land and building shelter out of any materials they could find.[85] Life for these individuals and other impoverished Guatemalans is precarious at best. Many have no running water or sewage system, and they work long hours for low wages. Some are unable to find permanent work in Guatemala City, and so they must seek seasonal work elsewhere. Alcoholism and physical and sexual abuse are pervasive, which leads to family disintegration. Outside of the home, violence perpetrated by common criminals and street gangs is a regular occurrence, and authorities have done little to stop it.[86] For the youth in these areas, life is bleak. Most have limited educational, recreational, and skilled employment opportunities. For some, gangs offer a sense of power, protection, identity, and importance that has been missing in their daily lives.[87]

For those who made it to the United States, the difficulties have been similar. [88] Without legal status, parents work low wage jobs which often require them to toil long hours away from home. They move to the only places they can afford, which are often high crime neighborhoods where gangs thrive. In Los Angeles, young immigrants and the children of those who fled have been drawn to two gangs in particular, Mara Salvatrucha (MS-13) and the 18th Street Gang (Barrio 18 or M-18).

Mara Salvatrucha (MS-13)

El Salvadoran refugees in Los Angeles founded the Mara Salvatrucha gang in the 1980s. Although it was originally comprised of El Salvadorans fleeing from the civil war, MS-13 soon began accepting other nationalities. It also began expanding out of Los Angeles and into other cities. MS-13's power increased when it joined into an alliance with the Mexican Mafia (La M). Being in partnership with La M gave the MS-13 more protection, and Mara Salvatrucha showed their solidarity by adding the number 13 to their name (M is the 13th letter of the alphabet.)

MS-13 is organized into semi-independent cells called cliques (*clicas* in Spanish). [89] Although there are mid-level and national leaders of the gang, the local leaders are largely autonomous. They are allowed to decide how they want to raise money, whether through extortion, contract killings, drug sales, and/or contracting with organizations like the Zetas to protect cocaine that is transiting through Guatemala en route to Mexico and the United States. Some of the money the cliques earn is channeled back to El Salvador where the top leadership resides. [90]

Extortion is a primary source of income for gangs, and it is also a deadly one. In 2010, 130 bus drivers and 53 helpers who collect bus tolls were murdered in Guatemala. [91] This was despite the fact that bus companies and drivers paid over 1.5 million dollars to organized crime "for protection" during that same year.

MS-13 now stretches from the United States through Central America. It has at least 30,000 members, of whom at least 8,000 are active in forty states and the nation's capital. On October 11, 2012, the U.S. Treasury Department designated MS-13 a transnational criminal organization (TCO). [92] Treasury Under-Secretary for Terrorism and Financial Intelligence, David S. Cohen explained, "MS-13 is an extremely violent and dangerous gang responsible for a multitude of crimes that directly threaten the welfare and security of U.S. citizens, as well as countries throughout Central America." [93] With such a designation, it is now illegal for Americans to engage in business transactions with MS-13, and they are no longer allowed to have property or other assets in the United States.

18th Street Gang

The 18th Street Gang (also known by other names such as M-18, Calle 18 or Barrio 18) was created in Los Angeles during the 1950s by Mexicans who were not accepted into other gangs because of their ethnicity. M-18 quickly began taking members from other countries. Like MS-13, M-18 is divided into cliques that operate semi-autonomously. It stretches throughout much of the United States and down through Central America. Similar to MS-13, M-18 also has an alliance with the Mexican Mafia.

MS-13 and M-18 Come to Guatemala

In 1996, Congress passed the Illegal Immigration Reform and Immigrant Responsibility Act (IIRIRA) in part to address the problem of MS-13 and M-18.[94] Before IIRIRA, a legal immigrant could not be deported unless he had been convicted of an aggravated felony. IIRIRA expanded the crimes that qualified for deportation and applied the law retroactively. In addition, IIRIRA made it easier to deport illegal immigrants. As a result of IIRIRA, the U.S. began aggressively deporting immigrants. This included Guatemalans who were members of MS-13 and M-18. Once they were back in Guatemala, gang members had a difficult time reintegrating. Many had grown up in the United States (indeed some had been legal permanent residents), and so Spanish was not their native language. Without skills, community connections, or language proficiency, these mostly young men had a difficult time being accepted. Many had highly visible gang tattoos, which made acclimation that much more difficult. As a result, even if they might have wanted to leave the gang life behind, some found that there were no other options.[95]

Although experts acknowledge that there were already members of MS-13 and M-18 in Guatemala before 1996, most agree that the population increased dramatically once systematic deportations began. Not only were hardened members of MS-13 and M-18 forced into Guatemala, but also they increased their ranks by recruiting youth from other gangs as well as those who had never before been gang members.

Ironically, the efforts of the Guatemalan government to combat gangs have only made them stronger.[96] The government responded to societal outrage over surges in gang violence and criminality by instituting *mano dura* policies that attempted to eradicate gangs by sending members to prison for long periods.[97] Unfortunately, this had the opposite effect as prison turned into a place for gangs to solidify their power, allowing them to recruit new members and increase the fidelity of those who already claimed membership.

In 2012, the U.N. Office on Drugs and Crime (UNODC) estimated that Guatemala had 5,000 MS-13 and 17,000 M-18, meaning that there were 146 gang members per every 100,000 population.[98] El Salvador had almost as many gang members as Guatemala (8,000 M-18 and 12,000 MS-13), but with a population less than half the size, there were 318 gang members per 100,000 inhabitants. Although Honduras had fewer total gang members than either country (5000 M-18, 7.000 MS-13), its population meant that it had 151 gang members per 100,000.

These numbers do not include separate criminal groups who operate with the gang's permission. Recently, ten people were sent to prison for extorting over 125,000 dollars from bus owners and drivers over a four-year period.[99] Two other extortion groups have also been recently convicted. Although these groups did not identify as gang members, they were paying the gangs for the right to engage in criminal activity. This technique of "taxing" those who want to engage in criminal activity in a certain area is reminiscent of tactics long used by the Mafia, and it reflects the gangs' increased power and control.

THE FIGHT TO CONTROL GUATEMALA'S LUCRATIVE DRUG TRAFFICKING ROUTES

At the same time that the number of L.A. style gang members was dramatically increasing, Guatemala was becoming more of a hub for criminal activity due to the effectiveness of the U.S. war on drugs in Colombia and then Mexico.[100] Colombian cartels used to transport cocaine directly to the United States because they were able to reap higher profits by

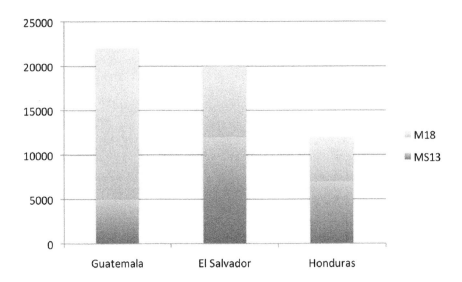

Figure 4.1.   Street Gangs in Guatemala, El Salvador, and Honduras. Source: United Nations Office on Drugs and Crime, Transnational Organized Crime in Central America and the Caribbean: A Threat Assessment, September 2012.

avoiding having to pay a middleman to transport the drugs. This practice changed when the United States began to aggressively combat the cultivation and exportation of drugs overseas. The U.S. began offering huge financial incentives for the Colombian government to implement its drug control policies, and it also provided logistical support and firepower.

Although the United States was successful at weakening the Colombian drug cartels, America's appetite (and that of other countries) for cocaine remained strong. With a multimillion-dollar market to supply, the cartels devised other methods of meeting America's need. No longer able to transport cocaine directly from Colombia to the United States, they turned to Mexican drug cartels to help with the trafficking. Initially, Mexican drug traffickers transported the drugs by water or just stopped in Guatemala for refueling en route to the United States, but this changed when Mexican president Felipe Calderón (2006–2012) started to vigorously combat trafficking in 2006. Since then thousands of Mexicans have been killed as the cartels battle the state and fight each other for control of the lucrative drug market. As with Colombia, Mexico has been successful enough at constraining the Mexican drug cartels that they can no longer easily transport drugs directly from Colombia to Mexico.[101]

At this point, Guatemala came to take on a more pivotal role in the trafficking of cocaine and other drugs. According to the United Nations Office on Drugs and Crime (UNODC), ". . . downward pressure from the Mexican security strategy . . . has virtually suspended direct shipments to Mexico and forced as much as 90 percent of the cocaine flow into the bottleneck of Guatemala."[102] The UNODC estimated that 330 tons of cocaine transited through Guatemala in 2010, more than any other Central American country.[103] The estimated value of the cocaine exceeded four billion dollars, which equaled 14 percent of the Gross Domestic Product of Guatemala. Those transporting the cocaine can collect 2000 to 2500 dollars per kilo.[104] That means that over 600 million dollars is at stake.

Guatemala is also appealing because the price of cocaine is still relatively low as compared with how much it costs in Mexico or the United States.[105] This creates an incentive for narco-traffickers who cannot buy the drug straight from the suppliers in Colombia, Bolivia, or Peru to obtain it in Guatemala because they can double their profits once they get the drug to Mexico.

In addition to cocaine, Guatemala is involved in other drugs. Poppy and marijuana are cultivated there, and it has become important in the methamphetamine trade. Large shipments of both methamphetamine and the precursors for making it have been seized leaving Guatemala for Mexico.[106] More recently, the necessary chemicals have been seized as they are being transported into Guatemala, which suggests that methamphetamine is now being produced there.

With so many millions of dollars' worth of cocaine and other contraband passing through Guatemala, criminal groups have battled to take control of the drug trafficking routes. Recently, the Maras have joined forces with the Zetas. The Zetas are now giving them paramilitary training and weapons in return for the Maras' support in transporting drugs.[107]

The battle over Guatemala's cocaine trade is in part responsible for its extremely high murder rate. The murder rate in Guatemala reached a high of 46 per 100,000 inhabitants in 2008, and in 2012 it was 34.5.[108] As a point of comparison, in 2012, the murder rate in Mexico was 22, and it was 4.7 in the United States. Furthermore, the recorded rate in Guatemala is kept artificially low because the recording agency most often cited in national and international statistics (the PNC) does not include those who were alive when they left the crime scene but succumbed to injuries later.[109] In contrast, the government agency responsible for keeping track of deaths in Guatemala records homicide rates 8–16 percent higher than those recorded by the PNC.[110]

Although the murder rate in Guatemala is extremely high, it is kept down by the fact that for the most part, the major trafficking organizations operate in different parts of the country.[111] The Zetas joined with the Lorenzanas, and they work in one part of the country as opposed to the alliance between the Mendozas and the Sinaloa Cartel, which works in another. In the regions where criminal groups are in direct competition, the homicide rate is significantly higher. The two departments of Guatemala that border with Honduras in the south, Zacapa and Chiquimula, have murder rates over twice the national average—74 and 89 per 100,000, respectively.[112] The departments that border on Mexico and Belize and Honduras in the north also have high murder rates, of 50 and 59.[113]

PROBLEM SOLVING

Ending the stranglehold that gangs and organized crime have over Guatemala is going to be difficult. In an interview with the *Observer*, President Pérez Molina gave a sense of both how hard the task will be and what is at stake. "'Drug traffickers have been able to penetrate the institutions in this country by employing the resources and money they have. We are talking about the security forces, public prosecutors, [and] judges. Drug money has penetrated these institutions and it is an activity that directly threatens the institutions and the democracy of countries.'"[114]

Effective law enforcement is one of the first steps. Criminals need to know that if they violate the law they will be punished. This requires investing resources into training and hiring more police officers, providing them with bulletproof vests and equal firepower to narco-traffickers, and paying them enough so that they will not be tempted to accept bribes. Prisons must also be reformed so that they are no longer another

arena for violating the law. This will take a significant financial investment. New and better machines are needed to screen for contraband,
especially drugs, weapons, and cell phones, and more guards, both better
trained and better paid, are required to maintain order and control.

In addition, the impunity that has been rife in Guatemala must end.
Narco-traffickers and gang members need to be arrested and tried with
due process and in a court of law. This requires brave prosecutors and
judges who are well paid and adequately protected. Unfortunately, the
most effective prosecutor in recent memory, Claudia Paz y Paz, has just
been ordered by the Guatemalan constitutional court to step down with
nine months remaining in her five-year term. Paz y Paz had been effective in arresting high-level Zetas and pressuring narco-traffickers. The
fact that she is being ordered to step down shows how at its core level,
the elites in Guatemala do not really want the country to change. [115] To
counter that message, Paz y Paz should be allowed to finish her term. Of
course, buttressing the criminal justice system also requires a dramatic
overhaul of the prisons. It does not matter how successful Paz y Paz is at
prosecuting criminals if those convicted are sent to a place where they
just continue their illegal activity.

In addition, the government needs to provide opportunities so that
youth have options other than gangs and organized crime. In 2010, 62
percent of the Guatemalan population were under the age of twenty-
four, and of these 20 percent were between fifteen and twenty-four. [116]
The Guatemalan government cannot afford to ignore these youth because
most criminologists agree that people are most likely to commit violent
crimes in their late teens and early twenties. [117]

Mano dura policies are not the solution; instead, the government must
offer youth a sense of hope and identity that they are not getting from
their dysfunctional families and communities. [118] At a minimum, it must
provide better schooling. Guatemala spends only about 3 percent of GDP
on education, and adult illiteracy stands at 25 percent. For every ten
children that enter the school system in Guatemala, only four graduate
from primary school. By the time they reach secondary school, just 34
percent are enrolled. [119] Recreational space, parks, and sports are also
important. Youth must also believe that they can support themselves
without resorting to crime. To that end, the government should provide
job training and employment opportunities. Many of Guatemala's roads,
for instance, are badly in need of paving. A major road and transportation project would provide desperately needed jobs.

All of these proposals require resources, and Guatemala has one of the
lowest tax rates in the Western region. The top 10 percent enjoy 45 percent of total income, whereas the bottom 10 percent have just 1 percent. [120] In 2012, total tax revenue was just 10.6 percent of GDP—a rate
that was lower than even Haiti. [121] This leaves insufficient resources for
the state to do its job. Thus there is not enough money to pay police

officers or prison guards, which leads to more corruption. Although violence hurts elites as well as the poor, they are more impervious since they can afford to build high walls and hire private bodyguards.

Strengthening Guatemala's institutions requires more than money; it also demands that Guatemalans be treated in a way that makes them feel invested in these institutions. People need to not just be protected from organized crime; they must feel that the government offers them something better.

Although life is comfortable for some Guatemalans, for most it is extremely difficult. In terms of income distribution, Guatemala is one of the most unequal in the world.[122] Over half the country lives below the poverty line, 13 percent in extreme poverty.[123] Infant mortality stands at 25 per 1000, and chronic child malnutrition is the fourth highest rate in the world—50 percent.[124] Although the minimum legal age for employment in Guatemala is fourteen, in 2010, UNICEF estimated that 21 percent of children between the ages of five and fourteen worked, and much of it was forced.[125] Things are even worse for the indigenous who have systematically been deprived of land, fair working conditions, and political power. Eighty percent live in poverty.[126]

Since the United States is at least partially responsible for Guatemala's situation, it should help to pay the costs for the above-mentioned reforms. In addition, it should provide a financial incentive to Guatemalan businesses to hire former gang members and at-risk youth so they have options outside of a gang. Regardless of whether the United States government feels any sense of responsibility for the problems it has helped to create, it should provide this funding and support because it will help to increase regional stability.

Ultimately, however, part of the solution should be ending the losing war on drugs[127] and allowing a regulated market instead.[128] The United States has spent over 200 billion dollars on counter-narcotics efforts over the past decade, and that's not including the enormous cost for policing, prosecuting and incarcerating those violating drug laws in the United States.[129] Of even greater concern are the 70,000 Mexicans[130] and thousands of Central Americans who have been killed since Mexico's former president, Felipe Calderón, declared a war on drug traffickers in 2006.[131] Because the demand for drugs remains strong, tapping down on supply in one country will just shift the problem to another, as what happened in Colombia, Mexico, and Central America.[132] Guatemala's poverty, its location, and its weak institutions allow organized crime to flourish. Should Guatemala somehow find a way to effectively fight drug traffickers, they will depart, only to wreak misery and mayhem elsewhere.

NOTES

1. John Mulholland, "Guatemala's President: 'My country bears the scars from the war on drugs,'" *The Guardian*, January 19, 2013. http://www.theguardian.com/world/2013/jan/19/otto-molina-war-drugs-guatemala

2. United Nations Office on Drugs and Crime, *Transnational Organized Crime in Central America and the Caribbean: A Threat Assessment*, September 2012, 39.

3. Edward Fox, "Jailed Gangs Behind Killing of Guatemala Prison Director," *InsightCrime*, July 23, 2012, http://www.insightcrime.org/news-briefs/jailed-gangs-behind-killing-of-guatemala-prison-director .

4. In February 2014, Jose Vidal Sarceño Lemus, the warden of a maximum security prison in Guatemala, was shot and killed as he was driving with his nephew who was uninjured in the attack. The prison houses fifty members of MS-13, and the week before the shooting, inmates reportedly tried to organize a riot to protest searches of their cells by prison guards. Authorities do not yet know who committed the killing. Agencia EFE, "Prison Warden Slain in Guatemala," Fox News Latino, 2/26/2014, http://latino.foxnews.com/latino/news/2014/02/26/prison-warden-slain-in-guatemala/

5. Arthur Brice, "Slayings of Four Guatemala Officials Blamed on Drug Trade," *CNN.com*, September 8, 2009, http://edition.cnn.com/2009/WORLD/americas/09/08/guatemala.officials.killed/

6. Julie Lopez, "Guatemala's Crossroads: Democratization of Violence and Second Chances," in Organized Crime in Central America: The Northern Triangle Woodrow Wilson International Center for Scholars, ed. Cynthia J. Arnson and Eric L. Olson (Washington, D.C.: Woodrow Wilson International Center for Scholars, 2011), 3–4.

7. Stephen Schlesinger and Stephen Kinzer, *Bitter Fruit: The Story of the American Coup in Guatemala* (Cambridge: Harvard University David Rockefeller Center for Latin American Studies, 2005).

8. "According to the most recent agricultural census (1979), only 2.5 percent of Guatemala's farms control 65 percent of the agricultural land, while 88 percent of the farms control only 16 percent of the land. The GINI Index for land distribution was calculated to be 85.9. This unequal distribution dates back to the colonial era when the Spanish crown granted large extensions of the land to colonizers." "Guatemala: an Assessment of Poverty," *Worldbank.org*

9. "Forced disappearance was a systematic practice even in rural areas, where people frequently were disappeared during military operations or, after being detained by clearly identified perpetrators . . . Living with this type of loss is much more difficult, even in cases where it is clear that the victim was ultimately killed. Disappearance creates a sense of ambiguity and heightened distress and anxiety over what actually happened and the whereabouts of the body." Human Rights Office of the Archdiocese of Guatemala. *Guatemala Never Again* (Maryknoll: Orbis Books, 1999), 19.

10. David F. Schmitz, The United States and Right Wing Dictatorships, 19665-1989 . (Cambridge: Cambridge University Press, 2006).

11. Commission for Historical Clarification, Guatemala: Memory of Silence, Report of the Commission for Historical Clarification, 19 (1999).

12. Human Rights Office of the Archdiocese of Guatemala. *Guatemala Never Again* (Maryknoll: Orbis Books, 1999).

13. Human Rights Office of the Archdiocese of Guatemala. *Guatemala Never Again* (Maryknoll: Orbis Books, 1999).

14. Commission for Historical Clarification, "Guatemala: Memory of Silence," Report of the Commission for Historical Clarification, Conclusions and Recommendations (1998), 17, 20.

15. "Four Convicted in Murder of Bishop Gerardi," *Famvin.org*, accessed March 9, 2014, http://famvin.org/en/2001/06/08/four-convicted-in-murder-of-bishop-gerardi/ .

16. Kate Doyle, "Monsignor Juan Jose Gerardi: A Martyr for Truth," America's *Quarterly*, accessed March 17, 2014, http://americasquarterly.org/monsignor-juan-jose-gerardi-a-martyr-for-truth; Associated Press, "Guatemala Frees Ex-Colonel who killed

campaigning Bishop," *theguardian.com,* July 14, 2012 http://www.theguardian.com/world/2012/jul/14/guatemala-frees-colonel-murder-bishop .

17. "Man Convicted of Killing Bishop Juan Gerardi in 1998 Granted Early Release," *hispanicallyspeakingnews.com,* July 14, 2012, http://www.hispanicallyspeakingnews.com/latino-daily-news/details/man-convicted-of-killing-bishop-juan-gerardi-in-1998-granted-early-release-/17116/

18. Associated Press, "Gen. Romeo Lucas García, 85, Former Guatemalan President, Dies," *New York Times,* May 29, 2006, http://www.nytimes.com/2006/05/29/world/americas/29garcia.html?_r=0

19. Associated Press, "Rios Montt From General to Dictator to Preacher to Courtroom Charged with Genocide," *Foxnews.com,* May 10, 2013, http://www.foxnews.com/world/2013/05/10/rios-montt-from-general-to-dictator-to-preacher-to-courtroom-charged-with/ .

20. Lauren Carasik, "Rios Mott Edges Closer to Escaping Accountability for Genocide," *Al Jazeera America,* November 14, 2013, http://america.aljazeera.com/opinions/2013/11/rios-montt-guatemalagenocidetrial.html .

21. "Claudia Paz y Paz Ousting Puts Spotlight on Guatemalan Justice System," *theguardian.com,* accessed March 9, 2014, http://www.theguardian.com/global-development/poverty-matters/2014/feb/19/claudia-paz-y-paz-guatemala-justice-system

22. It is no surprise that organized crime and gangs have taken root in Guatemala. Not holding General Montt and others like him accountable has serious implications for the rule of law. "(A) deep-seated culture of violence has taken root in Guatemala. Military regimes, army units and police squads have set an awful example, teaching entire generations that terror and murder are appropriate ways to achieve both political and personal ends. For their crimes, they have enjoyed nearly complete immunity, as the police and judicial systems exist to serve the unjust ruling order." Stephen Schlesinger and Stephen Kinzer, *Bitter Fruit: The Story of the American Coup in Guatemala* (Cambridge: Harvard University David Rockefeller Center for Latin American Studies, 2005).

23. Human Rights Watch, "World Report 2013- Guatemala," accessed March 9, 2014, http://www.hrw.org/world-report/2013/country-chapters/guatemala

24. International Crisis Group, Police Reform in Guatemala: Obstacles and Opportunities, Latin America Report No. 43 (July 20, 2012), 1.

25. Geoffrey Ramsey, "Police Withdraw from Key Drug Zones of Guatemala," *InSightCrime,* October 19, 2012, http://www.insightcrime.org/news-analysis/police-withdrawals-guatemala-drug-trafficking

26. Geoffrey Ramsey, "Police Withdraw from Key Drug Zones of Guatemala," *InsightCrime,* October 19, 2012, http://www.insightcrime.org/news-analysis/police-withdrawals-guatemala-drug-trafficking .

27. Natalie Southwick, "Escuintla: Guatemala's New Murder Capital," *InsightCrime,* November 18, 2013, http://www.insightcrime.org/news-briefs/escuintla-guatemalas-new-murder-capital

28. Drug Enforcement Administration, "High Ranking Guatemalan Police Officers Arrested For Conspiracy to Import Cocaine into The United States," (Press Release, Washington, D.C., November 16, 2005, accessed March 9, 2014), http://www.justice.gov/dea/pubs/pressrel/pr111605.html; Reuters, "Former Guatemalan Drug Czar Sentenced," *New York Times,* September 9, 2009, http://www.nytimes.com/2006/09/09/us/09brfs-006.html .

29. Associated Press, "Guatemalan Police Chief, Anti-Drug Czar Arrested," *Cannabis Culture,* March 5, 2010, http://www.cannabisculture.com/content/2010/03/05/Guatemala-Police-Chief-Anti-Drug-Czar-Arrested.

30. James Bargent, "Assault on Police Station Leaves Eight Dead in Guatemala," *InsightCrime,* June 14, 2013, http://www.insightcrime.org/news-briefs/assault-on-police-station-leaves-8-dead-in-guatemala .

31. International Crisis Group, "Police Reform in Guatemala: Obstacles and Opportunities, Latin America Report N°43 – 20 July 2012, http://www.crisisgroup.org/~/

media/Files/latin-america/Guatemala/043-police-reform-in-guatemala-obstacles-and-opportunities.pdf

32. International Crisis Group, "Police Reform in Guatemala: Obstacles and Opportunities, Latin America Report N 43–20 July 2012, 11 http://www.crisisgroup.org/~/media/Files/latin-america/Guatemala/043-police-reform-in-guatemala-obstacles-and-opportunities.pdf .

33. International Crisis Group, "Police Reform in Guatemala: Obstacles and Opportunities, Latin America Report N 43–20 July 2012, http://www.crisisgroup.org/~/media/Files/latin-america/Guatemala/043-police-reform-in-guatemala-obstacles-and-opportunities.pdf.

34. Michael Lohmuller, "Corruption Fueling Black Markets in Prisons" *InSight Crime* 2/4/2014 http://www.insightcrime.org/news-briefs/corruption-fueling-black-markets-in-guatemala-prisons

35. Nina Lakhani, "Claudia Paz Y Paz Ousting Puts Spotlight on Guatemalan Justice System," *theguardian.com*, February 19, 2014 http://www.theguardian.com/global-development/poverty-matters/2014/feb/19/claudia-paz-y-paz-guatemala-justice-system .

36. International Centre for Prison Studies, "World Prison Brief," *prisonstudies.org*, accessed March 9, 2014, http://www.prisonstudies.org/country/guatemala

37. "Cablegate: Merida Initiative: Guatemalan Prison Conditions," *Scoop Wikileaks*, accessed March 9. 2014, http://www.scoop.co.nz/stories/WL0808/S01525/cablegate-merida-initiative-guatemalan-prison-conditions.htm.

38. International Centre for Prison Studies, "World Prison Brief," *prisonstudies.org*, accessed March 9, 2014, http://www.prisonstudies.org/country/guatemala.

39. José Elías, "The Time Bomb Waiting to Explode in Guatemala's Prisons," El Pais, 10/14/2013, http://elpais.com/elpais/2013/10/14/inenglish/1381776230_182763.html

40. Mike McDonald, "Caging In Central America, "globalpost.com, May 14, 2012, http://www.globalpost.com/dispatch/news/regions/americas/120513/honduras-prison-fire-central-america-jail-crisis .

41. Mike McDonald, "Caging In Central America, "globalpost.com, May 14, 2012, http://www.globalpost.com/dispatch/news/regions/americas/120513/honduras-prison-fire-central-america-jail-crisis .

42. New York Times, "Coordinated Guatemalan Prison Riots Leave 31 Dead", 8/16/2005 http://www.nytimes.com/2005/08/16/world/americas/16iht-web.0816guat.html?_r=0

43. Marc Lacey "Guatemala Gains Control of Notorious Prison," *New York Times*, October 26, 2006, http://www.nytimes.com/2006/10/26/world/americas/26iht-prison.html .

44. JOSÉ ELÍAS, "The Time Bomb Waiting to Explode in Guatemala's Prisons,"El Pais, 10/14/2013, http://elpais.com/elpais/2013/10/14/inenglish/1381776230_182763.html

45. Jose Elias, "The Time Bomb Waiting to Explode Inside Guatemala's Prison System," *El Pais*, October 12, 2013, http://elpais.com/elpais/2013/10/14/inenglish/1381776230_182763.html .

46. Jose Elias, "The Time Bomb Waiting to Explode Inside Guatemala's Prison System," *El Pais*, October 12, 2013, http://elpais.com/elpais/2013/10/14/inenglish/1381776230_182763.html .

47. Lorena Baires and Sergio Ramos, "Gang Members Extort from Within Central American Prisons," *inforsurhoy*, December 4, 2013, http://infosurhoy.com/en_GB/articles/saii/features/main/2013/12/04/feature-01.

48. Jose Elias, "The Time Bomb Waiting to Explode Inside Guatemala's Prison System," *El Pais*, October 12, 2013, http://elpais.com/elpais/2013/10/14/inenglish/1381776230_182763.html

49. Harriette RWI, "Prisons in Guatemala- A focus on Rehabilitation," Roots and Wings International, May 28, 2012, http://rootsandwingsintl.org/blog/2012/05/prisons-in-guatemala-a-focus-on-rehabilitation/.

50. "UNODC Assists Guatemala to Tackle Organized Crime," United Nations Office on Drugs and Crime, accessed March 17, 2014, https://www.unodc.org/unodc/en/frontpage/2010/March/unodc-assists-guatemala-to-fight-organized-crime.html.

51. United Nations Office on Drugs and Crime, *Transnational Organized Crime in Central America and the Caribbean: A Threat Assessment*, September 2012.

52. Claire O'Neill McCleskey, "Guatemalan Officials Identify 54 Drug Trafficking Groups," *InSightCrime*, June 12, 2013, http://www.insightcrime.org/news-briefs/guatemalan-officials-identify-54-drug-trafficking-groups .

53. Julie Lopez "Guatemala: The Changing Face of Drug Trafficking," *InSightCrime*, July 30, 2013, http://www.insightcrime.org/news-analysis/guatemala-the-changing-face-of-drug-trafficking

54. "Sinaloa Cartel Guatemala," *InSightCrime*, accessed March 10, 2014, http://www.insightcrime.org/groups-guatemala/sinaloa-cartel.

55. United Nations Office on Drugs and Crime, *Transnational Organized Crime in Central America and the Caribbean: A Threat Assessment*, September 2012.

56. U.S. Department of the Treasury, Press Release, "Treasury Designates Sinaloa Cartel Members under the Kingpin Act," accessed March 31, 2014, 12/15/2009 http://www.treasury.gov/press-center/press-releases/Pages/tg444.aspx

57. U.S. Department of the Treasury, Press Center, Treasury Sanctions Key Sinaloa Cartel Network, 2/27/2014, http://www.treasury.gov/press-center/press-releases/Pages/jl2298.aspx.

58. "Sinaloa Cartel Guatemala," *InSightCrime*, accessed March 10, 2014, http://www.insightcrime.org/groups-guatemala/sinaloa-cartel.

59. United Nations Office on Drugs and Crime, *Transnational Organized Crime in Central America and the Caribbean: A Threat Assessment*, September 2012, 22.

60. E. Eduardo Castillo and Sonia Perez, "Mexico Meth Production Extends to Guatemala," *Huffington Post*, December 13, 2011, http://www.huffingtonpost.com/2011/12/31/mexico-meth-production-_n_1177735.html .

61. Steven Dudley, "Guatemala's new Narco Map: Less Zetas, Same Chaos," *InSightCrime*, September 16, 2013, http://www.insightcrime.org/news-analysis/guatemalas-new-narco-map-less-zetas-same-chaos.

62. "Zetas Guatemala," *InSightCrime*, accessed March 11, 2014, http://www.insightcrime.org/groups-guatemala/zetas.

63. "Zetas Guatemala," *InSightCrime*, accessed March 11, 2014, http://www.insightcrime.org/groups-guatemala/zetas. The Kaibiles

64. "Zetas Guatemala," *InSightCrime*, accessed March 11, 2014, http://www.insightcrime.org/groups-guatemala/zetas.

65. Exec. Order No. 13581, 3 C.F.R. 1589 (July 14, 2011).

66. Exec. Order No. 13581, 3 C.F.R. 1589 (July 14, 2011).

67. Adele Ramos, "Peten Massacre by Zetas too Close for Comfort!" *Amandala*, May 22, 2011, http://amandala.com.bz/news/peten-massacre-by-zetas-too-close-for-comfort/ .

68. Steven Dudley, "Guatemala's new Narco Map: Less Zetas, Same Chaos," *InSightCrime*, September 16, 2013, http://www.insightcrime.org/news-analysis/guatemalas-new-narco-map-less-zetas-same-chaos .

69. Steven Dudley, "Guatemala's new Narco Map: Less Zetas, Same Chaos," *InSightCrime*, September 16, 2013, http://www.insightcrime.org/news-analysis/guatemalas-new-narco-map-less-zetas-same-chaos .

70. Julie Lopez, "Plaza Publica: The Decline of Guatemala's Drug Dynasty," *InSightCrime*, June 7, 2011, http://www.insightcrime.org/news-analysis/plaza-publica-the-decline-of-guatemalas-drug-dynasty.

71. Claire O'Neill McCleskey, "U.S. Treasury Targets Guatemala's Lorenzana Crime Family," *InSightCrime*, November 15, 2012, http://www.insightcrime.org/news-briefs/us-treasury-kingpin-guatemala-lorenzanas .

72. Julie Lopez, "Plaza Pública: The Decline of Guatemala's Drug Dynasty," *InSight-Crime*, June 7, 2011, http://www.insightcrime.org/news-analysis/plaza-publica-the-decline-of-guatemalas-drug-dynasty.

73. Claire O'Neill McCleskey, "U.S. Treasury Targets Guatemala's Lorenzana Crime Family,"*InSightCrime*, November 15, 2012, http://www.insightcrime.org/news-briefs/us-treasury-kingpin-guatemala-lorenzanas.

74. Marguerite Cawley, "US Treasury Blacklists Guatemalan Trafficker Working for Zetas," Insight Crime, 8/21/2013, http://www.insightcrime.org/news-briefs/us-treasury-blacklists-guatemalan-trafficker-working-for-zetas.

75. Hannah Stone and Miriam Wells, "Zetas to Face Trial for 2011 Farm Massacre in Guatemala," *InSight Crime*, March 1, 2013, http://www.insightcrime.org/news-briefs/zetas-to-face-trial-for-2011-farm-massacre-in-guatemala.

76. Steven Dudley, "Guatemala's new Narco Map: Less Zetas, Same Chaos," *InSightCrime*, September 16, 2013, http://www.insightcrime.org/news-analysis/guatemalas-new-narco-map-less-zetas-same-chaos.

77. Steven Dudley, "Guatemala's new Narco Map: Less Zetas, Same Chaos," *InSightCrime*, September 16, 2013, http://www.insightcrime.org/news-analysis/guatemalas-new-narco-map-less-zetas-same-chaos .

78. U.S. Department of the Treasury, Press Center, "Treasury Designates Guatemalan Trafficker Allied with Los Zetas" 8/20/2013, http://www.treasury.gov/press-center/press-releases/Pages/jl2145.aspx

79. United Nations office on Drug and Crime, "The Importance of Territorial Groups in Central America," *United Nations*, accessed March 18, 2014, http://www.unodc.org/documents/toc/Reports/TOCTASouthAmerica/English/TOCTA_CACaribb_territorialgroups_centralamerica.pdf.

80. United Nations office on Drug and Crime, "The Importance of Territorial Groups in Central America," *United Nations*: 23, 25, accessed March 18, 2014, http://www.unodc.org/documents/toc/Reports/TOCTASouthAmerica/English/TOC-TA_CACaribb_territorialgroups_centralamerica.pdf.

81. United Nations office on Drug and Crime, "The Importance of Territorial Groups in Central America," *United Nations*: 23, 25, accessed March 18, 2014, http://www.unodc.org/documents/toc/Reports/TOCTASouthAmerica/English/TOCTA_CACaribb_territorialgroups_centralamerica.pdf , 24.

82. United Nations office on Drug and Crime, "The Importance of Territorial Groups in Central America," *United Nations*: 25, accessed March 18, 2014, http://www.unodc.org/documents/toc/Reports/TOCTASouthAmerica/English/TOC-TA_CACaribb_territorialgroups_centralamerica.pdf.

83. Nora Hamilton and Norma Stoltz Chinchilla, "Central American Migration: A Framework for Analysis" 26 Latin American Research Review 75–110 (1991).

84. Linda Green, The Fear of No Future: Guatemalan Migrants, Dispossession and Dislocation, 51 Anthropologica 327–341 (2009).

85. Gisela Gellert, "Migration and the Displaced in Guatemala City in the Context of a Failed National Transformation" Chapter 7, Journeys of Fear: Refugee Return and National Transformation in Guatemala (Liisa L. North & Alan B. Simons, Eds. McGill-Queen's University Press, 1999).

86. Caroline & Cathy McIlwane, Violence in a Post-Conflict Context: Urban Poor Perceptions from Guatemala (The World Bank, 2001).

87. Alisa Winton, "Young peoples' views on how to tackle gang violence in post-conflict Guatemala," *Environment and Urbanization*, Vol. 16 No. 2, October 2004, http://www.crin.org/docs/QMC_Gangs_Guatemala.pdf 87.

88. Cecilia Menjívar, "Liminal Legality: Salvadoran and Guatemalan Immigrants' Lives in the United States," 111 American Journal of Sociology (2006).

89. Douglas Farrah, "Central American Gangs and Transnational Criminal Organizations," *ibiconsultants.net*: 6, accessed March 18, 2014, http://www.ibiconsultants.net/_pdf/central-american-gangs-and-transnational-criminal-organizations-update-for-publication.pdf.

90. http://www.treasury.gov/press-center/press-releases/Pages/tg1733.aspx

91. Talea Miller and Christa Bollmann,"Buses Targeted by Guatemala City Gangs," *PBS Newshour*, June 7, 2011, http://www.pbs.org/newshour/updates/latin_america-jan-june11-buses_03-08/.

92. http://www.treasury.gov/press-center/press-releases/Pages/tg1733.aspx

93. http://www.treasury.gov/press-center/press-releases/Pages/tg1733.aspx

94. Mary Helen Johnson, "National Policies, and the Rise of Transnational Gangs," *Migration Policy Institute*, April 1, 2006, http://www.migrationinformation.org/usfocus/display.cfm?ID=394 .

95. Douglas Farrah, "Central American Gangs and Transnational Criminal Organizations," 11 *Ibiconsultants.net*, accessed March 18, 2014, http://www.ibiconsultants.net/_pdf/central-american-gangs-and-transnational-criminal-organizations-update-for-publication.pdf.

96. Clare Ribando Seelke, Congressional Research Service, Gangs in Central America, February 20, 2014, 7.

97. Clare Ribando Seelke, Congressional Research Service, Gangs in Central America, February 20, 2014, 9–10.

98. World Bank Population Data, accessed March 18. 2014, http://data.worldbank.org/indicator/SP.POP.TOTL . (The populations are as follows: Guatemala: 15,082,831; Honduras: 7,935,846; El Salvador: 6,297, 394) http://www.unodc.org/documents/data-and-analysis/Studies/TOC_Central_America_and_the_Caribbean_english.pdf , Page 29, Figure 20.

99. Michael Lohmuller, "Guatemala Bus Extortion Case: Maras Adopting Zetas Methods," *InSightCrime*, February 3, 2014, http://www.insightcrime.org/news-briefs/guatemala-bus-extortion-case-hints-maras-adopting-zetas-methods.

100. United Nations Office on Drugs and Crime, *Transnational Organized Crime in Central America and the Caribbean: A Threat Assessment*, September 2012, 31-32.

101. Daniel Sachs, "Los Zetas Southward Expansion," *Forbes.com*, August 27, 2013, http://www.forbes.com/sites/riskmap/2013/08/27/los-zetas-southward-expansion/ .

102. United Nations Office on Drugs and Crime (UNODC), Transnational Organized Crime in Central America and the Caribbean: A Threat Assessment, September 2012, page 39.

103. United Nations Office on Drugs and Crime (UNODC), Transnational Organized Crime in Central America and the Caribbean: A Threat Assessment, September 2012, page 43, Figure 34.

104. Steven Dudley, "Guatemala's new Narco Map: Less Zetas, Same Chaos," *InSightCrime*, September 16, 2013, http://www.insightcrime.org/news-analysis/guatemalas-new-narco-map-less-zetas-same-chaos.

105. Steven Dudley, "The Zetas in Guatemala," *InSightCrime*, accessed March 11, 2014, http://www.countthecosts.org/sites/default/files/Zetas_in_Guatemala.pdf

106. United States Department of State Bureau of Diplomatic Security, "Guatemala 2013 Crime and Safety Report," accessed March 18, 2014, https://www.osac.gov/pages/ContentReportDetails.aspx?cid=13878.

107. Romina Ruiz-Goiriena, Associated Press, "Mara Salvatrucha, Zetas Joining Forces? Guatemala Authorities see disturbing evidence," *Huffington Post* 4/7/2012 http://www.huffingtonpost.com/2012/04/07/mara-salvatrucha-zetas_n_1409814.html.

108. United States Department of State Bureau of Diplomatic Security, "Guatemala 2013 Crime and Safety Report," accessed March 18, 2014, https://www.osac.gov/pages/ContentReportDetails.aspx?cid=13878.

109. United States Department of State Bureau of Diplomatic Security, "Guatemala 2013 Crime and Safety Report," accessed March 18, 2014, https://www.osac.gov/pages/ContentReportDetails.aspx?cid=13878.

110. United States Department of State Bureau of Diplomatic Security, "Guatemala 2013 Crime and Safety Report," accessed March 18, 2014, https://www.osac.gov/pages/ContentReportDetails.aspx?cid=13878.

111. Daniel Sachs, "Los Zetas Southward Expansion," *Forbes.com*, August 27, 2013, http://www.forbes.com/sites/riskmap/2013/08/27/los-zetas-southward-expansion/.

112. Elyssa Pachico "Mapping Guatemala's Murder Hotspots," *InSightCrime*, January 31, 2013,http://www.insightcrime.org/news-analysis/guatemala-murder-hotspots-mapping.

113. Elyssa Pachico "Mapping Guatemala's Murder Hotspots," *InSightCrime*, January 31, 2013,http://www.insightcrime.org/news-analysis/guatemala-murder-hotspots-mapping.

114. John, Mulholland, "Guatemala's President: 'My country bears the scars from the war on drugs,'" *The Guardian*, January 19, 2013, http://www.theguardian.com/world/2013/jan/19/otto-molina-war-drugs-guatemala .

115. Michael Lohmuller, "Early Removal of Guatemala's Prosecutor Shows Power of Elites," *InSightCrime*, February 14, 2014, http://www.insightcrime.org/news-briefs/early-removal-of-guatemala-ag-shows-power-of-corrupt-elites.

116. United Nations Department of Economic and Social Affairs/Population Division, World Population Prospects: The 2012 Revision, Volume II: Demographic Profiles http://esa.un.org/unpd/wpp/Demographic-Profiles/pdfs/320.pdf

117. Alfred Blumstein and Jacqueline Cohen, "Characterizing Criminal Careers" Science Vol. 237, 985–991 (1987).

118. United Nations Office on Drugs and Crime, "Crime and Development in Central America," *United Nations*, May 2007: 24, http://www.unodc.org/documents/data-and-analysis/Central-america-study-en.pdf.

119. United Nations Office on Drugs and Crime, "Crime and Development in Central America," *United Nations*, May 2007: 13, http://www.unodc.org/documents/data-and-analysis/Central-america-study-en.pdf.

120. International Monetary Fund, "Guatemala, Selected Issues and Analytical Notes," IMF Country Report No. 13/248, August 2013, http://www.imf.org/external/pubs/ft/scr/2013/cr13248.pdf

121. United States Agency for International Development, "USAID's Strengthening Public Financial Management in Latin American and the Caribbean," *USAID*, Jan. 2014:3, http://www.usaid.gov/sites/default/files/documents/1862/Summary percent20Analysis percent20of percent20Country-Specific percent20Revenue percent20Briefs percent20-percent201-17-14.pdf .

122. In 2007, Guatemala had a GINI index of 55.1 which ranked it the 13th most unequal country in the world. "Global GINI Index, Ranking by Country," *Mongabay.com*, accessed March 18. 2014, http://www.mongabay.com/reference/stats/rankings/2172.html.

123. Guatemala Overview, *World Food Program*, accessed March 11, 2014, http://www.wfp.org/countries/guatemala/overview.

124. Education, Situation Analysis, USAID, accessed March 11, 2014, http://www.usaid.gov/guatemala/education/

125. World Report 2013, *Guatemala, Human Rights Watch*, accessed March 11, 2013, http://www.hrw.org/world-report/2013/country-chapters/guatemala?page=2.

126. "State of the Worlds Minorities and Indigenous Peoples- 2011 Guatemala," The United Nations Refugee Agency, accessed March 11, 2014, http://www.refworld.org/docid/4e16d37246.html

127. War on Drugs: Report of the Global Commission on Drug Policy, June 2011, http://www.globalcommissionondrugs.org/wp-content/themes/gcdp_v1/pdf/Global_Commission_Report_English.pdf

128. Gary S. Becker and Kevin M. Murphy, Have we lost the war on drugs, WSJ, 1/4/2013, http://online.wsj.com/news/articles/SB10001424127887324374004578217682305605070

129. Eduardo Porter, "Numbers Tell of Failure in Drug War," *New York Times*, July 3, 2012,   http://www.nytimes.com/2012/07/04/business/in-rethinking-the-war-on-drugs-start-with-the-numbers.html?pagewanted=all . http://www.nytimes.com/2012/07/04/business/in-rethinking-the-war-on-drugs-start-with-the-num-bers.html?pagewanted=all

130. "Mexico to track drug war victims, compensate families, " Jan. 9, 2013, *Chicago Tribune*, accessed, 2014.

131. Eduardo Porter, "Numbers Tell of Failure in Drug War," *New York Times*, July 3, 2012,   http://www.nytimes.com/2012/07/04/business/in-rethinking-the-war-on-drugs-start-with-the-numbers.html?pagewanted=all .

132. John, Mulholland, "Guatemala's President: 'My country bears the scars from the war on drugs,'" *The Guardian*, January 19, 2013, http://www.theguardian.com/world/2013/jan/19/otto-molina-war-drugs-guatemala. Some commentators call this the "balloon effect."

FIVE

Haiti

Prisons, Organized Crime, and Drug Trafficking

Christa L. Remington and
Jean-Claude Garcia-Zamor

The Republic of Haiti, located on the island of Hispaniola, has been considered the poorest country in the Western Hemisphere for the past fifty years. Its complex history is one of both victory and tragedy, rife with corruption and political unrest. Haiti is famous for its resilience and the extreme levels of poverty and human suffering. Caught in a web of stakeholders and their conflicting interests, Haiti continues to struggle with the consequences of consistent socioeconomic underdevelopment and national instability. Marked inequalities in access to productive assets and public services have further stalled economic development and contributed to persistent poverty nationwide. Nationwide, more than 80 percent of Haiti's population lives on less than two dollars a day, making it the Western Hemisphere's most impoverished nation and placing it among the poorest countries on earth.[1]

A lack of security and intense economic desperation have made Haiti particularly susceptible to national and transnational organized crime, including the trafficking of cocaine, marijuana, weapons, and humans.[2] In an effort to reduce international trafficking, the United States, Brazil, and other UN member nations have intervened, subsidizing Haitian prisons, training law enforcement, and prosecuting international drug lords. Until the January 2010 earthquake further destabilized the security and infrastructure of the island nation, modest gains were being realized in the battle against drug and human trafficking. Yet since the disaster, much of that progress appears to have been lost. Haiti continues to serve as a refuge for criminals as well as a major shipment route for illegal drugs and human cargo.[3]

At the heart of these challenges is Haiti's historically weak and tumultuous justice system, which remains underfunded, inconsistent, and unaccountable. Serving as the physical emblems of this disjointed system are Haiti's seventeen prisons. This chapter examines the current state of these prisons and the larger series of systems in which they are embedded. It highlights the role that prisons play in Haiti's current conflict against drugs, gang violence, trafficking, and organized crime. This chapter also looks extensively to the nation's current culture of reforms and the barriers to progress.

HAITI IN CONTEXT

Once a wealthy French colony, the nation of Haiti gained its independence in 1804 through a successful slave rebellion, making it the second nation in the Western Hemisphere to gain independence and the first republic in the world to be governed by people of African descent.

Well known for its tumultuous past, Haiti has been subject to frequent coups, military takeovers, dictators, and decades of foreign influence and involvement. Over the course of the past twenty-five years, the country has had nine different heads of state and thirteen total transferences of power. Such a long-term, pendulum-like environment has had multiple repercussions on nearly every national domain—impacting human development factors, the national economy, and the devaluation of the democratic process.

For more than two decades, Haiti was also shaped by the constraining forces of dictatorship. From 1964 to 1986, François "Papa Doc" Duvalier and his son Jean-Claude "Baby Doc" Duvalier maintained power through their brutal militia, the *tontons macoutes*. Imprisonment, violence, and torture were frequent tools of intimidation. Dissidents were quieted and uprisings squashed. It is estimated that 30,000–60,000 civilians were exterminated during the Duvalier era, a time when the nation's population was little more than one-half of its current size.[4]

In 1986, grassroots efforts and American intervention resulted in the exile of Baby Doc and the establishment of democratic intent and an interim government. Successive reforms, along with international support, led to the disbanding of the Haitian army in 1995, the establishment of the Haitian National Police (HNP), and the enactment of legislation intended to improve the nation's criminal justice system.

Despite these reforms, corruption and abuses of power continued to flourish even under the reform-minded presidency of Jean Bertrand Aristide, the nation's first democratically elected president. Aristide's blatant cronyism filled many top positions in the new Haitian National Police with political allies, facilitating both political violence and drug trafficking.[5]

In 2004, following a coup which forced the resignation of Aristide, the United Nations Stabilization Mission in Haiti (MINUSTAH), arrived with a mandate to restore law and order, lay the groundwork for national elections, and train the HNP.[6] Yet the HNP has consistently remained one of Haiti's most troubled agencies, plagued by almost continual allegations of corruption and abuse. Of the nation's 8,500 officers, approximately two-thirds are deployed in the greater Port-au-Prince area.[7] Underpaid and ill equipped, many in the police force have already succumbed to temptations of corruption or, at minimum, have turned a blind eye to trafficking, coercion, and the accepting of bribes. In its most extreme forms, the Haitian National Police have been accused of everything from serving as paid assassins to acting as drug couriers and escorts, collecting drugs dropped off the Haitian coast by airplane, often in full uniform and in the full light of day. Haiti's strategic location in the Caribbean makes it an ideal shipment route between South America and the United States. Cocaine and marijuana are regularly transported from South America and then forwarded via freighter to other parts of the Caribbean, Europe, or the United States.[8]

The government has long been complicit in such activity, turning a blind eye to the drug trade. In 2004, the World Bank's Country Policy and Institutional Assessment Program ranked Haiti in the bottom 1 percent of all countries in terms of corruption and government effectiveness while Transparency International's corruption perception index consistently ranks Haiti among the top ten most corrupt countries in the world.[9]

Such a culture of corruption at the national level serves as the heartbeat of organized crime throughout the country. Citizens often complain of bribery, unpredictability, and injustice in everything from schools and healthcare to the highest offices of government. Access to government services becomes less about need or procedures and more about "whom" one knows or how much money can be offered to reach the head of the endless queue of needs. For citizens in one of the world's poorest nations, endemic corruption makes it extremely difficult for individuals to improve their own lives through economic mobility. According to the World Bank, 80 percent of the population of Haiti lives below the poverty line, with unemployment numbers staying consistently high from decade to decade.[10]

The majority of workers in Haiti have only temporary or transient jobs and successful national entrepreneurship remains stalled. According to the United Nations, it takes four years longer to start a business in Haiti than the world average and business loans are virtually unattainable. This also contributes to corruption. Because the odds are stacked against new business owners, there is even greater inequality in terms of wealth.

These economic barriers have kept poor Haitians from upward mobility, and have resulted in weak or negative economic growth. [11]

ORGANIZED CRIME

Organized crime has played an important role for much of Haiti's history, yet it appears that criminal organization in the island nation is endemic, though not necessarily systemic in nature. Haiti's internal organized crime can be roughly demarcated into four categories: urban gangs, militias hired by private businesses or drug traffickers, independent criminal networks, and the disbanded Haitian army (*Forces Armées d'Haïti*, or FAd'H), known as the ex-FAd'H. Despite these demarcations, the barriers around these groupings are often porous and unclear, with individuals moving in and out of several categories over a period of time.

While there is little empirical knowledge about the current formal organization and activity of Haiti's gangs, they continue to influence politics and daily life in Haiti's urban centers. During the Aristide presidency, gangs allegedly played an even more powerful role, as the president's prime bastions of support—allies with powerful tools of persuasion. These gangs, known as "bazes," were given firearms in exchange for supporting and defending the administration and had the means to establish control over their neighborhoods. After Aristide's departure, these "bazes" quickly became the dominant figures in Haiti's organized crime. Small and geographically isolated, these gangs not only controlled neighborhood activity and engaged in criminal enterprises, but also provided protection for their neighborhoods, something the HNP failed to do.

The newly formed HNP, inexperienced and ill-equipped, was unable to squelch this mounting tide of "organizing" crime and for more than a decade the power and influence of the local gangs proliferated. [12] By the early 2000s, the seaside slum of Cité Soleil, home to over 300,000 residents, had become a "no-go" area for both the HNP and MINUSTAH. [13] An unabashed refuge for organized crime, the unguarded coastline provided unfettered access to drug smuggling and the open carry of weapons and constant firefights ensured that police were unlikely to risk entering the area, even to follow the trail of kidnap victims or to apprehend suspected murderers and thieves.

In 2006, the HNP established an anti-gang unit, charged with the tasks of investigating and interrupting organized crime in urban areas. [14] Under the administration of President René Préval, anti-gang operations began taking place in an effort to reclaim Cité Soleil. The HNP and UN Police worked together to crack down on gang activity, make arrests, and impose harsh sentences on gang leaders. The system of 'parallel justice' in Haiti is a controversial one and a source of constant debate. Extrajudicial execution alone is a subject worthy of an extensive in-depth examination. With the figurative heads removed from many criminal organizations, drug trafficking and kidnapping began to decrease and security slowly improved in Cité Soleil.[15]

In 2013, urban gangs, such as Baz Labanye, Lame Ti Machete, and Bois Neuf play active, yet less visible roles in Haiti's cities. Since the 2010 earthquake, gang activity has been on the rise.[16] More than 1,000 of the inmates who escaped from the ravaged National Penitentiary were members of gangs with drug ties. Despite the efforts of the HNP, almost immediately after the escape, crime resumed with a vengeance, taking the form of rapes, assaults, murders, robberies, and other gang activity. Some inmates banded together, mobilizing into an armed militia known as the *Armée Federale*, hiding in the hills and strategically coordinating crimes.[17] Firefights ensued as escaped gang members attempted to reclaim their turf. The temporarily crippled police force had little capacity to recapture or restrict such actions and gang leaders who had been in prison exploited the situation, regaining control of their former neighborhoods.[18]

A less recognized, but equally potent, form of organized crime in Haiti can be seen in the secretive, private militias that operate at the behest of some of Haiti's elite families or powerful private businesses. Often comprised of former or current members of the police force, these armed militias are recruited to protect legitimate business interests and perform illegal activity—including kidnapping, extortion, political intimidation, coercion, and the trafficking of guns, drugs, and people.[19]

More formalized and less privatized, the Ex-FAD'H, (e.g., Revolutionary Artibonite Resistance Front, Cannibal Army, Group Zero) generally consists of armed members of the former Haitian military.[20] These members recruit young adults, training them to police the streets, and demonstrate and protest on command. Their current numbers remain unclear, with estimates ranging from several dozen to several hundreds. Historically, ex-FAd'H members have been involved in the overthrow of the government and have strengthened their footing in times of national instability.[21] This was most recently demonstrated in the post-earthquake chaos of 2010. Members of the ex-FAd'H assembled and occupied Haiti's historical forts and abandoned military facilities, demanding pensions and the reestablishment of the nation's armed forces.[22] This pseudo-authority was soon checked by MINUSTAH and the HNP, but their power to effectively organize and function, despite the seventeen-year gap since the army's dissolution, garnered national and international attention.

It is vital to note that Haiti's criminal networks are still operating. Loyalties shift quickly and organization and structure are often informal or intensely temporary. Members of urban gangs may also serve in private militias, be ex-FAd'H or even a member of the HNP. Alliances form, dissolve, and reform quickly and while anti-corruption policies may exist on paper, bribery is often considered a normative path for circumventing Haitian law. [23]

DRUG TRAFFICKING

Historically, the Haitian people have not been primary consumers of narcotics. Pervasive generational poverty has, in some sense, left most Haitians "priced out of the market." Yet Haiti's relationship to the drug trade is as close as it is infamous and the exigencies and consequences of its role in the global cocaine supply chain have profoundly influenced the nation's economic and political trajectory.

In the mid 1980s, Haiti emerged as a key player in the drug trade between the U.S. and South America. Failed international economic policies resulted in the destruction of Haitian agriculture and production, leaving thousands of Haitians in economic desperation. Such despair served as fertile ground to exploit vulnerabilities and create transshipment points between South America and the United States. [24] Haiti's more than 1,100 miles of mostly unpatrolled coastline and at least twenty-nine clandestine airstrips, made it particularly attractive to narcotics traffickers. Historic patterns of governmental corruption and a wealthy elite class fueled the "business" of cocaine. By 2006, at least 8 percent of the cocaine that entered the U.S. that year had passed through Hispaniola—more than 83 metric tons. [25] In 2000, U.S. Attorney General Janet Reno highlighted the island nation's role in international supply, calling Haiti an ideal target and staging area for the large and sophisticated international drug trafficking syndicates. [26]

These drug trafficking syndicates have famously found allies in multiple Haitian administrations. At least a dozen Haitian officials, including the former national police chief, the former head of presidential security and the former president of the Senate, have been convicted on drug charges in U.S. courts since 2004. [27]

In 2008, the U.S. pledged 7.9 million dollars as part of the Mérida Initiative, a multinational anti-drug aid package, aiming to combat drug trafficking and to fight transnational organized crime and money laundering by improving Haiti's coast guard and training law enforcement to join in the war on drugs. [28] The Préval administration also partnered with the United States, and in 2009, international criminal charges were brought against numerous Haitian drug lords, resulting in their extradition to stand trial in the US. Anti-gang crackdowns by UN Police and HNP resulted in the arrest and marginalization of many criminal networks. [29] Criminal organizations began to dissolve and drugs became much more difficult to find.

But in the wake of the January 2010 earthquake, in which twenty-eight of the twenty-nine Haitian ministerial buildings were destroyed, both crime and drug trafficking resumed with vigor.[30] In the weeks that followed the disaster, the nation's already overstretched police force had little resources and manpower to spend on combating the drug trade. By the time a semblance of normalcy had returned to the devastated nation, the increase in trafficking was an undeniable reality.

A brief overview of the HNP's interventions in 2012 alone reveal renewed and rising trafficking activities: "eight cocaine seizures totaled 337 kilograms (kg) with a single 302 kg shipment composing the bulk, the largest single seizure in Haiti since 2007. BLTS also seized 300 kg of marijuana in five actions. Enforcement actions in 2012 yielded 92 arrests, 95,647 dollars in cash, twenty-four weapons, twelve seized properties valued at more than 5 million dollars, and seven vehicles. Haitian authorities transferred four of the arrestees to U.S. custody."[31]

Such evidence combined with anecdotal accounts and journalistic inquiries, have led many to believe that Haiti, once again, is serving as a major platform for cocaine from South America and marijuana from Jamaica. According to a report by the U.S. State Department, drugs from Venezuela and Colombia are dropped off the Haitian coast by aircraft or speedboat, and retrieved and loaded onto freighters headed to Europe or through the Bahamas and on to Florida. These shipments are frequently forwarded to Puerto Rico before coming to the United States, as shipments between the commonwealth and the U.S. are subject to less stringent customs inspections.

According to some reports, uniformed police officers often act as the middlemen between the suppliers and distributors, retrieving the drugs from the water.[32] It is not unusual for local individuals to be informed of drug drops ahead of time, resulting in a race between police and locals to retrieve the drugs. This competition to be the first to retrieve the drugs often results in gunfights and violence.

In order to combat this increase in brazen trafficking, the Supreme Council of the National Police in 2013 approved a five-year plan that aims to increase the strength of the Haitian National Police force to 15,000 officers by the end of 2016 and to add 200 officers to the counter-narcotics unit.

PRISON CONDITIONS IN HAITI

It would be hard to overstate the role that both organized and individual corruption play within Haiti's disjointed system of justice. Like an unbroken thread, pervasive corruption runs rampant through the nation's tangled and catastrophic history. There is perhaps no segment of the justice system that has historically been more infused with corruption than that which is contained within the walls of Haiti's prisons. Notorious for their chaos, neglect, and brutality, for decades Haiti's prisons stood as paradigms of corruption—indiscriminate tools of vengeance and repression wielded by dictators, foreigners, the wealthy, and the strong. Prior to the Haitian Revolution of 1986, most prisons operated merely as extensions of the Haitian military and, as such, were the ultimate apparatuses of dictatorial power.

The well-documented abuses of the Duvalier regimes were typified in the seemingly arbitrary use of incarceration, most notably at "the Auschwitz of Haiti," Fort Dimanche.[33] The notorious Port au Prince prison housed thousands of political prisoners, more than 3,000 of which met their death inside. Gruesome torture, violent beatings, and outright starvation were common, while electrocution and maiming were oft used to secure pledges of fealty to the Duvaliers.[34] While the horrors of Fort Dimanche lessened under succeeding leaders, it was not until the tenure of President Jean Bertrand Aristide that the nation's prison system began to measurably improve. Prison oversight was removed from the Haitian military and transferred over to the justice system.[35] Government officials publicly visited prisoners, listened to complaints, and pledged change. Yet underfunding, lack of social infrastructure, and repeated political upheaval left most reforms in the most nascent of stages.

Since the 1950s, the nation's prison system retains an only slightly less sullied reputation for its general state of disorder and for perpetual allegations of human rights abuses. Poorly funded and relying almost completely on foreign assistance, Haiti's prisons remain chronic sources of international tension and debate. According to the International Centre for Prison Studies, Haiti's seventeen prisons currently house nearly 10,000 prisoners—more than 400 percent of the national capacity.[36] Often cramped and squalid, many of Haiti's prisons lack the most basic of necessities. The 12'x12' cells may hold 50–60 inmates, with standing room only. Poor sanitation, meager food, and close quarters result in frequent deaths of inmates from starvation and sickness. Observations of the U.S. State Department paint a dismal picture:

> Some prisons had no beds for detainees; some cells had no access to sunlight. Many prison facilities lacked basic services such as medical services, water, electricity, and medical isolation units for contagious patients. Many prisoners and detainees suffered from a lack of basic hygiene, malnutrition, poor quality healthcare, and illness caused by the presence of rodents. Some prisons did not allow prisoners out of their cells for exercise.[37]

According to Dr. John May, the founder of Health Through Walls and an expert in global correctional healthcare, Haiti's prisons are among the worst in the world in almost every measurable domain.[38]

In recent years, these challenges may be best exemplified in the nation's largest prison, the National Penitentiary. Built in 1918 by the U.S. during its occupation of Haiti, it was originally intended to hold no more than 1,000 prisoners, but over the years its population expanded dramatically. In just a six-year span (1995–2001), the nation's number of detainees had more than doubled with, by early 2010, at least 4,200 of these inmates were living behind the walls of the National Penitentiary.

Underfunded and under-resourced, the innocent and the guilty end up in the same prison cell for years. Some 70 to 80 percent of the nation's prisoners remain incarcerated without trial or without ever coming before a judge.[39] According to Article 26 of the Haitian Constitution, this is a violation of the constitutional rights of the Haitian citizen.[40] Yet many prisoners have languished for more than four years before ever attending pretrial proceedings or being formally charged with a crime. As a result, frustrations run rampant behind the prison walls. While religious liberties and access to priests (both Christian and Vodou) are formally the right of inmates, such religious services were rare in the best of times—and in the wake of the cholera epidemic were suspended entirely. During long detentions, many inmates are disowned by their family and friends while faithful friends and family may stand in line for hours to send in packages of food and toiletries in an effort to sustain the life of their incarcerated loved one.

However, there is no guarantee that such care will ever reach its intended recipient. Packages are frequently confiscated or stolen by guards and other inmates. An informal system of "bribery for survival" permeates the prisoner's life. Receipt of packages, protection from violence, and even lifesaving medical care must be "paid for" to guards or other inmates in the form of money, drugs, sexual favors, or loyalty. Drugs, alcohol, cell phones, and weapons easily find their way into the prisons and almost anything can be purchased if the desired "currency" is right.

The young, the naïve, and the innocent must quickly learn to participate in this prison economy if they want to survive, for few barriers exist between the egregiously guilty and the neophyte criminal or the falsely accused. Those in jail for petty larceny are frequently housed together with murderers, rapists, and drug dealers. In an effort to survive, networks are formed between inmates, and between inmates and their guards. These networks extend beyond prison sentences and serve as a recruiting strategy for organized crime. Upon their release, or in the case of the 2010 earthquake, escape from prison, inmates find themselves with no possessions, skills, or social networks. In an effort to survive, they often feel forced to turn (or return) to a life of crime and survival. Likewise, significant delays in charging and sentencing and poor recordkeeping make recidivism difficult to determine.[41]

Because of this, it is impossible to separate the human rights abuses of Haiti's prisons from the issues of drug trafficking and gang activity, since none of these factors exist within a social vacuum. While larger networks of organized crime certainly hold some sway within Haiti's prisons, this is far less integrated and systematized than in many other nations. Instead, such activity exists primarily in independent "webs of corruption," more localized and individualized than national or international in nature. Because gang activity is so often geographically isolated, specific gang loyalties may begin and end inside the prison walls. Yet the virulently languid nature of the justice system and the dangers associated with incarceration make it impossible for inmates to survive without engaging, to some degree, with patterns of criminal activity and their associated networks.

ATTEMPTED REFORMS

Haiti is embedded in a complex ecosystem. For better or worse, its challenges and successes are noticed and influenced by the rest of the world. Over the years, the international community has significantly invested in both Haiti's physical and social infrastructures. International actors, in tandem with non-governmental organizations (NGOs) and the Haitian government have made gradual, albeit modest, progress towards security sector reform. International stakeholders continue to call for increased accountability and transparency for the billions of private and public funds that have been given for institution building and security and stability in Haiti. Such pressures from international governments and NGOs have led to various reforms aimed at improving Haiti's justice and security sectors.

In 2010, authorities permitted the International Committee of the Red Cross, Haitian Red Cross, and human rights groups to enter prisons in order to monitor conditions and provide medical and legal aid to inmates. Haitian authorities took measures to improve prison conditions and advocated for the human rights of inmates. Ministry officials began unannounced prison visits to the women's prison in Petionville and the National Penitentiary. The monitoring NGOs recommended changes to the prison authority to improve access to water, food, and sanitation. While some improvements to sanitation and healthcare were made, the government did not adopt many of the recommended changes and prison conditions remain a point of international contention and concern.[42]

In recent years, the Haitian Ministry of Justice has attempted to take responsibility for the numerous cases of violations to inmates' constitutional rights. Investigations were initiated into the cases of many defendants who had been held without charge for long periods of time. Beginning with the Petionville Women's Prison, a pilot program was launched which established a special correctional tribunal to deal with those awaiting formal charges.

During this tribunal, fifteen cases were heard which resulted in the release of fourteen detainees, including an inmate who had served her full sentence but had never been released. At the National Penitentiary, the Ministry of Justice also held hearings in an effort to reduce the pretrial detention backlog. By the end of 2010, an estimated 15 percent of detainees in the National Penitentiary had been convicted or released.[43]

With bilateral support, the Haitian government constructed a new prison in the Croix-de-Bouquets area. In addition to this new prison, which aligned with international human rights standards, the Haitian government also made significant improvements to prisons in Cap-Haitien, Arcahaie, and Delmas 33 in Port-au-Prince, Petit-Goave, and Fort-Liberte.[44]

Yet while these reforms were under way prior to the earthquake, the 2010 disaster revealed the government's limited capacity and the fragility of Haiti's internal security. By 2011, it was clear that much of the previous progress had been eliminated. The UN Office of the High Commissioner for Human Rights (OHCHR) reported that the HNP "have not made sufficient progress towards investigating allegations of extrajudicial killings, arbitrary arrests, and ill-treatment of detainees by police."[45]

In response to international scrutiny and funded by donors and foreign governments, the Ministry of Justice and Public Security initiated reforms intended to reshape the HNP. In conjunction with MINUSTAH, the Inspector General's Office began more aggressively investigating reports of criminal activity and corruption within the HNP.[46] Prior to the disaster, multiple reforms had occurred which were designed to target and reduce corruption within the HNP and the justice system. Under President Préval, MINUSTAH had already been vetting members of the Haitian National Police for human rights abuses and corruption and investigating reports of police corruption in participation with a large number of kidnappings.[47] However, in the wake of the earthquake, these investigations were halted and the number of kidnappings skyrocketed once again.[48]

As the international community responded to the disaster, many actors seized the opportunity to assist in developing Haiti's internal security. Foreign governments, including the U.S. and Canada, provided training and equipment intended to strengthen both autonomy and competency. Bilateral aid funded upgrades to police stations, human rights training to new and existing officers, and the provision of vehicles, computers, and communications equipment to the Anti-Kidnapping Unit.[49]

In 2013, MINUSTAH, the UNDP, and the Haitian Ministry of Justice and Public Security developed a joint program that seeks to maximize the impact of the UN assistance to justice, corrections, police, and violence-reduction programs. Despite these modest gains and attempts at change, security sector reform in Haiti remains extremely slow.

With this in mind, it is impossible to separate the troubles of Haiti's prison system from the nation's larger woes. Haiti's pervasive poverty, history of instability, and lack of governance capacity are the context in which the nation's prisons are embedded. National demographic data tells a startling story. Not only is Haiti the Western Hemisphere's poorest nation, but its infant mortality, life expectancy, rates of disease, literacy, and education rank among the world's most tragic.[50] Malnutrition remains a national norm and healthcare and education precious commodities. For every 4,000 Haitian citizens there is only one qualified Haitian doctor, while more than 400,000 six to eleven-year-old children remain completely outside of the educational system.

It is within this complex, high-stakes environment that Haiti's prison system exists. As mentioned above, Haiti's prisons are well known for their human rights abuses. Starvation, sickness, overcrowding, violence, corruption, confusion, and significant delays in justice are common. Parallel challenges exist in nearly all of the nation's other national services. Education, healthcare, electricity and water, security, social services, and transport all face similar dilemmas. As a whole, the nation simply does not have the fiscal and human resources to adequately fund and direct successful servicing for its ten million citizens. A nation still seeking to ensure access to the most basic of human needs has little left with which to reform and manage a justice system and guarantee humane and ethical treatment for its malefactors.

CONCLUSION

As this chapter has attempted to explain, organized crime in Haiti is part of a vast and complicated set of systems where everything from the nation's tragic history to its present culture of corruption play an influential role. Prisons, gang violence, and trafficking are concurrently both products of the nation's challenges and powerful drivers of them.

This complexity is nowhere more visible than in Haiti's tumultuous relationship to international aid. Dissonance between the priorities of international donors and the priorities of the Haitian government not only lead to confusion, but also serve as triggers of the cycle of corruption—something inevitably tied to organized crime. While donor scrutiny is an inherent part of receiving aid, donor funding must be aligned with government priorities. Those providing bilateral and multilateral aid must make reforming the police, justice system, and prisons a priority.

Additionally, security sector reform must continue for Haiti to effectively generate an environment that encourages innovation, investment, and entrepreneurship. As long as corruption and unpredictability remain national constants, economic growth will continue to be repressed.

While there was progress in Haiti's prison systems prior to the earthquake, the government must not be content with simply restoring the justice system to its pre-disaster state. Haiti must modernize existing prisons to meet international human rights standards and ensure that

Haitian citizens receive the full benefit of their constitutional rights. Human rights organizations should continue to monitor and report on the situation in Haiti's prisons and work with MINUSTAH and the Ministry of Justice and Security to ensure that international standards are being met. While there have been improvements in the nation's police force, MINUSTAH continues to lead the way in Haiti's law enforcement. This inverted relationship is a reflection of the HNP's current capabilities. Continued training on human rights standards, leadership, ethics and anti-drug and anti-gang practices will significantly help MINUSTAH achieve its goal of turning over security operations to the HNP in 2014.

No discussion of Haiti would be complete without acknowledging the prodigious role of NGOs. Haiti is home to anywhere from 3,000 to 10,000 aid organizations, the second highest number of NGOs per capita in the world, famously earning it the nickname the "Republic of NGOs."[51]

Foreign assistance is embedded in almost every level of society—from education, to housing, to medical care. NGOs currently provide many public services that the government has been incapable of providing. Because of this, many Haitians look to NGOs to meet basic needs and provide services, something that perpetuates the lack of confidence that Haitians have in their own government. Mistrust of the Haitian government and its lack of capacity have caused the majority of international aid to be funneled through these NGOs rather than through the Haitian government. For example, in 2007, all of the 300 million dollars spent in Haiti by USAID was directed through foreign NGOs.[52]

After decades of embezzlement by Haitian political leaders and blatant mismanagement of funds, international donors have had legitimate reasons to steer away from directly funding the Haitian government. However, this active mistrust has had powerful, unintended consequences. The Haitian government has been slow to develop the institutional capacity to effectively deliver services, while NGOs neither possess the authority nor the capacity to nationally and cohesively fill that gap.

Because of this, a quiet yet fervid rivalry for both funding and loyalty runs as an undercurrent beneath the relationship between Haiti's government and its NGO sector—neither trusting the other, yet each unable to ignore the other's influence. It is this deficiency in institutional capacity that undermines the legitimacy of the Haitian government in the eyes of its own citizens. Additionally, an internationally imposed security sector reform agenda has inhibited local ownership of the justice system. While donor scrutiny must continue, Haitian law enforcement and justice officials must begin to take ownership and responsibility of both priorities and process if lasting improvements are to be made.

While MINUSTAH has been successful in the broader stabilization of Haiti, stabilization is not synonymous with development. Haiti continues to suffer from a severe deficiency in capacity. Fragile institutions, ill-equipped security forces, and a corrupt justice system are constant reminders that renewed destabilization is only one disaster away.

Haiti's national legitimacy will never be firmly established until it has developed to the point of being able to provide security and basic infrastructure services to its people. Organized crime, with all of its many expressions and interconnectivities, are more than challenges faced by a struggling nation. Instead, they are symptoms of massive capacity gaps and a national government that lacks both internal and external credibility.

NOTES

1. Haiti Data. *The World Bank.* Retrieved November 8, 2012, from http://data.worldbank.org/country/haiti.

2. "Haiti's revolving door: Human trafficking and smuggling in Latin America." Alterpresse. 30 October 2012. http://www.alterpresse.org/spip.php?article13616#.Umqyr5FDGxL.

3. Ibid.

4. Paul Christopher Johnson, "Secretism and the Apotheosis of Duvalier." *Journal of the American Academy of Religion,* Volume 74, Number 2 (June 2006), pp. 420-445.

5. U.S. Department of State. "Haiti: Bureau of Democracy, Human Rights, and Labor." U.S. Department of State. http://www.state.gov/j/drl/rls/hrrpt/2004/41764.htm (accessed October 5, 2013).

6. "Security Council boosts force levels for military, police components." UN Department of Public Information, News and Media Division. 19 January 2010.

7. *Haiti Crime and Safety Report.* (2013) https://www.osac.gov/pages/ContentReportDetails.aspx?cid=14000.

8. Robinson, Linda. "The cocaine connection." *U.S. News & World Report* 128, no. 21 (May 29, 2000): 38. *Academic Search Complete,* EBSCOhost (accessed February 6, 2014); Arthur, Charles. 2001. "RAISING THE STAKES." *NACLA Report on the Americas* 35, no. 1: 42. *Academic Search Complete,* EBSCOhost (accessed February 6, 2014).; Chris, Hawley. 2010 "Drug trafficking likely to rise in quake aftermath." *USA Today,* n.d. *Academic Search Complete,* EBSCOhost (accessed February 6, 2014).

9. "Haiti Corruption." Transparency International. http://www.transparency.org/country#HTI (accessed October 26, 2013).

10. "Haiti Overview." World Bank. http://www.worldbank.org/en/country/haiti/overview (accessed October 26, 2013).

11. Economic Commission for Latin America and the Caribbean. "Haiti." Preliminary Overview of the Economies of Latin America and the Caribbean. http://www.eclac.org/publicaciones/xml/3/27543/Haiti.pdf (accessed September 30, 2013).

12. U.S. Department of State. "Haiti." Country Reports on Human Rights Practices. http://www.state.gov/j/drl/rls/hrrpt/1999/391.htm (accessed October 10, 2013).

13. Small Arms Survey (2010) Small arms survey: global gangs Cambridge: Cambridge University Press.

14. "Money Laundering and Financial Crimes Country Database." State Department. http://www.state.gov/documents/organization/211396.pdf (accessed October 8, 2103).

15. UN. "Haiti: UN pushes on with anti-gang crackdown; 59 suspects arrested so far." UN News Center.

16. "Dozens of additional UN Police start work in Haiti to help local officers." UN News Center. http://www.un.org/apps/news/story.asp?NewsID=21659&Cr=haiti&Cr1#.Umk_-RbvwzZ (accessed September 27, 2013).

17. Peace brief 2010. US Institute of Peace http://www.eisf.eu/resources/item/?d=4097.

18. Delva Joseph and Tom Brown. "Gangs return to Haiti slum after quake prison break." *Reuters.* http://www.reuters.com/article/2010/01/17/us-quake-haiti-gangs-sb-idUSTRE60G0CO20100117 (accessed October 3, 2013).

19. Athena Kolbe, "Revisiting Haiti's Gangs and Organized Violence." *Humanitarian Action in Situations Other Than War* 4 (2013): 2–35.

20. Ibid., 3.

21. Human Rights Watch. "World Report 2013." Haiti. http://www.hrw.org/world-report/2013/country-chapters/haiti?page=3 (accessed October 1, 2013).

22. Ibid.

23. Athena Kolbe, "Revisiting Haiti's gangs and organized violence." *HASOW* 5 (2013): 1–35.

24. "Money Laundering and Financial Crimes Country Database." State Department. http://www.state.gov/documents/organization/211396.pdf (accessed October 8, 2103).

25. Roberto Perito and Greg Maly. "Haiti's Drug Problems." *USIPEACE Briefing* 1 (2007): 1

26. Frank Loy and Janet Reno. "International Narcotics Control Strategy Report (INCSR)." *The DISAM Journal,* Spring (2000): 33–44.

27. Athena Kolbe. "Revisiting Haiti's gangs and organized violence." *HASOW* 5 (2013): 1–35.

28. Clare Ribando Seelke. "Mérida Initiative for Mexico and Central America: Funding and Policy Issues." *Congressional Research Service* 7 (2009): 1–28.

29. Robert Muggah, "The Effects of Stabilisation on Humanitarian Action in Haiti," *Disasters,* vol. 34 (2010), S444–S463.

30. "Money Laundering and Financial Crimes Country Database." State Department. http://www.state.gov/documents/organization/211396.pdf (accessed October 8, 2103).

31. "2013 International narcotics control strategy report: Haiti." U.S. Department of State. http://www.state.gov/j/inl/rls/nrcrpt/2013/vol1/204049.htm#Haiti (accessed October 26, 2013).

32. Stephen C. Johnson, *Caribbean Basin Security Initiative: Choosing the Right Course.* Testimony of the former deputy assistant secretary of defense for western hemisphere affairs, December 9, 2009.

33. Patrick Lemoine. *Fort-Dimanche: Dungeon of Death.* Freeport, N.Y.: Fordi9, 2011.

34. There is extensive empirical and anecdotal evidence documenting the abuses of Fort Dimanche. It was a place so horribly ingrained on the Haitian consciousness that many refused to go near the building years after its abandonment. For a comprehensive look at the "Auschwitz of Haiti," read Patrick Lemoine's *Fort-Dimanche: dungeon of death*

35. Marquez-Diaz, Nestor. "The Aristide Government's Human Rights Record." The National Coalition for Haitian Refugees and Caribbean Rights. http://www.scribd.com/doc/15026661/The-Aristide-Governments-Human-Rights-Record (accessed October 10, 2013).

36. "Haiti." International Centre for Prison Studies. http://www.prisonstudies.org/info/worldbrief/wpb_country.php?country=65 (accessed September 8, 2013).

37. U.S. Department of State. "Country Reports on Human Rights Practices for 2012." Haiti. http://www.state.gov/j/drl/rls/hrrpt/humanrightsreport/index.htm?dlid=186522 (accessed October 2, 2013).

38. Antigone Barton (2013). More than a decade of countering disease and disaster in Haiti penitentiary yields results as donors turn attention to prisons.

39. Minustah. "Prolonged pretrial detention creates overcrowding in Haitian prisons." (Accessed October 2, 2013).

40. *Constitution de la République d'Haiti, 29 mars 1987.* Port-au-Prince, Haiti: République d'Haiti, 1987. The Article clearly reads: "No one may be held in detention

who has not appeared before a judge authorized to rule on the arrest's legality within 48 hours of the arrest . . ."

41. Minustah, "Prolonged pretrial detention creates overcrowding in Haitian prisons." (Accessed October 2, 2013).

42. Human Rights Watch. "World Report 2013." Haiti. http://www.hrw.org/world-report/2013/country-chapters/haiti?page=3 (accessed October 1, 2013).

43. US Department of State. Haiti Human Rights Report. 2011.

44. For more, see http://www.state.gov/j/drl/rls/hrrpt/humanrightsreport/index.htm?year=2012&dlid=204458

45. For more, see the International Crisis Group http://www.crisisgroup.org/en/regions/latin-america-caribbean/haiti/028-reforming-haitis-security-sector.aspx

46. Ibid.

47. U.S. Department of State. "Haiti." Country Reports on Human Rights Practices. http://www.state.gov/j/drl/rls/hrrpt/1999/391.htm (accessed October 10, 2013).; "Reforming   Haiti's   Security   Sector."—International   Crisis   Group.   http://www.crisisgroup.org/en/regions/latin-america-caribbean/haiti/028-reforming-haitis-security-sector.aspx (accessed October 26, 2013.)

48. According to the US Department of State's Bureau of Diplomatic Security (OSAC), there was one kidnapping every three days in Haiti in 2010. See: OSAC. *Haiti Crime and Safety Report.* (2012) https://www.osac.gov/Pages/ContentReportDetails.aspx?cid=12152

49. Ibid.

50. Pardee Center for International Futures. Haiti. 2013.

51. Daniel Trenton. "Bill Clinton Tells Diaspora: 'Haiti Needs You Now.'" *The Miami Herald,* August 10, 2009.

52. Kristoff, Madeline, and Liz Panarelli. "Haiti: A Republic of NGOs?." United States Institute of Peace 23 (2010): 1–3.

SIX

Retribution vs. Reintegration

The Trinidad and Tobago Reality

Dianne Williams and Randy Seepersad

The Trinidad and Tobago Prison Service (TTPrS) is a product of Spain's colonization of the West Indies in the fifteenth century. In 2002, the then government outlined strategies to adapt the Restorative Justice Philosophy as the ideal concept to guide the country's penal policies and practices. In essence, the Prison Service was to commit itself to providing effective rehabilitation and reintegration services by adopting a Reintegrative Penal Policy and utilizing a shared responsibility model of rehabilitation. To date, neither the reforms nor the policy solutions have been implemented. This chapter will discuss the current state of prisons in Trinidad and Tobago including trends in recidivism, the impact of organized crime, and the cost of housing prisoners relative to the cost of providing correctional intervention services. Finally, this chapter will evaluate the intervention strategies for the development and transformation of the Trinidad and Tobago Prison Service.

COUNTRY OVERVIEW

The Republic of Trinidad and Tobago is an English-speaking twin island state in the Eastern Caribbean, which gained independence in 1962, and became a Republic in 1976. The *2011 Population and Housing Census, Preliminary Count*, estimated the population at 1,324,699.[1] The labor force participation rate, as of 2012, was 51.5 percent for females and 72.5 percent for males.[2] The country has an overall primary and secondary education attainment rate of 91.4 percent and, according to the Human Development Atlas, the life expectancy in Trinidad and Tobago ranges between 67.7 and 76.8 years.[3]

THE CURRENT STATE OF PRISONS IN THE COUNTRY

The Trinidad and Tobago Prison Service (TTPrS) was established in 1592, under Spanish rule. The physical structure was relocated in 1757, destroyed by fire in 1808 and reconstructed in 1812.[4] The TTPrS is an enforcement arm of the criminal justice system of Trinidad and Tobago and is funded and administered by the Central Government. It is a division of the Ministry of Justice; prior to 2010, it came under the purview of the Ministry of National Security. The TTPrS is headed by the Commissioner of Prisons who has delegated powers under the Constitution of the Republic of Trinidad and Tobago, and who is ultimately responsible to the Ministry of Justice.

There are currently nine prison facilities in Trinidad and Tobago; (1) Port of Spain Prison, (2) the Golden Grove Prison, (3) the Maximum Security Prison, (4) the Remand Prison,[5] (5) the Carrera Convict Prison, (6) the Youth Training Facility, (7) the Women's Prison, (8) the Tobago Convict Prison, and (9) the Eastern Correctional Rehabilitation Centre. The Carrera Convict Island Prison was established in 1877 off the northern coast of the island. It was initially used as a Maximum Security "convict depot" for long-term prisoners who were utilized to quarry limestone.[6] It is currently the sole offshore prison facility and is scheduled to be closed within the next year.

The Young Offenders' Institute was established in 1926 and was relocated to a seventeen-acre site, declared an Industrial Institution, and renamed the Youth Training Centre in 1949.[7] The remaining prison facilities were opened much later in the twentieth century, beginning with the Golden Grove Prison in 1947. During colonial times, Her Majesty's Royal Navy occupied the compound upon which the Golden Grove Prison is currently situated. In 1947, the site was formally converted to a Penal Institution for men. At the time of commissioning of the Golden Grove Prison in 1947, the initial facilities comfortably accommodated three hundred inmates. The Remand Prison at Golden Grove was subsequently opened at the Golden Grove Prison Complex in 1974, while the Maximum Security Prison was built and finally occupied in 1998.[8] The Golden Grove Prison is currently the only medium security prison in the country. Table 6.1 shows the total number of inmates in Trinidad and Tobago Correctional Institutions as of July 2013.

The first female prison was established in 1854, followed by another Women's Prison housed in the Royal Jail in 1886. The Eastern Correction-

Table 6.1.   Total number of inmates as of July 2013

Prison	Total Number of Inmates	Total Convicted	Total Remand
Carrera Convict Prison	291	291	0
Eastern Correction and Rehabilitation Center	105	105	0
Golden Grove Prison	461	461	0
Maximum Security Prison	1089	701	388
Port of Spain Prison	490	95	395
Remand Center	1051	0	1051
Tobago Convict Depot	47	23	24
Women's Prison	115	47	68
Total	3649	1723	1926

Source: Trinidad and Tobago Prison Service

al Rehabilitation Centre is the most recent addition, opened in 2011 to house individuals detained under the 2011 State of Emergency.

In the late nineteenth century, there were a variety of minor crimes for which citizens could be and were, charged, convicted, and incarcerated, such as non-payment of fines, riding a bicycle without lights or license, and non-payment of debts. There were also those who were imprisoned for more serious offenses, such as murder, theft, disturbing the peace, assault, and indecent behavior. During this period, the major prison facilities were the Royal Gaol and the Carrera Prison Depot. The main issue that existed at that time was the lack of classification of inmates. All prisoners were warehoused together, regardless of the type of crime committed. For the most part, this was unavoidable given the constraints of accommodation. Only the Royal Gaol was able to effectively segregate prisoners as it contained individual cells. The other depots, in contrast, were comprised of large buildings in which prisoners could mix freely. Although the smaller depot on Carrera Island was underutilized at the time, it was reserved for long-term prisoners who were being used to mine the stone quarry that existed on the island.

This convict depot served as a Maximum Security Prison for long-term criminals to provide the required *hard labor*. The labor involved was described as sufficiently severe and quite suitable for long-term offenders as they were made to work 309 days per year. The depot initially housed thirty to forty inmates and was intended to improve the deterrent effect of imprisonment.

Interestingly, in the late nineteenth century, incarceration was not viewed as negatively as it is today. Many offenders perceived imprisonment as a pleasant "vacation" indicating that the prison system, as it existed, was not a deterrent to crime.[9] This perception frustrated the police and prison authorities who faced three challenges: (1) changing the way in which the prison system was perceived such that the possibility of imprisonment became a deterrent, (2) instituting a proper classification system for prisoners, and (3) the institution of prison rehabilitation and reform. To this end, the then Inspector of Prisons made several recommendations including the following: a) the separation of the goal into two distinct departments, a house of corrections and a prison, and b) a change in the elements of hard labor. Notwithstanding these recommendations, during that period there was more of a focus on the punishment of prisoners rather than the rehabilitation of prisoners. As such, the recommendations were never implemented, which set the tone for the status of the TTPrS today.

OVERCROWDING

Historically, prison facilities in Trinidad and Tobago have fallen critically short of internationally accepted minimum standards. One of the primary challenges has been, and continues to be, overcrowding. Although no systematic data are available, from as early as the 1960s and 1970s, there have been accounts by prisoners and prison officials of cramped living conditions.[10] According to the Caribbean Human Development Report (2012), the official prison capacity in 2006 was 4,386 with a population density of 87.8 percent or approximately 3,800 inmates. In 2010, with eight facilities, figures suggest a decrease in the overall inmate population to 3,591, which is a rate of 276 per 100,000 including of pretrial detainees and remanded prisoners. In 2012, with nine facilities the International Centre for Prison Studies (ICPS) estimated that 3,800 prisoners were behind bars, including pretrial detainees and remanded prisoners,[11] a rate of 281 per 100,000, bringing the occupancy level based on official capacity to 77.8 percent.

Despite these statistics, overcrowding remains a serious concern in the nation's prisons. Statistics on overcrowding for the period January to June 2011 show that the Port-of-Spain Prison, Carrera Convict Prison, Tobago Convict Prison, and the Remand Prison have all exceeded their official capacities.[12] The Port-of-Spain Prison, built to house 250 inmates was at 140 percent of capacity, while Carrera Convict Prison built to house 185 inmates was at 181 percent of capacity. The Tobago Prison, built to house 30 prisoners, was at 130 percent of capacity, and the Remand Prison was at 169 percent of its 665 inmate capacity.

In a 2012 annual report, the Inspector of Prisons noted, with concern, that over 50 percent of the total prison population was still awaiting trial.[13] Additionally, a growing judicial trend of longer sentences for nonviolent offenses, combined with harsher sentences for violent and gang-related offenses, was also contributing to overcrowding. Given that the infrastructure of these prisons dates back to colonial times and the fact that each facility was expected to house much smaller inmate populations, it is not surprising that cells built to house one or two inmates are now housing as many as ten inmates in the Port of Spain Prison, Carrera Prison and Remand Prison (Golden Grove). It is also noted that some remand prisoners are held in facilities that were originally utilized to house voting machines used in elections in 1961.

Hygiene, Food and Clothing

The central government is responsible for the administration of the prison system. Yet the fact that under the existing Prison Rules prisoners endure an archaic system of provision of needs is not news.[14] It is also no secret that conditions in the nation's prisons are inhumane, degrading and unacceptable.[15] The 1945 Wright Report, the 1963 Garratt Report, the 1973, 1974 and 1975 Interim Reports, the 1977 Memorandum on Remand Prison, the 1980 Abdullah Report, the First and Final Reports of the 2002 Task Force, the 2003 Deosaran Report, and, most recently, the 2012 Prison Inspector's report[16] and 2013 Deosaran Report[17], have all made hundreds of recommendations to improve the horrific conditions under which the Remand population live.

The 2002 three-part task force report noted that, given the government's national policy emphasis on social sector delivery and consequential empowerment, the report should be the framework of reference for modernizing the Penal System in Trinidad and Tobago.[18] One of the key recommendations advanced by the Task Force was the implementation of a restorative justice philosophy. Ten years later in the 2012 Inspector of Prisons report, the Inspector stated:

> Conditions for getting rid of bodily waste and for performing basic hygiene routines are unbecoming. Pails which are used to urinate and defecate share crowded and unlit cells with cots and hammocks that can barely meet what passes for rooms.

This is a testament to the fact that nothing had changed in the ten-year period. The majority of the recommendations in each of these reports were never implemented. The Inter-American Court of Human Rights Report on the Conditions of Detention in Trinidad and Tobago[19] further corroborates these findings.

Conditions at Remand Yard are widely known by the public. The media has covered stories telling of the prisoners cleaning out buckets[20] of their own and their cellmate's faeces with their bare hands, and of roaches crawling into prisoners' orifices as they sleep at night, among other horrors.[21] These accounts are the day-to-day reality of Remand

Yard. With no proper toilet facilities, inmates are forced to use slop buckets (pails) in the cells which deprive them of privacy. The pails are emptied twice daily and washed, however during periods where water is unavailable, these remain unwashed after emptying, or are not emptied at all. In each case, prisoners face serious health risks, foul smells, and infestation by vermin such as flies and cockroaches.

Prisoners are allowed one shower per day, with all other functions such as the washing of hands performed over the pails in the cell. Death row inmates are confined for up to twenty-three hours per day and are allowed a meager fifteen minutes to empty their pails, shower, and drink their quota of water each day. These conditions are primitive and subhuman at best. As of January 2014, there were approximately 1,400 individuals (accused, not yet found guilty) in Remand and, because of inefficiencies in the criminal justice system, an accused can spend several years in Remand simply awaiting trial.

The theory behind the practice of holding individuals for a prolonged period of time, without the possibility of release on their own recognizance or bail is that being held indefinitely without bail is a deterrent to future criminal activity. In fact, there are currently discussions about removing bail altogether for certain categories of offenses, such as weapons offenses and offenses involving large quantities of controlled substances.

The current discussion about removing the possibility of bail for certain crime categories is a reflection of the central government's attitude toward criminal justice. Efforts by individuals in the field of prison reform to work with the government and urge them to see their role as a restorative one have not been successful. Academics have tried to convince legislative authorities that correctional institutions must be humane in order to actually *reform* criminals while serving their time. Although there is a move toward a more rehabilitative/restorative approach on paper, government officials continue to focus on imprisonment as a means of rehabilitating offenders and addressing the underlying problems causing criminality. Additionally, government officials by and large continue to subscribe to a retributive/punitive approach, which views imprisonment strictly as a means of punishing undesirable behavior.

Former Commissioner of Prisons, John Rougier, urged a move toward restorative justice,[22] so much so that some felt that he received negative pressure from all sides of the government to abandon this campaign and was pushed into retirement for this very reason. He has accused his successor, the current Commissioner, Martin Martinez of being a firm advocate of a retributive model of criminal justice.[23]

The conditions in Remand therefore reflect the position of the government regarding the purpose and benefit of the prison system. The government is aware of the conditions in Remand and has the financial resources to alleviate many of the problems. However, the government has not taken any meaningful steps to address the conditions in Remand,

and has been accused of lacking the political will to do so.[24] In fact, the absence of political will supports the idea that individuals in Remand are deserving of punishment, and the atrocious conditions that exist there will further that goal.

Unfortunately, the problems in Remand have been in existence for several years and continue to deteriorate daily. More importantly, as the crime rate in Trinidad and Tobago rises, the government has not allocated any additional funding to address the growing prison population. Consequently per capita spending on the prison system has actually decreased, even as Trinidad's oil wealth continues to grow. This is unsurprising given the country's retributive attitude toward criminal justice. Moreover, rising crime only increases popular support for greater and harsher punishment of perceived wrongdoers.

The failure of a prison reform bill known as the Prisons (Amendment) Act,[25] repeatedly proposed in the legislature of Trinidad and Tobago, is another example of the lack of will to effect any changes to this current reality. While the bill passed the Senate, it has effectively been stalled in the other house of Parliament because it is not the government's priority to push the bill through. Furthermore, the "reforms" that were to be a part of this legislation did not address the inhumane conditions of prisons, indicating that reforms of this nature are not even on the government's radar. Instead, the proposed "reforms," reflective of the retributive philosophy of criminal justice embodied by the government, were merely additional provisions to regulate the inmates, such as the institution of mandatory drug testing. Human rights elements addressing the inhumane conditions and abuses experienced by inmates were entirely absent from this legislation.

Another manifestation of the retributive attitude of the Trinidad and Tobago government can be seen in the quality of medical care—or rather lack thereof—offered in Remand. There is minimal medical attention provided in Remand, and the services that are provided are beyond substandard. As a comparison, public healthcare in Trinidad and Tobago, in general, is condemned as being substandard. Everyone but those of the lower strata of the country's population seeks out private healthcare and avoids public hospitals at all costs. But the services in Remand are below even this—it is the worst of the worst.

This subpar service is seen as appropriate in the Remand setting because of the intent to punish, which, in and of itself, drives the political attitude regarding the prison system. Not only are the services substandard, but they are only made available to those individuals who are blatantly in need of immediate medical attention, such as from a severe or obvious injury. Only then, when someone is literally bleeding on the floor, will the prison system be forced to provide treatment. That means, however, that there is absolutely no treatment or attention given to less readily obvious medical needs, in particular mental illness.

The government is well aware that only the most obvious of physical ailments receive medical treatment in Remand, and that there are many inmates, such as those with mental illness, who remain without treatment. Despite this awareness, they have not taken any concrete steps to remedy the problems, perhaps because the consensus of the general population is that those in Remand should not be getting medical care at all, because providing such care would be contrary to the punitive purpose behind imprisonment.

In the final analysis, the current status of the TTPrS is perhaps a reflection of the deeply entrenched resistance to change which exists more generally within the Trinidadian prison system. This resistance even bleeds into proactive support of the prisons' status quo. It is notable that TTPrS employees are vocally opposed to any change that would put the best and most capable people into positions of power in the prison system. Changes in the prison system are unlikely to happen because there is no constituency among the country's population that will demand this through the political process. In contrast, there is a major constituency pushing for greater crime control, and thus the government finds support for any measures that could be seen as more punitive. And with no pushback from any direction based on the lack of healthcare for the mentally ill, the government will not change that reality anytime soon.

THE COST OF HOUSING PRISONERS

Financial Cost

The housing and maintenance of prisoners weighs heavily on the pocket of the taxpayer and the state. In 2011, a former Minister of National Security revealed that the daily cost of maintaining an inmate was 312 dollars.[26] Given that there were approximately 3,800 prisoners being detained during that period, the total expenditure amounted to a staggering 43 million dollars annually. The budgetary allocation for the Ministry of National Security was 4.762 billion dollars for the 2010/2011 fiscal year; prisoner housing and maintenance accounted for around 11 percent of the total budget. It is also worth noting that the Ministry of National Security received the third highest budgetary allocation, surpassed only by the Ministry of Education and the Ministry of Infrastructure. Similarly in 2012, the then Minister of Justice pointed out that prisoner maintenance cost 315.57 dollars per day.[27] This translates into almost 44 million dollars per year, a 6 percent increase from 2011 (given the increase in the number of inmates), and 8.5 percent of the 2012 National Security budget of 5.2 billion dollars. National Security continued to receive the third highest budgetary allocation.

These figures bring some critical issues to light. Firstly, the housing and general care of inmates consume a massive portion of the public purse. While it can be argued that 11 percent of the total budget is moderately small, and the country can easily afford it, steady increases in the daily and annual expenses of the correctional system, as well as the myriad of other agencies under the purview of the Ministry of National Security, make it clear that the cost to maintain prisoners must be controlled and reduced. Secondly, and perhaps more importantly, National Security budgets facilitate mainly reactive techniques and measures to control crime, such as incarceration, "tough-on-crime" initiatives, and crime suppression. The massive budgets allocated greatly surpass those of other Ministries which offer social services, housing, and health as alternatives to punitive methods. Based on the figures for 2011 and 2012, the cost of housing and sustaining prisoners is increasing and, while there is a benefit to incapacitating violent prisoners, increased expenditure in this sector does not translate into a reduction in crime or fear of crime. Crime is the manifestation of a deeper social problem. Trinidad and Tobago cannot afford the persistent and rising costs of housing prisoners, which is, in effect, allocating millions of dollars to fight the symptoms of the problem without adequate budgetary allocations to address the problem itself.

Social Cost

The gender, ethnicity, age and crime-type dimensions of inmates in local prisons have remained largely unchanged in the last decade or so. The 2012 Ryan report[28] points out that the majority of inmates are male (98 percent), of African descent (55 percent), between the ages of 17 to 41 (80 percent), charged with narcotic-related offences (64.7 percent) and 50 percent first-time offenders.

These findings illustrate that a large proportion of the prison population is comprised of males in the prime of their lives, held for minor offenses, and who are not seasoned criminals. It can be argued, therefore, that the social cost of housing these inmates is depriving them of opportunities for true rehabilitation and restoration. Placing young, first-time offenders of minor crimes in overcrowded prison facilities with convicted re-offenders and career criminals greatly diminishes their chances of successful reintegration and contributing to society. The country is also divesting itself of a pool of young citizens who have the potential to contribute to the wider economic, social, educational, and vocational society.

THE RECIDIVISM RATE

Recidivism faces definitional challenges from the local perspective. International literature has sought to define and measure this concept but there are divergent opinions as to whether or not recidivism includes committing a new crime only, being arrested for the same crime only, violating parole or a combination of these.[29] Recidivism also has been found to exhibit particular characteristics such as (1) the likelihood that it will increase with age, (2) being more common in males than females and (3) increasing with the number of prior arrests and/ or convictions.[30] Ramdhanie[31] in his study of recidivism defined it as being incarcerated in any of the nation's prisons more than once. The Prison Reform Taskforce Report (2002) indicated that re-offending rates stood at 65 percent for both 1999 and 2000, while more recently, Seepersad[32] measured a rate of 49 percent.

In recent years, recidivism has become a major concern of Prison Authorities, especially given the shift from a retributive to restorative correctional paradigm. The recidivism rates remain high, strongly suggesting that incarceration is a failed policy. This is especially true in the Trinidad and Tobago context given that in 1958 there were four correctional facilities and 1,043 inmates and in 2012 there were nine facilities and 3,656 inmates.[33] A former Minister of National Security noted that:

> Our typical responses [to crime] have been arrests, trial and incarceration. As a consequence, our prison populations are on the increase. Given that a substantial number of crimes are committed by repeat offenders, it is critical that the prison services and penal systems focus on rehabilitation and reintegration. Such an approach would not only reduce the degree of recidivism, but also assist in effective crime management and would counteract the revolving door syndrome.[34]

Bronstein and Gainsborough,[35] drawing on the standards and goals of the National Advisory Commission on Criminal Justice, found that prisons have failed to reduce crime, act as punishment rather than a deterrent, offer only short-term protection for the community and, in fact, makes the offender more likely to engage in deviant behavior and more likely to reoffend over time. In other words, prisons continue to be used as punishment rather than rehabilitative centers, which perpetuate the problem of high recidivism rates.

REFORMS

The call for penal reform has been ongoing since the early 1960s, when nuns and priests, ministering in prisons, pleaded for the prison authorities and the public to treat prisoners in a more humane and civil manner and to embrace them as brothers. In more recent years, due to public demand and a deteriorating penal system, penal reform has been high on the agenda of prison authorities. However, penal reform has and continues to be a contentious topic with two main perspectives emerging. The first is the retributive perspective where proponents argue that the penal system be utilized for punishment. Persons who perpetrate crimes against society should be denied some basic human rights. Therefore, their freedom should be taken away and they should be made to endure the atrocious conditions of prison as a consequence of having committed a crime. Under this approach, retribution is believed to be a deterrent because it discourages criminal activity.

The second perspective argues that retributive justice is neither humane nor cost-effective. The cost to taxpayers of maintaining prisoners each day could be better spent delivering justice.[36] It is arguable that the majority of offenders can conform to social norms and laws and do not require physical confinement, particularly those convicted of nonviolent crimes. While total incapacitation is necessary for some offenders, these are in the minority. The main premise is that both society and the offender must be held accountable for the crime and are therefore obligated to provide restitution. A restorative justice approach also aims to rehabilitate and reintegrate ex-offenders. Such an approach is based on compassion, support and patience. Offenders are encouraged to admit their wrongdoing, seek forgiveness and make reparation to victims.

The shift in paradigm from retributive justice to restorative justice officially began in 2002 coming out of a report on the Penal Reform System in Trinidad and Tobago.[37] One of the primary recommendations was the adoption of restorative justice to transform the prison system. The TTPrS described restorative justice as "focusing on the harm or wrongs and promoting engagement and participation to put things right. It attempts to address harms and causes, while balancing concern for all."[38] Under the restorative system, as elaborated by the TTPrS, offenders are: (1) held accountable and responsible for their offence, (2) provided with mentors, teachers and coaches, (3) empowered, retooled and encouraged, (4) rehabilitated and reintegrated in society, (5) trained as mentors to other inmates, (6) given compassion, support and shown patience, (7) allowed to work, train, learn, earn and repay, and (8) encouraged to admit, seek forgiveness and pay reparations to victims.[39] In tandem with this new approach, five strategic objectives have been operationalized for prison reform: (1) protect, (2) correct, (3) relate, (4) reintegrate and (5) restore.

Additionally, the Penal Reform and Transformation Unit was established in 2007 to transform the "Criminal Justice System using a Restorative Justice Philosophy and Reintegration Penal Policy. The Unit assists in reforming the Penal System of Trinidad and Tobago,[40] the rehabilitation of offenders and supporting justice for victims."[41] There are also correctional education programs such as technical/vocational skills, life skills, sports, and agriculture. However, these programs continue to face a number of challenges with respect to funding, assessment, and customization for individual prisoner needs.

Additional efforts have been made by the government of Trinidad and Tobago to advance penal reform. One of the principal means has been the proposed revision of Prison Rules that govern the management of prison facilities in Trinidad and Tobago. It has long been argued that the rules are archaic and do not fulfil the needs of inmates in modern times. Indeed, since these rules were established in 1943, the prison system has made no changes. Ryan[42] noted that:

> The new rules, when given legislative approval, will focus more on the prisoners and less on prison officers . . . [and] will make prison officers more aware of the health challenges and status of prisoners, their gang affiliations, if any, their blood types and the level of risk which each constitutes, all this in order to better allow the authorities to stratify them on entry into prison. Prisoners will also be required to wear uniforms which will reduce the risk of contraband . . . as of right now prisoners on remand, i.e. charged but not yet sentenced, wear street clothing (p.265)

The latest action by the government was the signing of a memorandum of understanding (MOU) with Correctional Service Canada (CSC) for intervention in particular areas of the Prison Service. Some of the targeted areas are correctional policies and programs that focus on attitudes and behaviors that increase or decrease the inclination to offend, use of information technology in the correctional facilities, and employing more scientific methods for the management of prisoners.[43] The ultimate aim of the interventions would be to reduce the recidivism rate. Outside of these measures, the government has put forward a number of recommendations such as conjugal visits and cable television, both of which were criticized by the public.

Based on these proposed reforms, the question of implementation arises. Putting these measures into effect would be difficult, if not impossible, given the infrastructure of the prison system. Overcrowded prisons with poor conditions that are managed by antiquated rules would not support any attempt at rehabilitation or restoration. This would also impact the provision of educational programs due to insufficient space, poor delivery and low morale among inmates. Perhaps the most outstanding issue is the lack of concrete and modern policies focused on penal reform. While policymakers have been active in developing policies to bring about the required changes in the Prison Service, there has been opposition to approval, full implementation, obtaining additional personnel, training, and funding. Penal reform seems to be an elusive goal for the local prison system. However, with the escalating crime rates, growing prison populations, and increasing costs of housing prisoners, penal reform is no longer an option but a necessity with respect to the nation's security and economic well-being.

THE RELATIONSHIP BETWEEN ORGANIZED CRIME AND PRISONS

Over the last decade, crime and violence have adopted new dimensions and characteristics that were previously associated with larger and more developed countries. Apart from a proliferation of criminal gangs, organized crime has become a major concern for authorities in many Caribbean nations, including Trinidad and Tobago. Criminal gangs or street gangs have received substantial attention in academic, law enforcement, and public fora. However, organized crime has only recently begun to acquire the same attention. According to the Caribbean Human Development Report 2012:

> Organized crime is characterized by enterprise activity, the use of violence (actual and/ or threatened) and corruption as typical means and exploitable relationships with the upper world. In this regard, enterprise activity involves the provision of illegal goods or services to individuals. Traditional examples revolved around trafficking in drugs, guns and people, as well as extortion. [44]

The Report elaborates on the two types of organizational structures of organized crime groups. In the corporate form, there is a recognized hierarchy with definite lines of authority. The relational form is constructed on often pre-existing personal and social networks in a particular area or community. In a population of 1.3 million, this is easy to maintain. Another distinguishing feature of organized crime is that it is driven strictly by economics and tends to focus on large-scale distribution of activities such as drug trafficking.

While the existence of organized crime groups has been evident in several Caribbean countries such as Barbados, Guyana, and Trinidad and Tobago, systematically examining their prevalence and other defining characteristics specific to the Caribbean region is difficult. Only in Jamaica were the most comprehensive examinations of organized crime ever done. It is estimated that there were twelve groups, up from the seven identified by Moncrieffe in 1998. Harriott believes twenty such groups existed in Jamaica. Interestingly, he also points out that organized crime is "now more active, powerful and entrenched and perhaps more well tolerated by the people and their political representatives than ever before." [45] This statement may offer some insight into organized crime groups in other Caribbean countries but it is challenging to ascertain such in the absence of empirical evidence.

In a similar manner, the relationship between organized crime and the prisons is difficult to establish since the linkages are based largely on anecdotal evidence. Locally, murder and assault have been reported both within and outside of the prisons as a result of disputes between rival gangs who are housed together. Unlike criminal gangs, the activities of organized crime groups tend to be less discernible to the public eye.

However, it is believed that drug trafficking is perhaps the most prominent and lucrative enterprise within the Caribbean region for organized crime groups. Drug trafficking can lead to increased criminality and violence such as gang killings, escalation in property crimes, growth of the illegal firearm trade and corruption among public officials who "turn a blind eye." However, there is no concrete evidence linking organized crime groups to the prison system in Trinidad and Tobago. Nonetheless, anecdotal data suggest that, as organized crime becomes more influential, stable, and engrained in countries like Trinidad and Tobago, there will be an escalation of violence and corrupt practices. Inevitably, the consequences could result in an increased prison population, containing more individuals with connections to organized crime. These persons may pose a double threat in that they can recruit new members from the prison population as well as influence prison officials, through threats and/or the promise of economic gain, in order to conduct their illegal activities from behind prison walls. Although the relationship between organized crime and the prisons remains truly unknown, the potential ramifications of such are cause for concern.

RELATIONSHIP BETWEEN DRUGS AND CRIME

According to a 2013 study of 623 inmates,[46] 74 percent indicated that they had used marijuana at some point in their lifetime, 12 percent had used cocaine and 8 percent crack cocaine. Some 91 percent of those sampled have used at least one drug within their lifetime (including alcohol and tobacco), with 16.9 percent having used one drug, 20.4 percent having used two drugs, 38.7 percent having used three drugs, 10 percent having used four drugs, and 5 percent having used five or more drugs at some point in their lifetime. Of the sample, 6.6 percent indicated that they had already tried marijuana by the age of ten. By the age of fifteen, 1.2 percent of the sample had already tried cocaine, and 0.6 percent had already tried crack. Inclusive of alcohol, and tobacco, 66.5 percent of inmates had used drugs while in prison. With respect to the number of drugs used in prison, 22.5 percent of the sample indicated that they used one drug, 30 percent used two drugs, 13 percent used three drugs, and 1 percent used four drugs. When overall drug usage was considered, 69 percent of males and 22.9 percent of females indicated that they have consumed drugs in prison, while 63.6 percent of convicted persons and 69.8 percent of remanded persons have used drugs while in prison. The most widely used drugs within prison are marijuana, tobacco, and alcohol. A surprising 49.8 percent of respondents indicated that they use marijuana while in prison, while 54.3 percent use tobacco and 17.5 percent use alcohol. A small minority of respondents (2.6 percent) use prescription medication for purposes other than that for which such medication was intended, while the use of cocaine, crack, heroin, inhalants, and other drugs in prison is negligible. The lowest levels of drug use in prison occurs in the Women's Prison where 20 percent of remanded women and 25 percent of convicted women indicated that they have used drugs within prison. This is followed by the Carrera Convict Prison (45 percent), Eastern Correctional Rehabilitation Center (ECRC) (50 percent), convicted persons at the Port of Spain Prison (POSP) (65.1 percent), and remanded persons at the POSP (68.2 percent). The prison with the highest prevalence of drug use is the Tobago Prison with a rate of 87.5 percent of remanded persons and 100 percent of convicted persons indicating usage. The prisons with the highest prevalence of marijuana usage within the prison system are the POSP (remand—56.8 percent), Maximum Security Prison (remand—58.5 percent) and Tobago Prison (remand—75 percent). [47]

Not surprisingly, 30.7 percent of all respondents indicated that the crimes they committed were related to drugs. 46.1 percent of convicted and 13.1 percent of remanded prisoners and 30.1 percent of males and 40 percent of females indicated that the crimes they committed were related to drugs. The crime that was most closely linked to drugs was malicious damage, followed by stealing, attempted murder/manslaughter, and robbery. More specifically, of the persons who committed malicious damage, 57.1 percent indicated that their crime was related to drugs in some way. With respect to stealing, 40.6 percent indicated that there was a relationship between their crime and drug use, while 26.7 percent indicated that there was such a relationship for attempted murder/manslaughter and 25.8 percent indicated that there was such a relationship for robbery. The crimes with the weakest association to drug use were physical assault and sexual offences, with 22.3 percent of convicted persons and 13.1 percent of remanded persons indicating that they were under the influence of drugs when they committed the crime for which they were currently incarcerated. Of the convicted persons, 71.6 percent indicated that they would not have committed the crime if they were not under the influence of drugs, while 20.3 percent indicated that they would have committed the crime even if they were not under the influence of drugs. In the case of remanded persons, 56 percent indicated that they would not have committed the crime if they were not under the influence of drugs. Another 28 percent, however, indicated that they would have committed the crime even if they were not under the influence of drugs. Over 14 percent of convicted persons indicated that the crimes which they committed were done in order to get drugs for their personal use, while 2.1 percent of remanded persons answered similarly. When the sample was considered as a whole, 8.7 percent of all respondents committed crimes in order to acquire drugs for personal use.

The crimes that respondents committed were cross-referenced against their responses to determine if there were some crimes that were more likely to be associated with getting drugs for personal use. Sexual offences, physical assault, malicious damage, and kidnapping were unrelated to getting drugs for personal use. The crimes with the strongest linkage to the procurement of drugs were stealing, robbery and drug-related crimes. When the sample as a whole was considered, 6.3 percent of persons consumed drugs in order to boost their courage to commit crimes for which they were currently incarcerated and 9.3 percent of convicted persons indicated that they consumed drugs to boost their courage, while 2.7 percent of remanded persons did the same. Seventeen point two (17.2) percent of respondents indicated that the crimes for which they were convicted were linked to the production or trafficking of drugs.[48] When these results were disaggregated by offender status, it was discovered that 26.5 percent of convicted prisoners and 6.5 percent of remanded persons committed crimes which were linked to the production or trafficking of drugs, while 9.3 percent of respondents indicated that the crimes for which they were convicted were linked to activities to maintain the drug market such as turf fights between traffickers, the settling of accounts between traffickers, and confrontation between traffickers and the police. When these results were disaggregated by offender status, it was discovered that 13.6 percent of convicted prisoners and 4.5 percent of remanded persons committed crimes which were connected to activities to maintain the drug market, while 8.3 percent of respondents indicated that the crimes for which they were convicted were linked to activities such as money laundering, or the illicit purchase, sale or handling of chemical precursors, and 13 percent of convicted prisoners and 3.1 percent of remanded persons committed crimes which were linked to these activities. Given the crime situation at the time of this writing,[49] it is not surprising that 37.1 percent of the sample indicated that they were aware of gang-related activity which supports the drug trade, with 38.1 percent of males and 20 percent of females and 38.3 percent of convicted persons and 35.7 percent of remanded persons indicating the same.

CONCLUSION

According to the Prison Service mission statement:

> The Trinidad and Tobago Prison Service, as an arm of the Criminal Justice System, is committed to the protection of society and crime prevention by facilitating the opportunities for habilitation/rehabilitation of Offenders while maintaining control under safe, secure and humane conditions.[50]

Baptiste et al.[51] note that this mission statement advocates that the best way to protect society is to ensure the successful reintegration of prisoners into society so that they become law-abiding citizens. He further notes that the rehabilitative efforts of the TTPrS are founded on a model that incorporates correctional education, cognitive development and spiritual restoration. It should be a surprise, therefore, to note that Trinidad and Tobago has a recidivism rate of over 50 percent.[52] This means that every other ex-offender will reoffend and be reincarcerated.

Despite claims of a rehabilitative approach, the present penal system operates primarily according to a retributive model. According to the *2002 Final report of the Cabinet appointed Task Force on Prison Reform and Transformation*, the current prison system is characterized by a "tense setting . . . which is the result of fragmentation, useless coercion, and obsolete and outdated policies."[53] The philosophical concept of the prison as a rehabilitative instrument has not materialized, and an analysis of the world's prison population rates ranks Trinidad and Tobago at number 38 out of a total of 216 nations. Currently, Trinidad and Tobago has a prison population rate of 275 per 100,000 inhabitants which suggests that there is a need to devise mechanisms to address the level of incarceration and recidivism within our society.

Cid (2009)[54] examines the effects of custodial versus non-custodial sentences on recidivism. His findings reveal that prison sanctions do not reduce recidivism more effectively than suspended sentences. However, the risk of recidivism increases when the offender is imprisoned. He argues that the results of his research are compatible with labeling theory, which proposes that prison is likely to lead to higher rates of recidivism compared to a suspended sentence. In order to reduce recidivism it seems reasonable to replace prison with non-custodial sentences. This, Cid argues, is especially important when the offender has no previous conviction or no previous imprisonment. With high-risk offenders, in contrast, the risk of recidivism increases if the penalty is imprisonment and the re-offending rate is also very high when the penalty is a suspended sentence. Cid also differentiates between the high-risk offender who has a higher risk of reoffending whether incarcerated or not, and those with no exposure to imprisonment. He is essentially advocating discretionary sentencing or alternative sanctions for first-time offenders to reduce the possibility of recidivism among this category of offenders.

This introduces a necessary discussion for Restorative Justice. Restorative Justice is defined as a vision, a public policy, and a criminal justice model that links social justice and criminal justice, with the ultimate goal of keeping people out of prison, by dealing with them in the community without compromising public safety.[55] The process proposes to heal torn relationships and to restore justice. This means promoting responsibility, safety, and peace so that offenders become stakeholders in society. The Trinidad and Tobago Prison Service admits on its website that there is an ongoing challenge to move its operations, objectives, policies, rules and culture from retributive to restorative justice. They are nevertheless committed to ensuring its complete implementation.

The concept of restorative justice was further embraced by the state when the Prime Minister at the time of writing, the Honorable Mrs. Kamla Persad-Bissessar, in an article in the *Daily Express* dated 2/2/2011 announced that the Ministry of the People will be seeking to issue grants of 5000 dollars per person to former inmates for faster rehabilitation and reintegration back into communities and curb the revolving door syndrome.

Only over the last decade, has the Trinidad and Tobago Prison Service been engaged in the process of attempting to reform its culture, goals, and methodology from a retributive to a restorative orientation. The challenges in its implementation are made evident by the high recidivism rate. With the change in government and their stated support for the restorative approach it is hoped that the Prison Service will achieve its goals of reforming its organization and contributing to the rehabilitation of individuals within the system.

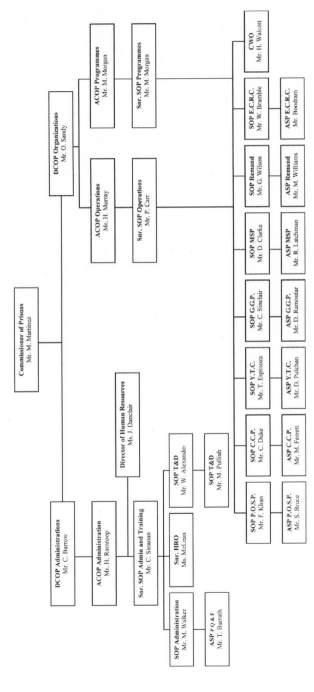

Figure 6.1. Organizational Chart of the Trinidad and Tobago Prison Service (2013). Source: Trinidad and Tobago Service

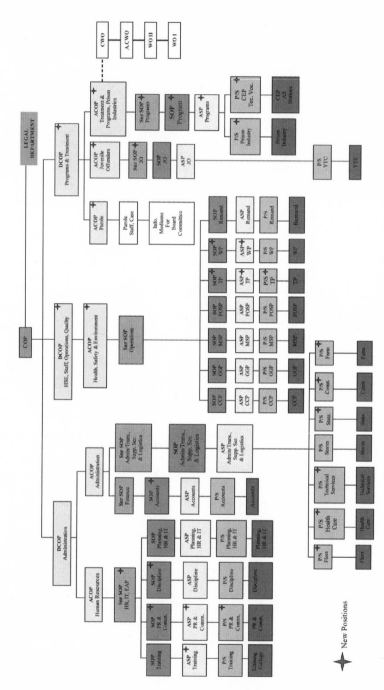

Figure 6.2. Proposed Organizational Chart of the Trinidad and Tobago Prison Service. Source: Trinidad and Tobago Prison Service

NOTES

1. Trinidad and Tobago Central Statistical Office (CSO) 2012 available at http://www.cso.gov.tt/.

2. Ibid.

3. Ibid.

4. Trinidad and Tobago Prison Service "Prison History" http://ttprisons.com/downloads/ttps1.pdf , n.d.

5. The prison system in Trinidad is divided into facilities for individuals who have been arrested and are awaiting trial and those individuals who are convicted and serving time in prison. In the Port of Spain region, the facilities for those individuals who have been arrested and pending trial are known as Remand Yard (or just "Remand").

6. Trinidad and Tobago Prison Service "About Carrera Convict Prison" http://ttprisons.com/2013/carrera-post/.

7. Youth Training Centre, Quarterly Report, January–March, 2010.

8. The Golden Grove Prison Annual Administrative Report, 2002.

9. Randy Seepersad, *Drug Use and Criminal Behaviour among the Prison Population in Trinidad and Tobago*, A report commissioned by the OAS, CICAD, National Drug Council, and Ministry of National Security of Trinidad and Tobago, 2013).

10. *Trinidad Express* "Prison Service moves towards penal reform" July 7, 2013; Selwyn Ryan, "Beyond the 'Pail': Towards Prison Reform" 2012

11. Figures from the U.S. State Department of Human Rights Report, 2012.

12. Ria Taitt, "Volney: Monitoring prisoners costly" *Trinidad Express Newspapers,* May 29, 2012.

13. Anna-Lisa, Paul, "Sweeping changes the only way forward" *Trinidad Guardian,* May 27, 2013.

14. Dana Seetahal, "Restorative Justice and the prisons" *Trinidad Express,* January 14, 2012.

15. Ryan, Selwyn "Beyond the 'Pail': Towards Prison Reform" 2012.

16. Inspector of Prisons 2012 report available at http://www.inspectorofprisonstt.com/wp-content/uploads/2013/08/IoP-Report-2012-Sans -Annex.pdf.

17. Ramesh Deosaran Special Prisons Committee Proposals for Early Urgently Needed Action, Special Report completed at the request of the Government of Trinidad and Tobago (2013).

18. Randy Seepersad and Dianne Williams, United Nations Development Programme *Caribbean Human Development Report: Human Development and the Shift to Better Citizen Security.* (UNDP, New York, 2012).

19. For more information, see *In the Inter American Court of Human Rights Report on the Conditions of Detention in Trinidad and Tabago.* Available at http://www.corteidh.or.cr/docs/casos/casoconso/gaietry.PDF.

20. This slop pail is approximately the size of a one-gallon paint bucket – Deosaran Report 2003, 87. Edghill v The Commissioner of Prisons and the Attorney General of Trinidad and Tobago No. 3178 of 2004 (Unreported). Judgement dated October 3rd 2008, at para 22(j).

21. Supra at 15.

22. Williams, Dianne, (2012). Interview with John Rougier Commissioner of Prisons of the Republic of Trinidad and Tobago *in Trends in Corrections: Interviews with Corrections Leaders Around the World.* Volume 3, 2012. Edited by Bruce Baker and Dilip Das. (33 pages) CRC Press, Taylor and Francis Group.

23. Ibid.

24. "Goverments lack political will," *The Guardian,* November 24, 2013, http://guardian.co.tt/news/2013-11-24/governments-lack-political-will.

25. LAWS OF TRINIDAD AND TOBAGO, PRISONS ACT, CHAPTER 13:01, available at http://rgd.legalaffairs.gov.tt/laws2/alphabetical_list/lawspdfs/13.01.pdf.

26. Anna Ramdass, "$400m a year to maintain prisoners," *Trinidad Express*, March 2, 2011.

27. Ria Taitt, "Volney: Monitoring Prisoners Costly," *Trinidad Express*, May 29, 2012.

28. Ian Ramdhanie, Prison Recidivism in Trinidad and Tobago in *Crime, Delinquency and Justice*: A Caribbean Reader, 2007, 368–397.

29. Ibid.

30. Ibid.

31. Ibid, 28.

32. 2002 Final Report of the Cabinet Appointed Task Force on Prison Reform and Transformation available at http://ttprisons.com/downloads/taskforcereport.pdf; Randy Seepersad, *Drug Use and Criminal Behaviour among the Prison Population in Trinidad and Tobago*, A report commissioned by the OAS, CICAD, National Drug Council, and Ministry of National Security of Trinidad and Tobago, 2013).

33. Inspector of Prisons 2012 report available at 1958 there were 4 correctional facilities and 1043 inmates and in 2012 there were 9 facilities and 3656 inmates.

34. Joel Julien,"Repeat offenders clogging prisons," *Trinidad Express*, February 6, 2011.

35. Alvin J. Bronstein, and Jenni Gainsborough (2004), *Using International Human Rights Laws and Standards for U.S. Prison Reform*, 24 Pace L. Rev. 811, 812 (2004) ("The prisoner rebellion and its aftermath at Attica in 1971 . . . served as an opening into the Dark world of America's prisons and became the catalyst for the development of the modern prisoners' rights movement.").

36. Selwyn Ryan, "Beyond the 'Pail': Towards Prison Reform," 2012.

37. 2002 Final Report of the Cabinet Appointed Task Force on Prison Reform and Transformation available at http://ttprisons.com/downloads/taskforcereport.pdf

38. Trinidad and Tobago Prison Service "Prison History" http://ttprisons.com/downloads/ttps1.pdf , n.d.

39. Ibid

40. Ministry of Justice, Penal Reform and Transformation Unit available at http://www.justice.gov.tt/about-us/units/penal-reform-and-transformation-unit/

41. Ministry of Justice, Government of Trinidad and Tobago "Penal Reform and Transformation Unit" http://www.justice.gov.tt/about-us/units/penal-reform-and-transformation-unit/ , n.d.

42. Supra at 35.

43. Trinidad Express "Prison Service moves towards penal reform," *Trinidad Express*, July 7, 2013.

44. Supra at 17.

45. Ibid.

46. Supra at 9.

47. Ibid.

48. In the case of remanded persons, this refers to previous convictions.

49. Peter Richards, "Trinidad premises to curb crime rate following nineteen murders in seven days." *Carribean 360.* January 8, 2014. http://www.caribbean360.com/index.php/news/trinidad_tobago_news/1105500.html#axzz2rivL DijN

50. Trinidad and Tabago Prison Service, http://ttprisons.com/

51. C. Baptiste. et al. *Final Report of the Cabinet Appointed Task Force on Prison Reform and Transformation.* 2002, http://ttprisons.com/downloads/taskforcereport.pdf

52. Supra at 39.

53. Supra at 19: p. 416.

54. Cid Jose (2009) Is imprisonment criminogenic?: A comparative study of recidivism rates between prison and suspended prison sanctions *European Journal of Criminology* 6(6): 459 –480.

55. Repubic of Trinidad and Tabago, *Final Reprot of the Cabinet Appointed Task Force on Prison Reform and Transformation,* 2002 http://ttprisons.com/downloads/taskforcereport.pdf.

SEVEN

Organized Chaos

Venezuela's Prison Crisis

Brian Fonseca and Pamela Pamelá

On the evening of January 6, 2014, Monica Spear, actress and former Miss Venezuela, and her husband were violently murdered along the Puerto Cabello-Valencia highway in Venezuela.[1] The murders sparked outrage and protests from Venezuelans across the country. In recent years, senseless crime and violence has become the norm in Venezuela. According to the Citizen Council for Public Security and Criminal Justice, Caracas is the second most violent city in the world, registering an alarming 134.36 homicides per 100,000 citizens in 2013.[2] Scholars and observers argue that violence in Venezuela stems from the destruction and distortion of institutions and the increasing prevalence of organized crime in the country—both of which intersect within the country's prisons. In Venezuela, prisons are illustrative of the government's inability to effectively execute domestic security and judicial policy.

Prisons in Venezuela suffer from overpopulation, overcrowding, decayed facilities, inadequate staff, a failed judiciary, widespread corruption, improper segregation of criminals, and extremely high levels of violence. Combined, these issues drive a complex criminal underworld seemingly isolated from the state and society. In most cases, inmates control prisons through informal hierarchies facilitated by corrupt officials and the inmates often outgun prison authorities. Inmates, with the explicit support from corrupt prison authorities and military personnel, routinely engage in organized criminal activities. In 2012, the *Economist* compared prisons in Venezuela, and other prisons in Latin America, to a journey into hell, arguing that prisons were perpetuating a culture of criminality.[3] Inmates that are incarcerated in Venezuela on relatively minor offenses return to society as hardened, experienced, and violent criminals.

Limited scientific research and the lack of comprehensive quality data make it difficult to truly assess the situation within the walls of Venezuela's prisons. Much of what has been published to date is largely anecdotal and journalistic in nature, and data from government and NGO sources often conflict with each other. The reality is that prison authorities do little to document, monitor, and assess prison activities, and often their data is inaccurate. The public's awareness of prison conditions often occurs when riots or protests break out within prisons, and these riots and protests usually indicate an escalation of turf wars among prison gangs or conflicts between corrupt officials and criminal organizations operating outside of the prisons.[4]

PRISONS: SEVERE STATE OF NEGLECT

Prisons remain at the center of Venezuela's penitentiary crisis and suffer from severe neglect by the state. Prisons are overpopulated, poorly maintained, and largely controlled by the inmates. Prisons have become synonymous with hell in Venezuela. To illustrate the deplorable conditions in prisons, former Tocorón and La Planta inmate turned TV personality Luidig Ochoa created a popular animated YouTube series titled "Jail or Hell" (*Carcel o Infierno*) in 2011; by 2014, the series had more than seven million views on YouTube.[5] Ochoa's series offers a unique and accurate look at the violent and inhumane conditions that exist in Venezuela's prisons. In the series' seven minute long first episode, Ochoa highlights prison overcrowding, the failed judiciary, extreme violence among inmates, and shows the National Guard's complicit involvement in promoting criminal activity.[6]

Overcrowding and overpopulation are the most critical issues driving Venezuela's inability to control its prisons. Venezuela's fifty-one imprisonment centers (including jails and detainment centers) have a capacity for 16,189 inmates, yet according to the NGO Observatorio Venezolano de Prisiones (OVP), Venezuelan prisons currently house 53,566 inmates, which is 231 percent overcapacity.[7] During the thirteen-year tenure of former President Hugo Chávez, the government built only one new prison and expanded the infamous Yare Prison, where Hugo Chávez was imprisoned after his failed military coup in 1992. During the same period, Venezuela's prison population more than doubled.[8]

In 2011, newly appointed Minister of Prisons Iris Varela declared overcrowding the most important factor driving Venezuela's prison crisis. In fact, Varela vowed to release 40 percent of the country's 50,000

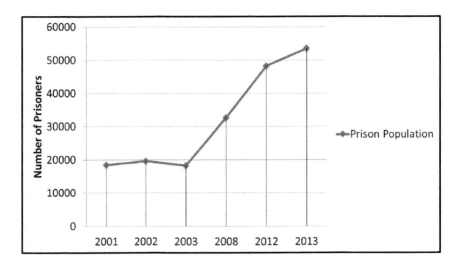

Figure 7.1.   Prison Population. Source: Observatorio Venezolano de Prisones

inmates, citing her intent to close prisons instead of building new facilities. However, Varela reversed her emphasis on closing prisons as a result of public backlash and the reality on the ground. Varela instead committed to building new facilities by 2012.[9]

Contributing to the overcrowding and overpopulation is Venezuela's inept judiciary. The inability of Venezuelan courts to effectively process pretrial detainees is leaving the overwhelming majority of the prison population in a judicial uncertainty, sometimes for years at a time. In 2014, OVP cites that only 29.89 percent of the prison population has actually been sentenced or convicted of a crime. That means nearly 75 percent of the country's prison population is classified as pretrial detainees.[10] Furthermore, Venezuelan penal laws call for the separation of pretrial detainees and convicts; however, because of limited prison facilities, prison authorities are left with few options but to integrate pretrial detainees with convicts. Making matters worse, prison authorities fail to appropriately separate inmates based on severity of the criminal offense. Nonviolent offenders are often imprisoned with violent criminals, causing many nonviolent offenders to re-enter society as hardened criminals.

Venezuela's prison population consists largely of lower-class young men, many of whom are first time offenders. Detailed demographic data is limited and recidivism rates are unavailable. However, 94 percent of the prison population is male, and according to surveys conducted with inmates, approximately 72 percent of the inmate population is between the ages of nineteen and twenty-nine years old—the vast majority between the ages of twenty to twenty-four years old.[11] Surveys also indicate that the majority of inmates between nineteen and twenty-nine years of age are first time offenders. High unemployment and lack of education in Venezuela are the primary reasons given by inmates for committing the crimes that led to their imprisonment.

Prisons in Venezuela are considered by many to be among the most violent in the world. Since 1999, when Chávez began his presidency, 6,163 inmates have died and 16,208 have been injured—1,300 deaths over the past two years alone. The increasing annual death rate inside prisons corresponds with the growing inmate population. According to OVP, the most violent Venezuelan prisons in 2013 were Sabaneta (79 deaths), Tocuyito (70 deaths), Uribana (63 deaths), Tocoron (51 deaths), and Penitenciaria de Venezuela (44 deaths). Scholars argue that prison violence is a result of two general considerations: the inability of the state to assert control over the country's prisons and inmate population, and the importance of illicit activities conducted inside prisons and in their surrounding communities. [12]

PRISONS AND ORGANIZED CRIME

Venezuelan prisons can be described as an organized, yet chaotic underworld; a violent hell that allows for relative order through hierarchically structured prison gangs. According to Venezuela's *Dirección Nacional de Servicios Penitenciarios* (National Directorate of Penitentiary Services), Venezuelan prisons are governed through *el carro* (the car), an informal authority structure that exists inside of all Venezuelan prisons. *El carro* is a phenomenon exclusive to Venezuela and is led by *pranes* and *luceros*.

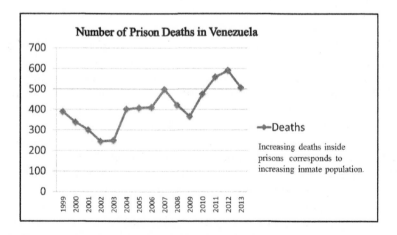

Figure 7.2.   Number of Prison Deaths in Venezuela, Source: Observatorio Venezolano de Prisiones

The *pran* is a prison gang leader that usually acquires control of a prison's inmate population by having a violent reputation and string of brutal crimes behind him—both inside and outside prisons. There is still a debate as to how the term *pran* emerged. According to journalist and author Patricia Clarembaux, author of *A ese infierno No Vuelvo* (I Won't Return to Hell), *pran* is an acronym for *preso, residente, asesino, nato,* meaning born murderer, resident inmate. During Clarembaux's field research, an inmate suggested that the term was derived from Puerto Rico's prison gangs and is a derivation of the word *pram,* or "small car."[13]

Luceros act as the *pran's* inner circle and soldiers, and can range upward to a few hundred per *pran,* depending on the size of the prison and inmate population. In Rodeo I, for example, the two main *carros* are made up of 500 *luceros* and control the lives of the more than 3,000 inmates housed in the prison.[14]

The social structure of the inmates is very hierarchical and normative. The *pran* asserts power through the monopoly of firearms and the application of violence. Gang leaders enforce what might seem like an excessive amount of rules, meant to minimize violence and maintain order within prisons. However, this is necessary, particularly in prisons where there are multiple *pranes* as power plays can lead to prison riots and clashes between gangs. This is precisely why every inmate is given a title, duty, and a set of norms to uphold, because the *pran* needs to control every aspect of the prison—from the means of generating funds to the removal of unwanted inmates.

Since the state has little to no control inside the prisons, experts proclaim that the current situation represents an undeclared truce or pact between inmates and the state. According to OVP, more than 80 percent of Venezuelan prisons are controlled by inmates. Inmates' complete control of the prison, inside and out, can be attributed to the state's consensual release of authority, most likely due to the explosion of the prison population in the 1990s, and their increased accumulation of weapons through smuggling.[15]

Weapons smuggling, informal economies, and other illicit activities allow for a *pran's* preservation of power. In these prisons, nothing is free; from a place to sleep to protection and a tax on drug sales, *pranes* charge inmates in the lower ranks for everything. In April 2013, a report was sent to a local newspaper in Venezuela from employees of the National Directorate of Penitentiary Services, the employees kept anonymity for political reasons. The report estimates that an average prison generates almost 14.5 million Bolivars a year from all the fees *pranes* collect—about 2.5 million USD (calculated by official exchange rates during that time).[16] These and other known activities lead experts to claim Venezuelan prisons have become banks, armories, and drug warehouses.

Inmates are known to conduct extortion, kidnapping, armed robbery, murder, and drug trafficking—both inside and outside the prison—to generate funds. In an interview with Roberto Briceño-Leon, an expert on crime and violence in Venezuela, an example was cited where the *pran* of a prison in the state of Anzoátegui is known to leave the prison to extort construction businesses.[17] Other accounts confirm previous reports of inmates habitually leaving the prison at night and coming back early in the mornings.[18]

The idea that prisons act as command centers for organized crime, then, is not hearsay or speculation anymore. The director of the NGO *Paz Activa* (Active Peace), asserts that the *pran's* control is nothing more than the same leadership that they may have had in a criminal structure outside, transferred into the walls of the prison. He argues, "the more powerful the pran becomes inside the jail, his leadership transcends into the street, since currently there have been organized mafias found to operate from the prisons with external ties of great reach."[19]

Strong links to drug trafficking exist, as inmates not only habitually use drugs but also store them inside the prisons. As Briceño-Leon corroborates, prisons are safe houses to store various types of illicit items. A number of prisons have been raided by police forces, and drugs and firearms are consistently seized.[20] He and other experts also assert that the trade of drugs permeates into the surrounding communities thanks to their extensive criminal networks and agreements with or payoffs to police forces guarding the prisons.

Drug trafficking through the command or participation of prisons is a factor not only within the country's borders but internationally. *Pranes* and these criminal groups work hand in hand with extensions of, or similar groups of organized crime. In this vein, San Antonio, the prison in Margarita Island, located in the Caribbean and home to the largest drug-trafficking inmate population, is considered by many to be a strategic trafficking route through the Caribbean. San Antonio's current *pran*, Teófilo Rodríguez, or *El Conejo* ("The Rabbit"), was a powerful narcotrafficker at the time of his arrest.[21]

Margarita's prison is not only a possible key link to transnational drug trafficking, but might also have connections to transnational organized crime actors such as the Mexican Sinaloa cartel and terrorist organization Hezbollah. According to former U.S. Permanent Representative to the Organization of American States (OAS) Roger Noriega, in a testimony before the House Committee on Foreign Affairs in March 2013, Margarita has become a safe haven for terrorists and drug smugglers. Citing his own research, he asserts that both the Sinaloa cartel and Hezbollah run operations in and through the island, particularly by drug trafficking and fund-raising activities.[22] Such assertions (with the caveat that Noriega's claims are partly anecdotal), lead one to question the possible connection that might exist between one of the island's most powerful narcotraffickers and other drug trafficking and transnational criminal organizations.

Finally, the implications surrounding government officials' illegal activities are enormous. Officials in control of the prisons' peripheries are complicit and collaborate with inmates in order to move illicit goods and persons in and out of prisons. Although neither side admits it, both the inmates and government actors negotiate and arrive at arrangements that benefit both sides—the inmates are granted passage of persons and items in and out of prisons, and government officials are paid off, all while ensuring control is maintained inside prisons. Riots and confrontations between inmates and officials rarely occur, but when they do occur it is largely associated with deals gone wrong.[23] Ultimately, the National Guard and authorities are fully aware of the activities going on inside and around the prisons, particularly when many of the weapons seized are military-grade.[24] Therefore, experts interviewed suggest that the real *pranes* are the corrupted officials (often National Guard leadership) that allow *pranes* to govern inside the prison.[25]

EVOLUTION OF POLICY

Venezuelan policies regarding the penitentiary system are characterized by inconsistency, inefficiency, and a lack of real political will to resolve the problems outlined throughout this chapter. While the government has argued that these problems are inherited from the mismanagement of previous administrations, others argue that current failure stems from the failed political will of former President Hugo Chávez (1999–2013) and current President Nicolás Maduro's administrations (2013 to present) in that have not done enough to address and improve conditions. The reality is that Venezuela's penitentiary policy beginning in 1999 does not diverge much from policies implemented during the previous four decades. The state has always strived to improve infrastructure and personnel, to reduce overcrowding, and to implement educational and employment programs, with the main goal being to reinsert the prisoner into society.

Beginning with the creation of the modern prison system following the ratification of the constitution in 1961, Venezuela maintained relatively humane prisons until the early 1990s.[26] During the 1990s, attempts were made to humanize the prisons and since then, numerous policies have been created, but not implemented successfully. Inhumane living conditions and levels of violence have continued to increase, leading to further deterioration.[27]

On the judicial side, in 1998 a new penal process code was enacted (*Codigo Organico Procesal Penal*) that expanded the two-stage process into four stages. Whereas previously the police would carry out nearly all of the *sumario* (summary) investigation and this would then be the basis of the *plenario* (full session), the new code: (1) designated the Attorney General (AG) to conduct the summary, (2) based on this evidence, a judge would decide whether to proceed to the plenario and if so to which court, (3) following the summary, the case would move to a separate, unbiased court, (4) and additionally, instead of one judge, most trials were now designed to be led by "mixed tribunals" (where citizens deliberate with the judge).[28] Since then, it has been reformed various times, to include the reduction or elimination of prison time for minor crimes and the elimination of mixed tribunals. Still under criticism, many believe it is to blame for the widespread judicial delay.

According to the Ministry of Justice and Interior, between 1999 and 2008, penitentiary policies were made in accordance with the constitution's mandates of article 272—establishing human rights and rehabilitation guarantees and administrative decentralization—and within the framework of *el Plan de Desarrollo Economico y Social de la Nacion 2001-2007 y el Primer Plan Socialista 2007-2013* (Economic and Social Development Plan of the Nation 2001-2007 and The First Socialist Plan 2007-2013). However, neither of these plans mention penitentiary reform.[29]

Since Venezuela's transition to a democracy in 1959, most policies do not constitute a major change from previous administrations. However, what began with Chávez can be categorized as a disoriented response when implementing programs to implement in order to gain control over the prisons:

- *Plan Estrategico de GestionPenitenciaria 1999-2000* (Strategic Penitentiary Management Plan 1999-2000): short-term plan to open inmates' participation to productive behavior, such as sports, cultural, and educational activities.
- *Plan Justicia 2000* (Justice Plan 2000): sought to classify inmates, streamline penitentiary benefits, and remodel various prisons.
- *Plan Nacional de Seguridad 2000* (National Security Plan 2000): sought to remodel and equip nine establishments, transfer the management of jails to municipal governments, and create the *Instituto Autonomo Penitenciario* (Autonomous Penitentiary Institute).
- *Politica Penitenciaria 2001-2003* (Penitentiary Policy 2001-2003): established guidelines for the modernization of the penitentiary system, which led to a series of ambitious projects and programs.

Following the declaration of a "prison emergency" in 2004, the Venezuelan government conducted a study of the problems plaguing the penitentiary system and activated its Prison Humanization Program the following year, aiming to promote ethical, moral, and social values through a series of comprehensive institutional and infrastructure projects.[30]

The following years are no different. The creations of the Superior Penitentiary Council (2008), the Penitentiary Symphonic Orchestra (2007), and the inauguration of the Penitentiary Center of Coro (2008), among others, showcase the abundance of generous, ambitious projects.

Nevertheless, the successes of all these policies have been limited, since the inmates' overall living conditions have not improved.

In fact, the simmering crisis during the 2000s led Chávez to create a new government ministry in June 2011, *Ministerio del Poder Popular para el Servicio Penitenciario "Hacia la Mujer y El Hombre Nuevo"* (The Ministry of Penitentiary Affairs "Toward the New Woman and Man"). This was also in response to the standoff between prison inmates and guards in the Rodeo prison, where the inmates held government employees hostage earlier the same year.

Since then, government forces have been intervening in prisons across the country to regain control from prison mafias, and to disarm and "humanize" the prison population.[31] The new ministry's policies seek to prevent corruption, renovate prison facilities, and reduce the backlog of prisoners' cases. Keeping with tradition, this "humanist" approach to reforming Venezuela's prison system is partly made up of the introduction of sports, music, and cultural programs meant to rehabilitate inmates. The ministry's 2011–2013 strategy consists of five major courses of action: the social transformation of inmates; the guarantee of the protection of human rights; adequate housing conditions; alternatives to the completion of sentences; and post-penitentiary support.[32]

The importance of humanizing the prison system also is emphasized by the creation of a separate section within The Ministry of Penitentiary Affairs webpage solely for the description of the "New Prison Models." Here, explicit appeals are made to the importance of the inclusion of the inmate in society through infrastructure that will allow for new activities and courses, adequate healthcare, recreational spaces, and individual rooms, with kitchens and sanitary facilities to share. As part of the Prison Humanization Program, the government wishes to reduce the negative impact resulting from incarceration.[33] The vision for the new Venezuelan Penitentiary system is summarized as a humane and modern one that assures opportunities for rehabilitation, supported by administration and ruled by ethical values and principles, within a framework that guarantees a speedy and appropriate judicial process.[34]

The government has reported on positive results from the new ministry and strategic plan. As of September 2013, according to the minister of Penitentiary Affairs, Iris Valera, over 100 National Guard soldiers and 62 ministry officials were under investigation for arms trafficking into prisons, and declaring that there are now prisons where there are no firearms.[35] Other positive developments include results from initiatives such as *Plan Cayapa*, created to attack delays in the judicial process, where last year officials stated, "33,000 prisoners have been helped by the plan, and as a result, the judicial backlog has significantly diminished."[36] However, the severely limited capacity of the government to effectively implement these reforms will ultimately lead to the inability to address Venezuela's prison crisis. This has led inmates to take matters into their own hands and attempt to humanize their spaces. Parties, concerts, and discotheques have been reported in several prisons, a process that has evolved from the early 2000s, stemming from the policy that made it legal for visitors to stay over the weekend.[37]

PERPETUATING A CULTURE OF CRIMINALITY AND VIOLENCE

Lucia Dammert and Liza Zuniga's report titled *Prisons: Problems and Challenges for the Americas* suggest that prisons are as much a driver of increased criminality as they are part of the solution.[38] In fact, prisons in Venezuela function more as incubators for criminals than they do rehabilitation centers, and prisons are a contributing factor to the high levels of violence plaguing the country. Pretrial detainees and sentenced criminals are often housed together, as are violent criminals and minor offenders. The inability to separate criminals forces minor offenders to adapt to high levels of criminality and violence. Once released, minor offenders reenter society more violent and connected than when they went into prison thanks to the exposure to extensive criminal activity and to violent behavior while incarcerated.

Making matters worse, Carlos Nieto Palma's, Director of the Venezuelan NGO *Una Ventana a la Libertad* (Window into Freedom), research indicates that inmates' families have a tendency to form small communities in close proximity to loved ones serving time. These communities are often drawn into a life of crime in order to sustain the financial burden required to pay *pranes* inside prisons for services rendered to their loved ones. Primary activities include armed robbery and *secuestro express* (express kidnappings).

Some experts argue that prisons act as safe havens for criminals.[39] Criminal groups and corrupted officials rely on prisons to manage and hide activities from public view. Gangs in prison are often given latitude by corrupt authorities to engage in illicit activities inside and outside of prisons; the latter is done often in partnership with criminal groups outside of prisons. Authorities are protected as well because inmates/criminals will not or cannot report them to authorities.

CONCLUSION: THE LONG ROAD AHEAD

Venezuelan prisons are illustrative of the general decay of Venezuelan institutions, and it is unlikely that things will change in the near future. Despite the Venezuelan Government's weak attempts to enact prison reform over the last decade, none of the reforms have been effective in addressing the fundamental issues facing the country's prisons. State resources, not just politically motivated rhetoric, must be dedicated to reverse the severe state of neglect of prisons throughout the country.

New facilities and improvements to existing facilities must be made to accommodate the existing prison population. The state must exercise enough force to regain physical control over the inmate population and subsequently provide adequate and sufficient personnel to maintain control inside the prisons. Once control is established and maintained, prisons must implement substantive employment and rehabilitation programs to keep inmates engaged and on a path to reintegration into society. Carlos Nieto Palma argues that the most detrimental factor affecting the condition of the prisons is the fact that inmates do not have any formal authority, sanctioned roles, or responsibilities inside prisons or programs to occupy their time.[40] Currently, inmates suffer from excessive leisure time, affording space for illicit trafficking, alcohol and drug abuse, and violence.

Additionally, improving prisons in Venezuela requires a mix of effective penitentiary and judiciary reforms to process criminals, classify and separate inmates, and enforce the rule of law in order to crack down on corruption and impunity. The latter, corruption and impunity is central to effectively addressing the prison crisis. Unlike other Latin American countries, resolving Venezuela's penitentiary crisis does not rest on decriminalization of certain crimes, such as drug legalization. According to official numbers, about 50 percent of arrests from 2000 to 2003 (no records available after that year) involved crimes against property, such as theft, with crimes involving narcotics only making up about 1 percent.[41] The state must reduce corruption among the National Guard, prison authorities, and administrative staff—as well as public officials. Decentralizing management according to article 272 of the constitution—which establishes the states, not the federal government as the ultimate authorities for their respective penitentiary systems—is necessary, along with a reassessment of the inmate processing and structure of trials.

Prisons play an important role in facilitating organized crime and perpetuating a culture of criminality, as illustrated in the country's high levels of violence. The Venezuelan government must retake control of the country's prisons, although it is likely that the state does not currently have the capacity to reform prisons with the current levels of corruption penetrating every aspect of government. Unless addressed, prisons will likely remain an important source of insecurity and add to the many considerations threatening the country's stability.

NOTES

1. "Former Miss Venezuela, Ex-Husband Shot Dead by Robbers" *Associated Press*, January 8, 2014.

2. The Justice in Mexico Project, "Report on 50 Most Violent Cities Worldwide Includes Nine Mexican Cities," January 24, 2014. The link to this report is http://

justiceinmexico.org/2014/01/24/report-on-50-most-violent-cities-worldwide-includes-nine-mexican-cities/.

3. "A Journey into Hell; Prisons in Latin America" *The Economist*, September 22, 2012.

4. Lucia Dammert and Liza Zuniga. "Prisons: Problems and Challenges for the Americas" FLACO Chile, January 2009.

5. Luidig Ochoa, "Carcel o Infierno," October 27, 2011. The link to the video is http://youtu.be/rhmM_mqKBbk.

6. Laura Weffer Cifuentes, "Luidig Ochoa no es Comiquita," *Ulitmas Noticias*, October 28, 2012.

7. For more on el Observatorio Venezolano de Prisiones, see http://www.ovprisiones.org/

8. A Posada and M Díaz-Tremarias, "Las cárceles y población reclusa en Venezuela," Rev Esp Sanid Penit 2008; 10: 22–27, esp, 33.

9. "The firth circle of hell," *The Economist*, July 14, 2011

10. http://www.ovprisiones.org/.

11. Humberto Prado, "Los Derechos Humanos y Debido Proceso de las Personas Privadas de Libertad" Observatario Venezolano de Prisiones, 2010.

12. Interviews with experts in Venezuela that asked to remain anonymous in February 2014.

13. "Conozca el reino de los 'pranes,'" *UltimasNoticias*, July 4, 2011.

14. Molina, T. "PENALES: El "pran" y su ejército de peones." *El Universal*, June 17, 2011.

15. Ibid.

16. "ESPECIAL: Conozca cuánto dinero genera una cárcel venezolana al año," *DiarioRepublica*, April 24, 2013.

17. R. Briceño-Leon (March 2014). Phone interview by authors. Caracas, Venezuela and Miami, FL, USA.

18. "Cicpc abatió a pran de Sabaneta que salió a pasear." *UltimasNoticias*, September 19, 2013. http://www.ultimasnoticias.com.ve/noticias/actualidad/sucesos/cicpc-abatio-a-pran-de-sabaneta-que-salio-a-pasear.aspx (accessed March 6, 2014).

19. Thabata Molina, "PENALES: El "pran" y su ejército de peones." *El Universal*, June 17, 2011.

20. "Incautan dinero y droga en cárcel venezolana donde sigue motín." *La Republica*, Junee 29, 2011. http://www.larepublica.ec/blog/internacional/2011/06/27/incautan-dinero-y-droga-en-carcel-venezolana-donde-sigue-motin/ (accessed March 6, 2014).

21. D. Mizrahi, "Venezuela: la prisión-resort, un paraíso para los delincuentes." *Las cárceles en América Latina, auténticas escuelas del delito*, November 19, 2013. http://www.infobae.com/2013/11/17/1524235-las-carceles-america-latina-autenticas-escuelas-del-delito (accessedMarch 15, 2014).

22. Roger, Noriega, "Hezbollah's strategic shift: A global terrorist threat." *Testimony before the House Committee on Foreign Affairs, Subcommittee on Terrorism, Nonproliferation, and Trade*, March 20, 2013. Retrieved from http://www.aei.org/speech/foreign-and-defense-policy/regional/middle-east-and-north-africa/hezbollahs-strategic-shift-a-global-terrorist-threat/

23. Girish Gupta "Prison uprising continues in Venezuela." *Global Post*, June 22, 2011. http://www.globalpost.com/dispatch/news/regions/americas/venezuela/110622/prison-uprising-venezuela-riot (accessed March 6, 2014).

24. "Cárcel venezolana: incautaron 105 armas y 22.767 municiones." *Infobae*, September 30, 2013. http://www.infobae.com/2013/09/30/1512447-carcel-venezolana-incautaron-105-armas-y-22767-municiones (accessed March 6, 2014).

25. Interviews with experts in Venezuela that asked to remain anonymous in February 2014.

26. Mark Ungar, "Prison Mayhem."*NACLA Report on the Americas.*Vol. 30, no. 2. 37 (January 1996).

27. Mitch Roth, *Prisons and Prison Systems: A Global Encyclopedia.* (Westport, CT: Greenwood, 2005), 286–287.

28. Mark Ungar, "Prisons and Politics in Contemporary Latin America." *Human Rights Quarterly.* Vol 25, 4 (2003): 909–934.

29. MG Morais, "Situacion actual de los derechos humanos en las carceles de Venezuela." October 2009. Observatorio Venezolano de Prisiones and Instituto Latinoamericano de Investigaciones Sociales.

30. Embassy of the Bolivarian Republic of Venezuela to the UK and Ireland.(n.d.). *Fact sheet: The Humanisation of Venezuelan Prisons.* Retrieved from http://embavenez.co.uk/sites/embavenez.co.uk/files/factsheets/fs_Humanisation_Venezuelan_Prisons.pdf.

31. Chris Carlson, "Massacre in Venezuelan prison reignites criticism of prison system." *VenezuelaAnalysis.com.* January 28, 2013. Retrieved from http://venezuelanalysis.com/news/7651.

32. Ministerio del Poder Popular para el Servicio Penitenciario, (2011). *Plan estratégico del sistema penitenciario venezolano 2011-2013.* Retrieved from website: http://www.ciudadccs.info/wp-content/uploads/PLAN_DEL_SISTEMA_PENITENCIARIO_230811_.pdf.

33. Ministerio del Poder Popular para el Servicio Penitenciario. (n.d.). *Nuevo modelo de prisiones.* Retrieved from http://www.fonep.gob.ve/institucion.php?ids=14.

34. Ibid.

35. Ewan Robertson, "Venezuelan government evacuates prison following deadly inmate clash." *VenezuelaAnalysis.com.* September 20, 2013. Retrieved from http://venezuelanalysis.com/news/10037

36. Ibid.

37. "Reos de la cárcel de Margarita inauguraron discoteca." *El Universal.* March 30, 2013. Retrieved from http://www.eluniversal.com/sucesos/130330/reos-de-la-carcel-de-margarita-inauguraron-discoteca

38. Lucia Dammert and Liza Zuniga. "Prisons: Problems and Challenges for the Americas" FLACO Chile, January 2009

39. Interviews with experts in Venezuela that asked to remain anonymous in February 2014.

40. C. Nieto Palma (2014, February). In-person interview by authors. Caracas, Venezuela.

41. "Detenciones efectuadas, según tipo de delito," *Venescopio,* http://www.venescopio.org.ve/estadisticasbasicasdevenezuela/detenciones-efectuadas-segun-tipo-de-delito.

EIGHT

Drugs and Prisons

The Slippery Road to the Criminalization of Drugs in Ecuador

Adrián Bonilla and Nashira Chávez

Latin America's position in the international economy of the drug trade is not new. Drugs such as coca, opium poppy, and marijuana are enduring features of the Andean landscape, yet they are exposed to ever-changing attitudes about their use. At the time of the Inca Empire, coca was consumed to increase work productivity and was also used in ritual ceremonies and as part of various cultural practices and exchanges of indigenous groups. The social role of coca continued during the Spanish conquest as a symbol of indigenous identity and it was used in religious ceremonies, food, medicine, and collectively consumed during labor in what is today Peru and Bolivia.[1] Until the twentieth century, coca consumption, and cocaine as its by-product, was considered legal. Perceptions regarding the use of coca have nevertheless left their traditional associations behind and are now securitized.

By the end of the twentieth century, security became the main point of reference to address drug-related activities, resulting in the criminalization of users and the overcrowding of the prison system. The U.S.–led "war on drugs" marks Latin America's shift from treating drugs as a health issue to a security issue. This work analyzes the relationship between drugs and crime, focusing particularly on the penitentiary system, in Ecuador. The analysis is divided into four sections. The first section traces Ecuador's role in the political economy of the international drug trade in the western hemisphere. The second section analyzes Ecuador's domestic policy efforts to reduce drug trafficking and consumption. In the third part, we discuss the criminal justice system, its norms, costs, and the criminalization of drug users. We conclude with reflections on penal policies implemented to combat drugs, analyzing their effectiveness and highlighting the growing problems that must be addressed in the near future.

A BRIEF HISTORY OF THE WAR ON DRUGS IN THE AMERICAS

Beginning in 1960, the international system, under U.S. leadership, began to define the "drug problem" in terms of consumption and the traffic of coca, marijuana and opium poppy. The 1961 United Nations Single Convention on Narcotic Drugs stated that chewing coca was a form of drug abuse. These plants have remained a high security priority because they are used to produce psychoactive drugs, cocaine in particular. The U.S. has been a crucial actor in the implementation of repressive policies against drugs. In 1971, Richard Nixon officially declared the war on drugs, which was further strengthened by Ronald Reagan in the 1980s. The proliferation of cocaine in the United States and its relation to violence in the streets prompted the declaration of drugs as a national security threat and the enforcement of increasingly repressive policies. At the end of the century, cocaine, heroin, and marijuana came to be considered a social problem despite relatively low addiction levels when compared to alcohol. The new approach relies on law enforcement, incarceration, and military strategies as policy tools. The offensive military arm of the war on drugs in particular, has attempted to curb drug production in source countries through crop eradication, efforts to dismantle organized crime, and seizures of illicit substances along transit routes prior to arrival on U.S. shores.[2]

The timing of the shift toward a security focus is associated with the end of the Cold War. The return to democracy and the collapse of ideological wars left a void in regional missions. In this context, the expansion of drug cartels and organized crime coincided with the last stage of the Cold War.

The war on drugs is based on the notion that crime must be addressed through the seizure of illegal drugs. The U.S. has focused on stopping the supply of drugs by implementing various counternarcotic measures in the Andean Region, which consists of Colombia, Ecuador, Bolivia, and Peru. The U.S. provided military and police assistance under the Andean Initiative program. Initially created under George H. W. Bush, the Andean Initiative is probably the most consistent and continuous U.S. policy in the region, and provides funding for military and police training, military equipment and transportation, installations and, to a lesser extent, law enforcement, development, and economic aid.

At the international level, the security approach is based on moral assumptions. Francisco Thoumi explains the link between drugs and crime and the perception of Washington, which views the war on drugs as the "continuous struggle of good and evil."[3] The standard presumption identifies the enemy as the consumer engaging with illegal products as well as organized crime cultivating, manufacturing, and transporting such noxious substances. Said differently, groups related to the production, transportation, and consumption of illicit drugs are criminals and the drug trade is the crime.

The aim of the security strategy has been the eradication of coca leaf production concentrated in Colombia, Peru, and Bolivia with the first two positioned as drug cartel havens. The emphasis on the source of coca leaves, cocaine and heroin production centered the strategy in producer countries under the assumption that eradicating the leading cartels would dismantle the drug trade.

The U.S. has provided financial resources to militarize the war on drugs in order to help the armed forces survey, search, and eradicate coca and other drugs, as well as to launch missions to patrol, arrest, and question civilians. In some countries, such as Ecuador, these initiatives included hosting a U.S. base known as Forward Operation Location (FOL).[4] Given Ecuador's role as a transit route and producer of precursor chemicals, U.S. funding has been concentrated on law enforcement programs with less money allocated for offensive initiatives. The counternarcotic policies in its initial stages sought to dismantle the large cartels and arrest leading drug lords. Victory was declared with the dismantling of the Medellín Cartel and the reduction of coca crops in Peru and Bolivia. Yet for the most part, success was short-lived as total coca production remains steady and even increased in Peru.

Counternarcotic initiatives in Ecuador are intrinsically related to its geographic position in the war on drugs as Ecuador is located between two major coca producers and sources of psychoactive drugs.[5] As of

Country	2011	2012	2013	2014	Country Total
Colombia	175,250,000	140,100,000	139,111,268	129,063,380	4,222,292,151
Peru	29,400,000	26,646,597	26,007,065	23,384,130	636,587,792
Bolivia	15,000,000	7,500,000	6,870,000	4,580,000	440,792,997
Ecuador	4,300,000	4,300,000	4,400,000		116,206,000
Venezuela					12,174,000
TOTAL	223,950,000	178,546,597	176,388,333	157,027,510	5,428,052,940

Figure 8.1. U.S. Military and Police Aid, 2001–2014. Source: Just the facts, accessed October 2, 2013, http://justf.org/Aid.

2013, Ecuador's security policies have focused on securing the northern border. The Ecuadorian government has focused on the collateral effects of Colombia's military initiatives pushing guerrilla organizations, such as The Revolutionary Armed Forces of Colombia (FARC), from the center of the country outward toward border areas. The effects of Colombia's conflict have become visible along the border with sporadic mobilizations of illegal groups on the margins of Ecuador, where they have sought shelter and assistance. Another key complaint has been with regard to the repercussions of aerial spraying programs undertaken in Colombia, which have not been effective in eradicating coca but have resulted in significant environmental damages. Socially speaking, fumigation of coca crops has strained relations due to health effects among northern communities. Yet Ecuador has traditionally refused any direct engagement in the Colombian conflict.

The drug trade also has impacted Ecuador's domestic politics. The political game between the center-left party of the presidency (*Izquierda Democrática*) and the right opposition (*Partido Social Cristiano*) in the 1990s was partially responsible for undermining counternarcotics efforts. The opposition criticized non-incarceration policies and the enforcement of health treatment for drug users under the 1970 and 1987 laws, and accusing them of being weak. The result was Law 108, a framework supporting punitive policies. [6] The end of Ecuador's territorial conflict with Peru further accelerated the transition toward the construction of illicit drugs as a threat. Previously, for more than fifty-seven years, security policies gravitated toward the adeptness of the Ecuadorian armed forces for a potential conflict with Peru. As a result, military deployment clustered in the southern region of the country.

A combination of international and domestic dynamics resulted in Ecuador's participation in the political economy of drug trafficking. The vast literature on the subject has offered a consistent argument on the correlation between the birth of the U.S.–led war on drugs and Latin American punitive approaches to illegal drugs. [7] Within the international structural pressure, the Andean countries produced diverse strategies according to their role in the drug trafficking networks. For Ecuador, both its transit position and the spillover of the Colombian conflict marked its participation in the regional agenda.

ECUADOR AS A TRANSIT COUNTRY: WHAT HAS CHANGED IN THE LAST TWENTY YEARS?

The dynamics of drug trafficking have evolved in the last twenty years cascading into a different role for Ecuador. The initial stage of the war on drugs led to the collapse of cartels in Colombia, which dominated the drug trade industry in the 1990s. [8] The approach emphasized eradication and interdiction. Bolivia and Peru as producing countries spotlighted most eradication missions. With the removal of the cartels, small-organized groups assumed leadership roles in the illicit trade. This implied the dispersion of the drug structure to multiple and fragmented groups. At the same time, coca now supported counterinsurgency groups and as a result drug-related activities moved beyond material profits. In Bolivia and Peru, the absence of a violent conflict, beginning in the 1990s, favored manual eradication complemented by aerial operations to shut down what has been referred to as the "air-bridge" toward Colombia.[9] Within the industry, Peru and Bolivia cultivated more coca than Colombia and, therefore, served mostly as suppliers in the supply-chain network. The division of labor within the drug industry was able to adapt to the relative success of coca suppression in Peru and Bolivia (coca crops increased again in Peru by 1999 despite a previous 50 percent decrease in production). The Andean region witnessed the expansion of drug flow along ground routes toward Colombia. At the same time in Colombia, violence and the lack of state presence in remote areas facilitated its position as a producer and transit country. Ecuador's role is determined by its geographic location flanked by Peru and Colombia as major producers: between 1995 and 1999 both countries had become the world's major coca leaf producers.[10] While there have been substantial military actions, such military initiatives have neither reduced the availability of illegal drugs nor the strategic position of the region.

Cultivation: Why Ecuador Is Not a Producer

Ecuador has traditionally been considered a relatively stable country within the international political economy of drugs in comparison to other Andean countries. There is no evidence of Ecuador as a large illegal drug producer or consumer according to the UN Office on Drugs and Crime. No more than twenty hectares of coca leaf production on average has been reported scattered along the northern border.[11] According to reports, in 2012 the government eradicated 61,056 coca plants, 1.8 million poppy plants, and 85,134 cannabis plants.[12] Located in a region which produces cocaine and marijuana, Ecuador has predominantly served as a transit point, a producer of precursor chemicals, and arguably a haven for money laundering (although the magnitude of the latter lacks evidence).[13] Transit operations occur along clandestine, sparsely populated, uncontrolled border routes and also via maritime routes toward the U.S.

According to the U.S. government, around 110 metric tons of cocaine transit Ecuador every year coming from Peru and Colombia.[14] In the last ten years, transportation tactics have become more sophisticated with semi-submersibles, speed-boats, and container ships. Another increasing trend has been the emergence of transnational organized networks working sporadically in Ecuador, such as Colombia's FARC, Los Zetas, and the Gulf Cartel from Mexico, as well as Russian and Chinese criminal networks. In this context, major Ecuadorian initiatives rely on the seizure of psychoactive drugs and the destruction of cocaine laboratories. Despite its location—situated between major producers Peru and Colombia— [15] Ecuador has successfully curbed drug production. The country represents an intriguing case because of its limited participation in drug trafficking given its strategic location and weak public institutions.

The answer to Ecuador's peculiar position in the political economy of drug trafficking can be found by analyzing the domestic socioeconomic determinants. At the time of the Spanish Conquest, two contradictory events unfolded. On the one hand, part of the struggle between the Spanish Conquest and the Inca Empire occurred along cultural confrontations based on religion and the use of coca in rituals associated with divinity and Mother Earth. [16] At the core of the conquest was the need to outlaw and eradicate coca in order to weaken an integral part of native Indian identity. On the other hand, the Spanish elite benefited from coca chewing among Indian miners because of its palliative effects on hunger and exhaustion. All in all, scant research on the topic argues coca chewing was not as ingrained in Quito as in other parts of the Inca Empire now known as the Andean region. [17] Second, the ban of coca during the colonial viceroyalty of Peru (comprising most of South America, including Ecuador) was inconsequential for Ecuador due to the lack of mines. While coca chewing was accepted along mining areas of the colonial viceroyalty, the lack of mines in Ecuador reduced its economic priority within the viceroyalty. This led to the expropriation of indigenous territory to be managed by the Catholic Church resulting in the decreasing use of coca as a social and labor practice among the indigenous Ecuadorian population. [18]

Beginning in 1828, Ecuador and Peru engaged in the longest territorial conflict in the region; a conflict which ended in 1998. The priority became securing the state and defending Ecuador's sovereignty. This in turn resulted in the containment of the drug trade, coca cultivation, and production during this period in which Peru was the major producer of coca. Moreover, the war on drugs also coincided with the oil boom and its strategic role in the economic development of Ecuador. The exploitation and control of oil in remote areas was supervised and led by the military and this obstructed coca production. To this date, Ecuador's compact geography allows Ecuadorian forces to control remote areas such as the forest. Notwithstanding the weak state presence along isolated areas, Ecuador's small size allows law enforcement easy access to those areas. Furthermore, by the end of the 1980s the Ecuadorian government distributed land tenure and titles among the indigenous population, which advanced the regularization of vast amounts of the territory.

In sum, Ecuador's divergent path from its neighbors is a result of domestic conditions. Ecuador's position in the drug trade is marked by the early eradication of coca crops in colonial times and the control of the territory during the conflict with Peru. Later, the agrarian reform, early settlements at the border and the projection of the state in remote areas furthered expanded control over the territory and thwarted production of psychoactive drugs.

ECUADOR'S DOMESTIC POLICY:

NATIONAL EFFORTS TO REDUCE DRUG CONSUMPTION AND DRUG TRAFFICKING

The aforementioned domestic conditions provide some lessons about Ecuador's role in the drug trade. As a transit route and precursor of chemicals, Ecuador has avoided much of the violence associated with the drug trade. There is no evidence that the drug trade supports domestic insurgency and cartels like in the case of Colombia. Because Ecuador has neither been a producer nor a country laden with violent conflict, its counter-initiatives are characterized by the surveillance of transit flows and consumption. Interdiction efforts emerged intensely at the end of the 1990s with the armed forces taking on the task. A clear sign of this was the elaboration of the security and defense white paper in 2002.[19] This promoted the redefinition of security threats in terms of organized crime and drugs four years after the peace agreement with Peru. In 1999, Ecuador's counternarcotics efforts progressed with the implementation of a ten-year cooperation agreement with the U.S., which provided resources from the U.S. Southern Command to detect drug shipments in the region. Part of the Ecuadorian security vision is the result of the U.S. policy of certification, under which trade benefits as well as security funding are contingent upon the country's willingness to comply with U.S. anti-drug policies.[20]

In 1970, the "Law of Control and Intervention in the Trafficking of Narcotics" set the stage for future national efforts to reduce consumption.[21] This was the first law that addressed illicit drugs and focused on the consumption of such substances. The Government focused on public health. Enforcement emphasized incarceration for those who grew illegal crops. However, drug users received treatment.[22] Ecuador's lack of history in coca leaf cultivation produced a low number of prisoners. A second stage in Ecuadorian legislation began with the passage of the "Law of Control and Intervention in the Trafficking of Narcotics and Psychotropic Substances," passed by the national Congress in 1987. The new law again did not advance punitive actions against consumers and instead mandated rehabilitation.[23] In any case, measures underpinning public order were equally enforced. Prison sentences up to sixteen years were first introduced at this time, but they were applied only under extreme circumstances upon evidence of drug production or trafficking.[24]

DRUGS: A SHIFT IN THE REGULATORY FRAMEWORK TO CRIMINALIZATION

The Andean Initiative facilitated the "Law of Narcotic Drugs and Psychotropic Substances" in 1991. Also known as Law 108, the legislation marks the shift toward punitive measures. Offenses including possession, transport, and production faced a mandatory minimum of twelve years compared to the sixteen years maximum sentence for murder. The criminalization of drugs was further expanded by the processes involving the law. Law 108 required the Supreme Court[25] to review sentencing in drug cases in order to monitor and review judges' verdicts. This put in place a clear-cut presumption of guilt for drug possession crimes. The system threatened judges with sanctions for ruling in favor of suspects resulting in a high proportion of guilty verdicts and imprisonment. In addition, Law 108 considers drug offenses an imprisonable crime, and therefore, grants detention. Third, U.S. certification of the counternarcotics program required a 12 percent annual increase in the incarceration and sentencing rates for drug-related crimes and a 10 percent increase in the interdiction of drugs.[26]

The criminalization dynamic resulted in setbacks. The shift from a public health focus to punitive measures did not allow for distinctions among types and levels of crime; drug consumers risked the same sentences that drug traffickers and leaders of organized criminal networks faced. Equal sentences for all types of drug offenses without bail resulted in the proliferation of drug-related arrests. In addition, the 12 percent requirement forced the government and law enforcement officials to increase not only the number of arrests but the number of incarcerations as opposed to focusing on treatment, education, and prevention.

OVERVIEW OF THE PRISON SYSTEM

Ecuador's historic role and position in drug trafficking sets the stage for a punitive policy that does not reflect the reality of the country. There are two important time lines that are necessary to mention when analyzing the Ecuadorian penal system. The first one goes from 1989 to 2008 and refers to the penal figures in the context of the war on drugs and Law 108. A second stage for the prison-drug dynamic began to unfold post-2009 in the wake of the 2008 Constitution and the 2009 closing of the Forward Operation Location in Manta. Reforms to the law and public policy after 2009 are still ongoing and the long-term effects remain to be seen.

Within the context of Law 108, the prison population more than doubled to 13,532 prisoners by 2008.[27] According to the Washington Office on Latin America report, "Drug Law Reform in Ecuador: Building Momentum for a More Effective, Balanced and Realistic Approach," between 1993 and 2007 the average proportion of detainees held on drug-related charges was 45 percent. By 2008, the latest Ecuadorian prison population census revealed that 34 percent of prisoners, numbering approximately 4,600 inmates, were in prison on drug-related charges.[28] Prisoners sentenced under Law 108 now constitute consistently the largest population cluster in Ecuador's penal system. This is followed by those convicted of crimes against property and far greater those held for crimes against persons (the latter constituting some 15 percent of the prison population). Around half of prisoners in urban prisons are held on drug charges.[29] Furthermore, the rate of people held in prison per 100,000 people was 161, comparatively higher than Colombia (117) and Peru (154).[30] These statistics also reveal an overcrowding of 157 percent. By 2011, the total prison population numbered 15,420, down from a high of 18,000 in 2010, in a system with a capacity for no more than 9,000 detainees.[31]

Current data reveals a connection between the enforcement of repressive policies under the auspices of the war on drugs and the proliferation of prisoners incarcerated for drug charges. Beginning in 1993, as the post-Cold War broadened the security agenda and Law 108 was enforced, Ecuador consistently had higher incarceration rates related to drug charges. In 1975, for example, Ecuadorian policy focused on health initiatives and imprisonment for property crimes constituted the highest percentage of prisoners.[32] As previously mentioned, this changed as a result of the shift in policy and the focus on incarcerating not only drug traffick-

Table 8.1.   Ecuadorian Prison Population Census (2008)

Type of Crime	Number of Prisoners	Percent (of total)
Drug Offenses	4,600	34
Crimes Against Property	3,924	29
Crimes Against Persons	2,029	15
Sexual Crimes	1,353	10
Other Crimes	1,626	12
Total	13,532	100

Source: El Universo, "Hoy se presentan los resultados del censo penitenciario," National Edition, Sucesos sec., accessed September 20, 2013, http://www.eluniverso.com/2008/07/31/0001/10/
1E6737433C0F45F1984ACB88ECA80A1E.html

ers but drug users, as opposed to treating drug problems as a public health issue. Overcrowding in the Ecuadorian prison system is a result of various factors, most notably the high percentage of individuals who have not received a sentence; 60 percent of inmates have not been sentenced.[33] In addition, the need to continue arresting and incarcerating people on drug charges has contributed to the overcrowding of the penitentiary system.

Ecuador has forty prisons, and approximately nine out of ten detainees are men (92 percent of total detainees are men and 8 percent women). Yet 80 percent of women are detained on drug charges.[34] According to a 2005 National Statistic report, most prisoners were between eighteen and thirty-nine years old.[35] Drug offenses also run high among foreign inmates, the majority of which are from neighboring countries. Two-thirds of foreign offenders are from Colombia, followed by Peruvian offenders.

Statistics on the prison system and drugs are for the most part incomplete and limited. However, the data available provides us with some information about how the criminalization of drugs affects the Ecuadorian prison system. Drug-related charges are the highest among both male and female inmates; for females, drug-related offenses are the most common, while for males it is the second most common.[36] Granted, this profile suggests most offenders are potentially consumers or low-level traffickers. Studies on gender, drugs, and prisons in Ecuador reveal that female inmates generally are non violent offenders that have engaged in low-level trafficking operations. Despite being 10 percent of the total pris-

Table 8.2.   Prison Figures

2007–2011	
Number of Prisons	40
Total Drug Offenses	34 percent
Total Drug Offenses in Urban Areas	45 percent
Number of Detainees Imprisoned for Micro-Trafficking	63 percent
Highest Age Interval Detainees for Drug Offenses	18–39
Number of Females Incarcerated	1,213
Number of Males Incarcerated	14,207
Number of Foreigners Incarcerated	1,946

Source: Jorge Nuñez, "La crisis del Sistema penitenciario del Ecuador" and Jenny Pontón and Andreina Torres, "Cárceles del Ecuador: los efectos de la criminalización por drogas."

on population, more than two-thirds of women are imprisoned for drug-related charges, mostly in urban areas.[37] Female offenders are at the lower end of the drug decision-making pyramid. At the same time, the youth rate and the rate itself of micro-traffickers suggest a significant proportion of drug offenders are either consumers or intermediaries.[38]

The enactment of Law 108 and the war on drugs appear to be a critical juncture for the current profile and overcrowding of the prison population. Starting with the criminalization of drugs between 1989 and 1991, the data reveals a drastic rise in the number of prisoners (see table 1.3). The criminalization of drugs through a combination of instruments, such as military initiatives and national legislation, established basic objectives to combat illegal drugs. That is to say, that it defined the centerpiece of crime in the manipulation of drugs, drug users, and traffickers as the enemies of the national interest. Yet as the profile of prison inmates demonstrates, the problem turned out to be more complex. Such repressive policies have resulted in overcrowding and have become a burden to the Ecuadorian government. Vast resources are needed to maintain such an expanding system.

The criminalization of drugs in Ecuador also expanded as a result of initiatives to increase public order and security. The delineation of crime under Law 108 does not distinguish among offenders and results in the punitive measures, including a twelve-year minimum sentence, from first time offenders to small-scale drug traffickers, mules, and cartel leaders. Nevertheless, the shift in the regulatory regime from a health policy to punitive measures seems to have failed to achieve the main objectives of

Table 8.3.   Prison Population Growth 1989–2011 (selected years)

Year	Population Growth	Cumulative Relative Frequency	Incarceration per 1,000 population
1989	6,978	0.45	NA
1992	7,884	0.51	74
1995	9,646	0.63	85
1998	9,439	0.61	79
2001	7,856	0.51	63
2003	9,866	0.74	91
2005	11,358	0.74	91
2008	14,628	0.95	118
2011	15,420	1.00	107

Source: Sandra Edwards, "A short history of Ecuador's drug legislation" and Elias Carranza, "Situación Penitenciaria en América Latina y el Caribe."

capturing the critical actors in the supply-chain of drugs. As previously mentioned, statistical evidence suggests that more than 60 percent of prisoners are low-level drug-traffickers. These types of offenders are traditionally nonviolent actors and indiscernible at the pinnacle of production cartels or organized crime networks. Yet they face the same penalties as violent offenders charged with rape or robbery. Likewise, the enforcement process itself criminalizes drug offenses, and as a result, the penal system prioritizes drug legislation since half of the cases in criminal courts are drug-related. Furthermore, all legal processes associated with drug offenses are revised and accepted for court. [39]

PRISON COSTS, CONDITIONS AND MANAGEMENT

Enforcement of security initiatives—which are distant from the reality of Ecuador's role in drugs—comes also at a cost in the structure of the penal system itself. The rising prison population has resulted in massive overcrowding. With the doubling of its population relative to its capacity, Ecuador's prison system experienced a critical overcrowding density of 145 percent in 2011, from a high of 161 in 2007. [40] These statistics are a result of the drastic increases in the number of people arrested and sentenced for drug crimes. Table 1.3 illustrates a steady growth rate beginning in 1992 with an acceleration tipping point around 2004 and continuing to the present. The Ecuadorian government is struggling with the cost of building new facilities and expanding the existing ones to accommodate the increasing prison population. International norms establish 20 square meters as the minimum space available per prisoner, a standard the government must meet. Currently, the penal system only allows half of that space. [41] In the case of female prisons, where 392 minors lived with their mothers in 2007, overcrowding leads to even more inadequate living conditions. [42] At one point, according to reports, three prisoners may share a single bed. [43]

Budget for personnel and the expansion of the physical infrastructure are lacking. Despite overcrowding, less than 10 percent of an already inadequate budget was used for infrastructure in the last decade while 70 percent was allocated to food. [44] An insignificant increase in the food budget for detainees—two dollars per prisoner in 2010—did nothing to improve conditions. [45] Furthermore, there is also evidence of fewer healthcare providers and guards, reducing adequate services. A 2006 report estimates the presence of one guard for 11.7 detainees, which is four times higher than the three to one ratio required. [46]

Overall, a weak institutional structure points to a bleak future ahead. There is a lack of current data for the number of medical, legal, and psychological personnel. The prison's poor living conditions suggest a system that fails to adequately incorporate offenders into society. The lack of adequate supervision facilitates the formation of violent groups of inmates who run the prison, establishing a subset of rules. Moreover, the lack of an adequate structure ensures a relapse rate.

THE CRIMINAL CONSTRUCTION OF DRUG USERS AND DRUG-RELATED OFFENDERS

Starting in the 1980s, there has been a drastic shift in the demographics of the prison population. In 1972, 3.5 percent of inmates were in prison for drug-related offenses. By 1980, the number had increased to 17 percent. A decade later, the number jumped to 45 percent, making drug-related activities the main criminal offense. The increase in the number of drug offenders in prison reflected the shift in the government's view regarding drugs. Government officials who once saw drugs as a health issue and placed offenders in hospitals, now began to criminalize drug activities. The criminalization of drugs within the domestic structure runs parallel to the war on drugs and the construction of drug users and traffickers as menaces to society that should be punished. The counternarcotic logic thus measures success in terms of quantity: the number of offenders imprisoned. Punitive policies shift the target to the often poor and uneducated males living in rural areas to the urban male or female more educated user or micro trafficker.[47] In sum, the prohibitionist argument defines the agenda.

At the state level, the judicial process predetermines a guilty verdict in the sentencing procedure. Drug suspects are immediately imprisoned without the possibility of bail regardless of the type of crime or the quantity of drugs involved; whether they are consumers, small-scale traffickers, or even major cartel leaders, all suspects fall in the same category and receive the same punishments.[48] Edwards and Youngers describe the Ecuadorian judicial process in terms of "the transfer of burden of proof onto the accused,"[49] and, as a result, there is an automatic assumption of guilt.

The lack of an independent judicial and legal defense for those arrested also contributes to the negative portrayal of those arrested. The judicial system traditionally stigmatizes judges who rule in favor of offenders as soft on crime. In particular, the Supreme Court revisions of the 1990s sparked fears of sanctions for judges encouraging them to be "tough on crime" and contributing to the presumptions of defendants' guilt. The negative portrayal of those arrested is another factor contributing to the increasing incarceration rates.[50] Moreover, the low numbers of public defenders ensured the lack of legal representations for the defendants. For example, in 2007, there were thirty-two public defenders for hundreds of defendants waiting for trial. Those who lack the resources necessary to hire a private attorney are guaranteed an unfair trial. In addition, even if defendants have the money many lawyers steer clear of drug cases as they fear being perceived as corrupt.[51] In sum, this reality, coupled with the construction of the war on drugs as a security issue has set the parameters for the criminalization of drugs.

THE SLIPPERY ROAD TO THE CRIMINALIZATION OF DRUGS

The regional drug trade displays multiple layers of complexity. Latin America's system of growers, producers, storage, and transit countries have expanded considerably, making the drug trade's political economy even more intricate. Military repression while effective in eradicating targeted spots, forces the drug trade to adapt and relocate within the region. The war on drugs, and consequently Ecuador's policies, have developed under the assumption that high incarceration rates are evidence of success in efforts to combat drugs. The fact that the Andean countries continue to be drug havens in the Western Hemisphere leads experts to conclude that drug policies have failed to achieve their objectives as drugs remain readily available. Ecuador, as well as other countries, must answer the question of who the "enemy" is. Is our struggle with consumers, producers, or traffickers of drugs? Moreover, how does one solve the drug problem? Ecuador and other countries in the Americas that are examined in the other chapters in this volume still have problems with drug trafficking and organized crime despite such efforts to punish drug offenders by incarcerating them. Clearly, the statistics reveal that this strategy has not been successful.

The criminalization of drugs in Ecuador and its results attest to fundamental flaws with the system and the identification of the problem. Law enforcement's main objective has been to arrest and imprison drug users although they are by far the least powerful actors in the drug trade. There is no evidence of the reduction of the drug supply as a result of these punitive efforts targeting the most vulnerable population in the drug chain. The Ecuadorian judicial system thus operates separately from the Ecuadorian drug reality, resulting in high levels of overcrowding in prisons as well as a backlog of cases in the penal system, which, in turn, have been quite costly as a result of the weak institutions in Ecuador. In addition to the cost for the state, there also has been an extremely high social cost associated with this policy. The eventual transition to life outside prison is made impossible by the current subhuman conditions, including the clustering of first-time offenders and small-scale traffickers with violent ones, the high number of minors living in female prisons, and the lack of educational opportunities. All of these conditions contribute to a vicious cycle of criminality.

CURRENT AND PROSPECTIVE POLICIES

The inconsistencies in Law 108 and the overcrowding of the prison system garnered attention in Ecuador at the end of the twentieth century. Beginning in 2000, the state advanced two initiatives to reduce overcrowding by cutting sentences in half for offenders with a record of good behavior and who had served a good portion of their time. Media coverage and attempts from academia to organize and report on the conditions within the penal system brought heightened attention to high rates of the drug-related incarceration. At the institutional level, the creation of the Ministry of Justice and Human Rights also increased political attention and scrutiny of the national penitentiary system.

In 2007, President Rafael Correa declared a state of emergency within the system of social rehabilitation. This raised the number of public lawyers to 220 to reduce the backlog of pretrial detainees. As a result, the rate of prison overcrowding dropped from 157 percent to 54 percent.[52] The drug crime-related population segment also went through a review, as did Law 108. In the meantime, the drafting of a new constitution created a window of opportunity for a national pardon of all drug crime-related prisoners who met specific criteria. Among other requirements, eligibility was limited to first-time offenders who had received a sentence, completed at least 10 percent of their sentence, and had been in possession of no more than two kilograms of illegal drugs. The result was the pardon of 2,300 prisoners with a recidivism rate of 1 percent.[53] The new constitution shifted the drug debate back to drugs as a public health problem. Overall, reforms under a new law are still ongoing and the results, therefore, remain to be seen.

Counternarcotic military initiatives continue to dominate public order. Coastal cities in Esmeraldas and Manabí are identified as strategic transit zones of drugs as well as centers of operation for organized crime. As recent as November 2013, more than 100 soldiers were deployed to the province of Manabí to look for clandestine routes. The Ecuadorian government acknowledges an increased presence of transnational organized crime, evidenced by the presence of the Rastrojos and the Sinaloa Cartel in the country, as it works to abate drug trade in Ecuador.[54]

Efforts to advance a comprehensive regulatory framework to decriminalize drug use were ongoing in 2013. The drug law reform would allow legal possession of 10 grams of marijuana, 2 grams of cocaine base, and 0.1 grams of heroin. The reform would potentially be one of the main tools used to distinguish between users and traffickers. The framework, if passed by Congress, will potentially alter the prison population and future dynamics.

CONCLUSION

The Ecuadorian case offers a comprehensive look at the historical gaps and inefficiencies in Latin America's counternarcotics policies. Despite a forty-year focus on eradication, seizure, and prosecution, the results of criminal and prohibitionist policies under the security logic have been dismal and should be, for the most part, considered failures.

Offensive initiatives emanating from the securitization framework have historically suffered a variety of transformations with pernicious and damaging effects that further burdens states with limited resources. Ecuador is an example.

Notwithstanding these security policies and the adaptation of the legal framework, Ecuador retains its position as a transit point and a small precursor center. The regional war on drugs has failed to modify Ecuador's role in the drug trade while adding costly and dreadful consequences at all levels of society. Furthermore, the regional war on drugs has, for the most part, strained Ecuador's relations with neighboring Colombia. The drug war has defined the terms of their interaction, resulting in problems related to the Colombian conflict, migration towards Ecuador, and an increase in organized crime. Simply put, despite the implementation of offensive policies, Ecuador continues to be vulnerable to organized crime as seen in the recent emergence of Mexican criminal groups in the country. Little has changed for the better over the twenty years of the criminalization of drugs.

One of the most important elements of counternarcotic efforts stressed by the United Nations and the United States was the consolidation of a criminal definition of drug offenses within the judicial systems in the region. Ecuador was not an exception and, in fact, prison sentences for drug offenses were more severe than punishment for murder in the country. A repressive logic is attached to a prohibitionist vision and, as such, constructs a special criminal framework that violates normal procedures within the Ecuadorian Criminal Code. The legal system targeted consumption; it never established a distinction between different types of drug-related activities or made exceptions for addicted users. This reasoning opened up the window for military and police cooperation with the U.S. for three decades although Ecuador received little aid compared to its neighbors. The nation funneled a large percentage of its domestic resources and efforts to fight the drug battle.

The enforcement system has misused and squandered the operability of institutions for public order. Offenses against persons and property are not subject to the same punitive measures nor are sufficient resources dedicated to them, despite the severity of offenses. Such distortion is acute in terms of the high rate of detainees held on drug-related charges and the prevalence within the system of small-time traffickers. The severity of sentences has not proven particularly efficient; no more than a few high level traffickers are imprisoned. The harsh penalties are reserved for small-time actors of little consequence in the drug networks.

Consistent criminal sanctions inserted in the legal and judiciary institutions have failed as instruments intended to reach the objectives of a regional agenda advanced by the U.S. for more than thirty years. The cause of such a failure cannot be found as a result of lack of investment, political will, or the influence of illegal organizations in state institutions. Instead, its abysmal failure lies in miscalculations inherent to the approach: the assumption that demand, now also emanating from Latin America itself and not exclusively from developed nations, can be regulated through security-oriented punitive and offensive strategies. Above all, drug consumption is related to human conduct and, as such, is predominantly related to cultural logic and public health. As long as the market remains profitable, drug trafficking networks will continue to find mechanisms to address existing demand. This is the reality in Latin America in general and as evidenced in Ecuador. Although Ecuador has so far eluded the extreme manifestations of the drug trade, it does not mean the country is immune.

NOTES

1. Francisco Thoumi, *Illegal Drugs, Economy, and Society in the Andes*, (Baltimore: Woodrow Wilson Center Press, 2003), 31.

2. Coletta Youngers, and Eileen Rosin, "'The U.S. War on Drugs'": Its impact in Latin America and the Caribbean," in *Drugs and Democracy in Latin America: The Impact of U.S. Policy*, eds. Coletta Youngers and Eileen Rosin (Boulder: Lynne Rienner, 2005), 3.

3. Thoumi, "Illegal Drugs," 20.

4. Adam Isacson, "The U.S. Military in the War on Drugs," *in Drugs and Democracy in Latin America: The Impact of U.S. Policy, ed.* Coletta Youngers and Eileen Rosin (Boulder: Lynne Rienner, 2005), 23.

5. Bruce Bagley, Adrian Bonilla, and Alexei Paez, *La Economía Política del Narcotráfico: El Caso Ecuatoriano* (Quito: Flacso: Ecuador, North South Center University of Miami, 1991).

6. Sandra Edwards, and Coletta Youngers, "Drug Law Reforms in Ecuador: Building Momentum for a More Effective, Balanced and Realistic Approach," *in Transnational Institute, Drugs and Democracy and Washington Office for Latin America,* no. May (2010), accessed October 3, 2013, http://www.tni.org/briefing/drug-law-reform-ecuador.

7. See, for example, Russell Crandall Guadalupe Paz, and Riordan Roett, *The Andes in Focus: Security, Democracy, and Economic Reform*, (Boulder: Lynne Reinner, 2005), Bruce Bagley, Adrian Bonilla, and Alexei Paez, *La Economía Política del Narcotráfico: El Caso Ecuatoriano*, (Quito: Flacso: Ecuador, North South Center University of Miami, 1991); Brian Loveman (ed), *Addiccted to Failure: US Policy in Latin America and the Andean Region*, (Lanham: Rowman and Littlefield, 2006).

8. Isacson, "The U.S. Military in the War on Drugs, 27.

9. Bruce Bagley, "Drug-Trafficking and Organized Crime in the Americas: Major Trends in the Twenty First Century," Woodorw Wilson for International Scholars, accessed January 23, 2014, http://www.wilsoncenter.org/sites/default/files/BB%20Final.pdf

10. Clifford Krauss, "Peru's Drug Successes Erodes as Traffickers Adapt." *New York Times*, August 19, 1999, National Edition, International sec, accessed September 21, 2013, http://www.nytimes.com/library/world/americas/081999peru-drugs.html.

11. Fredy Rivera, "Ecuador: Untangling the Drug War," in *Drugs and Democracy in Latin America: The Impact of U.S. Policy*, eds. Coletta Youngers and Eileen Rosin (Boulder: Lynne Rienner, 2005), 234.

12. United State Department of State, "International Narcotics Control Strategy Report: Drug and Chemical Control," Volume I, ed. Bureau for International Narcotics and Law Enforcement Affairs (Washington, D.C.: United State Department of State, 2013), accessed September 22, 2013, http://www.state.gov/documents/organization/204265.pdf.

13. Clare Ribard, "Ecuador: Political and Economic Situation and U.S. Relations," in Congressional Research Service: Report for Congress (Washington, D.C.: The Library of Congress, May 21, 2008), 133, accessed October 3, 2013 http://www.fas.org/sgp/crs/row/RS21687.pdf.

14. United State Department of State, "International Narcotics Control Strategy Report," 156.

15. Krauss, "Peru's Drug Successes Erodes as Traffickers Adapt."

16. Thoumi, *Illegal Drugs*, 33.

17. Ibid, 31.

18. Adrián Bonilla, "Ecuador: Actor Internacional en la Guerra de las Drogas," *in La Economía Política del Narcotráfico: El Caso Ecuatoriano*, eds. Bruce Bagley, Adrián Bonilla and Alexei Páez (Quito: Flacso-Ecuador and North-South Center of University of Miami, 1991).

19. Ministerio de Defensa Nacional, *Política de la Defensa Nacional del Ecuador*, (Quito: Ministerio de Defensa Nacional).

20. Isacson, "The U.S. Military in the War on Drugs," 22.

21. Sandra Edwards, "A short history of Ecuador's drug legislation and the impact on its prison population," *in Systems Overload: Drug laws and prisons in Latin America*, ed. Pien Metaal and Coletta Youngers (Amsterdam, Washington, D.C.: Transnational Institute and Washington Office for Latin America, 2011), 51, accessed September 22, 2013, http://reformdrugpolicy.com/wp-content/uploads/2011/09/Systems-Overload.pdf.

22. Sandra Edwards and Coletta Youngers, "Ecuador Memo: Drug Law Reform in Ecuador: Building Momentum for a More Effective, Balanced and Realistic Approach" (Washington, D.C.: Washington Office for Latin America, Transnational Institute, 2010), 2, accessed September 22, 2013, http://www.wola.org/drug_law_reform_in_ecuador.

23. Ibid, 3.

24. Ibid, 3.

25. The Supreme Court is the highest authority of the Ecuadorian judicial branch. Judges of the Supreme Court provide final rulings and are the last resource of the judicial process.

26. Edwards and Youngers, "Ecuador Memo: Drug Law Reform in Ecuador," 5

27. "Hoy Presentan Resultados del Censo Penitenciario", *El Universo*, July 31, 2008, National Edition, Sucesos sec., accessed September 20, 2013, http://www.eluniverso.com/2008/07/31/0001/10/1E6737433C0F45F1984ACB88ECA80A1E.html.

28. Ibid.

29. Edwards, "Edwards, "A short history of Ecuador's drug legislation," 54.

30. Elías Carranza, "Situación Penitenciaria en América Latina y el Caribe ¿Qué hacer?" in *Anuario de Derechos Humanos*, ed. Marianne González Le Saux, Volume 0 Number 8 (July 9, 2012), 34, accessed October 16, 2013, http://www.revistas.uchile.cl/index.php/ADH/issue/view/1970.

31. Ibid.

32. Edwards, "A short history of Ecuador's drug legislation," 52.

33. Comisión Ecumenica de Derechos Humanos. "Audiencia sobre la situación penintenciaria en Ecuador" (March 21, 2011), 1, accessed October 19, 2013, http://www.cedhu.org/index.php?option=com_content&view=article&id=40&Itemid=7.

34. Edwards, "A short history of Ecuador's drug legislation," 55.

35. Dirección Nacional de Rehabilitación Social, " El sistema penitenciario en Ecuador en cifras, "Boletín Estadístico" (Quito: DNRS).

36. Jenny Pontón and Andreina Torres, "Cárceles del Ecuador: los efectos de la criminalización por drogas" *in URVIO: Revista Latinoamericana de Seguridad Ciudadana*, (Quito: Flacso Ecuador, May 2007), 55–73.

37. Jenny Pontón and Andreina Torres, "Cárceles del Ecuador: los efectos de la criminalización por drogas," 66.

38. Ibid.

39. Sandra Edwards, "A short history of Ecuador's drug legislation," 52.

40. Carranza, "Situación Penitenciaria en América Latina y el Caribe."

41. Pontón and Torres, "Cárceles del Ecuador."

42. Pontón and Torres, "Cárceles del Ecuador," 60.

43. Edwards and Youngers, "Drug Law Reform In *Ecuador,"* 11.

44. Pontón y Torres, "Cárceles del Ecuador," 61.

45. Edwards, "A short history of Ecuador's drug legislation," 54.

46. Carranza, "Situación Penitenciaria en América Latina y el Caribe," 49.

47. Jorge Nuñez, *Cacería de Brujos: Drogas 'Ilegales' y Sistema de Cárceles en Ecuador*, (Quito: ABYA-Yala, Flacso- Ecuador, 2006).

48. Edwards, "A short history of Ecuador's drug legislation," 52.

49. Edwards and Youngers, "Drug Law Reform In Ecuador," 7.

50. Edwards, "A short history of Ecuador's drug legislation," 52.

51. Edwards, and Youngers, "Drug Law Reform In Ecuador," 7.

52. Edwards, "A short history of Ecuador's drug legislation," 56.

53. Ibid.

54. Charles Parkinson, "Ministro de Ecuador reconoce presencia de cartels narcotraficantes extranjeros," accessed 29 October, 2013, http://es.insightcrime.org/noticias-del-dia/ministro-de-ecuador-reconoce-presencia-de-carteles-de-la-droga-extranjeros.

NINE

A Special Kind of Hell

The Bolivian Penal System

Marten W. Brienen

Prisons in foreign countries hold a particular fascination. More than a few documentaries have aired in a variety of European countries exposing the relatively awful conditions in U.S. prisons, and some television networks have featured series detailing the plight of nationals in perhaps even more terrifying prisons throughout the developing world.[1] To some extent, these programs serve as entertainment, but the underlying message is clear: prisons in poor countries are terrifying places and when traveling, one should avoid them. Bolivia stands out as a shining example to the contrary: here, backpackers line up to enter prison.

The Bolivian prison system gained notoriety particularly as a result of the development of San Pedro Prison—located in the bustling heart of La Paz—as a somewhat popular tourist destination among backpackers.[2] The attraction lay in the novelty of visiting a prison in a poor country without the need for a conviction of one's own, the fact that the internal organization of the prison—which tourists would tour with a local guide (i.e., a prisoner)—was completely unlike what Westerners might expect, and lastly is that the prison was regarded as one of the safest and easiest places for tourists to purchase *pasta base* and cocaine.[3] The novelty factor of this particular Bolivian prison presents us with an odd duality. On the one hand, it has served to communicate to the world the conditions in at least one Bolivian penal institution. On the other hand, given the target audience of mainly backpackers from Europe, the United States, and Israel, it has served mostly as a somewhat perverse type of adventure tourism rather than as an accusation against the generally deplorable conditions of the Bolivian system. The result has been some publicity in the form of a book by the institution's one-time inmate Rusty Young, which details his misadventures in the Bolivian penal system, but which again serves more as adventure travel literature than as a serious attempt to bring to light the injustices and humiliations suffered by the many inmates who crowd this prison.[4] Or, to be more accurate, the many inmates *and their families*, who crowd this prison.

Aside from Mr. Young's account, the Bolivian penal system has occasionally made it into the international spotlight when foreigners from a variety of countries end up in its clutches. The most recent case to reach a broad audience, and perhaps the most widely publicized of all, was that of Jacob Ostreicher, a U.S. citizen who as a result of an exceptionally corrupt bureaucracy ended up in the country's Palmasola prison in the department of Santa Cruz, largely in an elaborate attempt at extortion and theft by high-placed functionaries in the patently broken judicial system.[5] On other occasions, both Spain and Germany have seen momentary glimpses of life within the walls of what can only be described as one of the most broken and dysfunctional penal systems in the Western Hemisphere—as it compares badly even to the already atrocious penal systems in other parts of the hemisphere, as described in detail in other chapters in this volume.[6] Again, those few reports that have appeared in the national presses of the United States, Spain, Germany, and a smattering of other developed countries whose citizens were unfortunate enough at one time or another to descend into the abyss of the Bolivian penal system, tend to emphasize either the nature of an extraordinary adventure or the personal travails of men and women unjustly held in exotic places. The atrocious nature of what exists between the walls of these institutions thus serves as a backdrop to a story of human interest that would appeal to audiences otherwise safely at home.

In this chapter, I intend to pull the true nature of the Bolivian penal system to the foreground, placing it front and center in an effort to provide some detail into the conditions found in Bolivia's many prisons. In addition, I will provide some detail into the operation of these institutions, and the bureaucracy behind them.

THE BOLIVIAN PENAL SYSTEM

The Bolivian penal system is overseen by the National Directorate of the Prison Regime and Supervision (DGRP), located in the Ministry of the Interior and Police. It operates a total of fifty-four penal institutions spread throughout the country with an annual budget of around 2.44 million dollars.[7] While some prisons serve both men and women, most prisons were built to house either male or female inmates. In mixed facilities, sleeping areas are generally segregated—though this is not always enforced. In addition, juveniles and adults are housed together.[8] The official capacity of the penal system stands at 5,000 as of 2013.[9] While the DGRP is responsible for the supervision of the prison system, Bolivia is somewhat unique in that it employs no trained prison guards: prisons are guarded by members of the national police, who receive no special training. "[The] administration has made no effort to see that members of the National Police responsible for penitentiary issues have specific preparation that would transmit to them a general idea that their functions within the prison have nothing to do with what they learned in their professional training in the police academy."[10]

Bolivia incarcerates a relatively small proportion of its population with an incarceration rate of about 140 per 100,000 inhabitants.[11] Compared to the rest of the Americas, that places it near the bottom, above only Haiti (96), Guatemala (105), and Paraguay (118). At most recent count, the total prison population (as of August 2013) stood at 14,770 inmates.[12] Given the relatively low rate of incarceration, it would appear that Bolivia does not at this time suffer from an apparent overreliance on incarceration as a means to control crime, although, as I discuss further on in this chapter, that appears to be changing. The apparently low rate of incarceration, however, rather obscures two important points with regard to the system. The first of these is that Bolivia's prison population is rapidly increasing. While the current rate of 140 is comparatively low, it is almost double the rate of 76 noted in 2005.[13] The second point to be made is that the Bolivian penal system is among the very worst in the Americas in terms of overcrowding and general conditions for inmates, as well as ranking at or near the bottom with regard to other key indicators, such as the percentage of inmates held in pretrial detention, the length of such detentions, and the generally arbitrary nature of the system, which has been highlighted in recent years by a number of high-profile corruption scandals involving judges and prosecutors.[14] Indeed, the office of the national ombudsman—the *defensoría del pueblo*—has condemned the conditions in the prisons on numerous occasions, as have international organizations ranging from the Organization of American States (OAS) to the United Nations Office for the High Commissioner for Human Rights.[15]

The most striking feature of the Bolivian penal system in recent years has been the massive growth in the total prison population, which has more than doubled from a total of 5,577 in 2001 to 14,770 in 2013.[16] It is of particular interest to note that this growth is almost entirely attributable to the massive increase in inmates held in pretrial detention. Indeed, the number of sentenced inmates remained almost entirely stable between 2001 and 2011, rising from 1,830 to 1,890. It has only been since 2011 that a sizable increase in the number of convicted inmates has occurred, rising to a total of 2,461 in 2013.[17] In the same period, the number of inmates in pretrial detention rose from 3,747 to 12,309, with the most significant growth taking place between 2008 and 2013. [18]

This very significant increase is further noteworthy due to the effects this has had on overcrowding. With an official capacity of 5,000, the system was reasonably well equipped to deal with the number of inmates held in 2001, when it was at 112 percent of capacity, whereas the system is currently at 269.8 percent of capacity, which places it ahead of only El Salvador (324.7 percent) and Venezuela (270.1 percent). [19] This very rapid expansion of the prison population, without commensurate increases in prison capacity, has exacerbated already profoundly inhumane conditions. The picture is especially stark in a handful of prisons in particular: Quillacollo prison (La Paz) houses 320 inmates in a facility with a capacity of 30, thus operating at 1,067 percent of capacity. San Roque prison (Chuquisaca), houses 420 inmates in a facility with a capacity of 60, thus operating at over 500 percent of capacity. Palmasola prison (Santa Cruz), which serves as one of the main prisons in the country, has an official capacity of 600, but is operating at 833 percent of capacity with some 5,000 inmates. [20]

It should further be noted that due to peculiarities in Bolivian law, many young children inhabit the prisons. Officially, children under the age of seven are allowed to remain with their inmate parents, though in reality—given that there generally is no place to send these children once they "age out"—most stay with their parents long after that. [21] Indeed, the warden of San Pedro prison in La Paz has publicly stated that he would not remove children above the age of six from the institution, given that this would make them homeless: if there were a better place for the children to be, they would be there already. [22] Since these children are not inmates—and may come and go as they please to attend school and other activities outside of the prisons—they are not included in statistics relating to the total inmate population, although they do physically share the space. [23] While estimates vary, some 2,000 children inhabit prison facilities, [24] and it is clear that our data on prison overcrowding necessarily understates the problem as a result of this phenomenon. Indeed, the number of children in San Pedro Prison alone exceeded the capacity that the institution was originally designed to house. [25]

While it may not be uncommon internationally for children to live with their parents in penal institutions, the Bolivian case is an oddity in that while the law limits this practice to children under the age of seven, in reality children and adolescents remain with their parents long after they have officially "aged out." [26] Moreover, it is common in a number of penal institutions to house not only the children, but the spouse of an inmate as well. The most well-known example is the San Pedro Prison in La Paz, where many women live along with their husbands and children despite the fact that the institution is a male prison. [27] Wives of inmates in this institution are free to come and go as they please, and many sell hand-made goods and other wares on the plaza on which the prison sits. As is the case with minors inhabiting the institution, the women—as they are not part of the penal system in any formal sense—are not counted in statistics relating to the penal population and consequently not taken into account when arriving at estimates of prison crowding.[28] San Pedro Prison in particular was designed to house 300 inmates, but now houses some 2,400 inmates along with approximately 250 children and a similar number of spouses, meaning that its population is near 1,000 percent of the original capacity.[29]

The presence of minors and spouses in the main prisons clearly creates the potential for abuse, and the prisons—San Pedro and Palmasola especially so—are quite frequently the subject of abuse scandals, including a recent scandal involving the rape of a twelve-year-old in San Pedro, which prompted the director of the DGRP to issue an order to remove all children over the age of six and eventually to close the prison altogether.[30] While dozens of children were removed in mid-2013, the prison that was supposed to house many of San Pedro's inmates after its intended closing proved to be uninhabitable and was closed down instead, sending prisoners back to San Pedro and resulting in the scuttling of the plan.[31] Moreover, plans to remove minors from the institution were canceled as a result of the inability to find suitable alternative shelter for the children involved.[32]

Other peculiarities have made the Bolivian penal system the subject of some debate in both academic and tourist circles. One of the most frequently noted oddities is the fact that in the major prisons, inmates are not assigned cells. Prisons such as Palmasola and San Pedro are divided into neighborhoods, and inmates can purchase cells from the internal prison authority—which is run by prisoners, not official authorities. Such cells range from 150 to 8,000 dollars where the more expensive ones are larger, sometimes multistory, and may have quite a few amenities—including private baths, televisions, kitchens, computer access, and other such desirables.[33] Those who do not have the money to buy a cell sleep in the hallways, corridors, and on the main plaza within the prison, often with their spouse and children. It is not only cells that are for sale or rent: the Organization of American States reported in 2007 that the gymnasium of Chonchocorro prison "[. . .] belonged to an inmate, who charged a membership fee of B. 20 a month for its use."[34]

With the exception of the rural prisons, prisons are operated and managed entirely by inmates. Guards are not present inside the major prisons, except to guard those in solitary confinement. It should be noted that solitary confinement is a punishment imposed by inmate-operated disciplinary committees.[35] Indeed, internal inmate authorities control most aspects of life inside prison walls, including discipline, security, and so on. The different neighborhoods are controlled by individual committees that are responsible for the creation and enforcement of regulation: indeed, the sale of a prison property—that is, a cell—requires a witness, a contract overseen by the neighborhood committee, and stamps provided by inmate authorities. The high level of social control has proven quite effective in maintaining a relatively low rate of crime within the penal institutions. The result of the relative order imposed by inmate authorities has also meant that the prisons have lively markets, restaurants, bars, and other amenities one might expect to find in general society. It should be noted that there has been discussion with regard to the "taxes" and "fees" extracted by the committees from inmates, with some arguing that this practice constitutes extortion, while official prison authorities and inmate authorities tend to defend the practice as necessary for the maintenance of the prison structure itself, given that the budget allocated to the DGRP does not allow for maintenance: when lightbulbs fail, for instance, inmates are expected to replace them. [36]

It has been noted, in particular with regard to San Pedro, that the structure of inmate governance appears to have created a prison society in which disputes can be settled, property rights can be maintained, and misbehavior is dealt with. A set of regulations governs the interior of the prison, while further regulations govern each of the neighborhoods. Indeed, inmates themselves have observed that the society within prison walls is relatively secure, and while not free of violence, even violence between inmates is regulated—for example, prisoners may not engage in physical altercations when a child is present. The presence of spouses in the institution can serve as further indication of the relative security of the space, since their presence is voluntary and requires that a spouse actively choose this environment over any alternative. Nevertheless, the larger prisons have on occasion been the site of riots, sometimes with grave consequences: the 2011 riot at Palmasola resulted in a fire that left thirty-five dead, including an eighteen-month-old infant. [37]

The very severe overcrowding has led to significant challenges with regard to the overall health of inmates. The DGRP budgets no more than about USD 0.80 per inmate for nutrition and healthcare, which obviously is not enough to meet the needs of inmates or their dependent children. [38] In rural prisons, in which the conditions are generally the most deplorable, no medical services are available to inmates. In the urban prisons, very few services are made available: Palmasola has one doctor to tend to the needs of the entire population, while the budget does not allow for the purchase of medications. As with most other needs, the internal market remains the primary mechanism through which both medical services and necessary medications are obtained. Just as incarcerated lawyers provide legal services to fellow inmates for a fee, incarcerated doctors and nurses provide the bulk of the medical care. [39] The severe overcrowding, of course, has produced a society in which a great level of vulnerability exists. Once communicable diseases enter the prison walls, they spread very quickly and inevitably overwhelm the ability of the inmate infrastructure to deal with the consequences.[40] Indeed, in 2013, San Pedro Prison was hit by an outbreak of meningitis, resulting in the deaths of a woman and a child.[41]

While any discussion in Bolivia about its penal system tends to be dominated by the San Pedro, Palmasola, and Chonchocoro prisons, which house the majority of the total number of prisoners, some fifty relatively minor institutions also exist, including around twenty in more remote rural areas. While the conditions in the main prisons has been described as unacceptable in terms of overcrowding, access to food, health resources, and other basic necessities, these much smaller institutions are in effect forsaken.[42] In a number of the rural prisons—known in Bolivia as *carceletas*—inmates have attempted to meet their nutritional needs by growing their own food.[43]

PRETRIAL DETENTION

As I stated earlier, the single greatest contributing factor to the severity of Bolivian prison overcrowding has been the excessive use of pretrial detention by authorities. The vast majority of inmates in Bolivian prisons are merely accused of criminal behavior, but have not been sentenced. Indeed, the zeal for pretrial detention is such that there are documented cases of individuals who have been held in pretrial detention for extended periods of time without any formal charges having been filed against them.[44] Under Bolivian law, individuals may be held for six months before defendants are notified of the charges filed against them, although extensions for up to eighteen months may be requested by prosecutors. Pre-trial detention may last, by law, up to thirty-six months—and even after that, house arrest or other measures restricting movement may still be imposed. It should be noted that this thirty-six month cap is often extended or simply not observed. Moreover, pre-trial detainees who challenge their detention are frequently subject to punitive action by judges who will then extend the length of pretrial detention.[45] The worst cases of excessive pretrial detention uncovered to date are those of Zacarías Navia Navia and Luís Córdoba Marca, who were released in 2013 after twenty-three and twenty-one years of detention, respectively, formal charges against them never having been filed.[46]

Although the Bolivian constitution and Bolivian law prohibit the use of pretrial detention except under certain circumstances, it is clear that these protections are not enforced. Rather, the government has issued orders to ensure that for "serious crimes," pretrial detention should always be imposed. Indeed, in at least two cases, the Public Ministry has incarcerated judges for failing to order pretrial detention—in clear violation of the law, of human rights, and of a variety of international treaties.[47] As a result, it is understandable that under the current regime, judges tend to impose pretrial detention whether they believe it is justified or not.

The failure of the Bolivian justice is such that the current government has passed the *Ley de Seguridad Ciudadana*, which was described by the responsible minister as "a law [. . .] with more drastic sanctions for delinquents and for the judges who allow them to go free."[48] Given the fact that the issue at hand is that of pretrial detention, this is rather shocking language, as it requires incarceration for accused individuals under the presumption that they are "delinquents," therewith effectively canceling the constitutional notion of the presumption of innocence. In addition to the threat of imprisonment made against judges who do not impose pretrial detention, even when doing so would violate both the letter and the principle of the law, it has been argued extensively—especially by Fujimura-Fanselow and Wicker—that the participants in the justice system are still caught in the mind-set of the inquisitorial system (known as the *Códigos Banzer*) that was created during the military dictatorships of the 1970s and remained in place until the judicial reforms of 1999.[49] This attitude among judges is especially visible during pretrial hearings, which more often than not result in discussions about the guilt of the defendant, even in the absence of evidence of any kind.[50] Pretrial detention is then imposed as a means to punish the defendant, effectively transforming the practice of pretrial detention—which, under international treaties as well as the Bolivian constitution, is intended to ensure that a defendant will attend his or her criminal proceedings—into a pre-sentence.[51]

With tremendous pressure on judges to impose these pre-sentences, lest they themselves be judged, and a relatively widespread misunderstanding of the intent of the 1999 judicial reforms, which had been intended to cement the notion of the presumption of innocence into the judicial system, it is not especially surprising that the gains of the 1999 reforms in terms of the tremendous reduction in the amount of pretrial detainees has now evaporated. Certainly, the speed with which new pretrial detainees have been added to the profoundly underfunded and overcrowded system has been nothing less than astonishing. As noted above, levels of overcrowding now exceeds the levels that in 1994 were considered so egregious that they resulted in the 1999 reforms in the first place.[52]

LEY 1008

Bolivia's prominence as one of the major producers of coca leaf—the raw material used in the manufacture of cocaine and other illicit substances—has played a significant role in the development of the Bolivian penal system over the past three decades, and has been widely regarded as one of the main factors contributing to prison overcrowding. While numbers vary a little from source to source, the most recent data made available by the *Instituto Nacional de Estadística* (INE)—covering the year 2011—indicates that some 29 percent of Bolivian inmates are held on charges related to drug trafficking.[53] That stands rather in contrast to data provided by the *Programa de Investigación Estratégica de Bolivia* (PIEB) that suggest that some 45 percent of pretrial detainees in the country were held on drug-related charges in that same year.[54] There is, however, clear indication that the percentage of inmates held on drug-related charges has declined somewhat over the past decade and a half from a peak of about 58 percent in 2000 to the current level of about 28 percent. However, this decline has not been the result of a change in the enforcement of drug laws, but rather of the increase in the number of inmates held on other charges. The total number of inmates held on drug-related charges has, in effect, remained fairly constant since 2001, ranging from a low of 2,517 in 2003 to a high of 3,205 in 2011.[55]

The Bolivian propensity for incarcerating individuals for the production, sale, and trafficking of cocaine and its variants has its roots in U.S. policies that resulted from Ronald Reagan's famous relaunch of the "war on drugs" in 1982. In the years immediately following, the United States became fully embroiled in the moral panic of the so-called crack epidemic, creating a political climate that required a forceful hard-on-crime approach as well as renewed attention for the producer countries held responsible for the scourge of drugs thought to be destroying inner cities across the United States.[56] Given that Bolivian production had increased significantly from the mid-1970s to the mid-1980s, making the country the second largest exporter of coca, U.S. interest in the country intensified,[57] leading to a series of efforts intended to resolve the problem at the source,[58] including U.S. support for the creation of Bolivian special forces to deal with the drug problem. In 1983, with significant U.S. material support, Bolivia created the *Unidad Móvil de Patrullaje Rural* (UMOPAR), which was followed by the creation of the *Fuerza Especial de Lucha Contra el Narcotráfico* (FELCN), which subsumed UMOPAR, in 1987. The FELCN was funded, trained, supported, and overseen by the United States, and especially the Drug Enforcement Administration (DEA).[59]

The most important U.S. effort to combat the cultivation of coca for the manufacture of cocaine came with the creation in 1988 of *Ley 1008*, which regulates the cultivation and sale of coca.[60] It should be noted, of course, that the cultivation of coca—notwithstanding the 1961 Single Convention—has always been legal in Bolivia, and plays an important role in indigenous traditions and religious practices.[61] While the cultivation of coca has a long history in the Bolivian Andes, *Ley 1008* limited the total acreage of coca cultivation to a total of 30,000 acres in the provinces of Nor and Sud Yungas, thereby prohibiting the cultivation of coca in the Chapare region of Cochabamba, which had become the site of a very

rapidly growing coca-based agricultural sector, largely composed of former miners due to the closure of many of Bolivia's famous tin mines in
the early 1980s. [62]

Moreover, *Ley 1008* was designed to impose especially harsh sentences on those suspected of trafficking illicit substances. Among its
many provisions, it established some thirty-two offenses that would fall
under the law, which instituted a fully parallel system of justice, with its
own regulations and institutions—effectively creating "drug courts" existing in a separate judicial space. [63] Among its more debated provisions
were those imposing sentences that far exceeded sentences for violent
crime, and in some cases resulted in sentences that exceeded the constitutionally permitted maximum of thirty years, and the imposition of effectively mandatory pretrial detention for extended periods of time, and an
inquisitorial system that was heavily tilted against defendants. [64]

It was *Ley 1008* which, due to its draconian nature, [65] was responsible
for the very rapid increase in the number of inmates held in Bolivian
prisons in the 1990s, leading to a crisis as a result of the very significant
levels of overcrowding and to what were considered at the time to be
unacceptable numbers of pretrial detainees. [66] As a result of pressure—
including from the United States—from internal as well as external
sources, based in large part on the overcrowded conditions and the excessive rates of pretrial detention, the judicial system underwent a significant reform in 1999, which drastically reduced the prison population and
the number of people held in pretrial detention. As I have shown, that
relief was to be short-lived. Indeed, under the tenure of President Evo
Morales, the overcrowding has grown beyond the level observed in the
1990s, which gave rise to the 1999 judicial reforms which were specifically intended to reduce the rate of pretrial detention and relieve the massive overcrowding. [67]

It should be noted that while *Ley 1008* did result in large increases in
the prison population, the political will to implement the law with regard
to the eradication of coca crops in the Bolivian tropics remained relatively
low for the first decade after its enactment. From the very beginning, the
public reaction to *Ley 1008* was exceptionally negative, as it was widely
regarded as an instrument that had been foisted upon the Bolivian people
by the United States, rather than responding to domestic needs. [68] The
fact that this foreign imposition was resulting in ever-increasing rates of
incarceration, especially of the poor, [69] only added to the sense that the
law worked against Bolivian national interests: Bolivia itself did not experience high levels of criminality nor did it have a significant problem of
drug abuse.

Moreover, strict enforcement of the law put Bolivia in an awkward
position with regard to its economic needs, as the late 1980s and 1990s
were marked by the aftermath of structural adjustment, which caused
significant pain to the Bolivian economy and to Bolivians themselves.

While the dependence on multilateral organizations—such as the IMF and the World Bank—during this period meant that the Bolivian governments of that era were in effect obligated to cooperate actively with U.S. strategies on drug production and trafficking. It was well understood that the income generated by illicit coca provided a sorely needed boost to a struggling economy. Thus, not only was the implementation of *Ley 1008* exceptionally unpopular, but it was also regarded as harmful to the Bolivian economy.[70]

While the law had been unpopular from the very moment it was introduced, it was not until its full implementation by President Hugo Bánzer Suárez, roughly a decade after it was first enacted, under the banner of *coca cero* ("zero coca") policy that the effects became fully felt. In his enthusiastic embrace of U.S. drug policies, the Bánzer regime undertook the eradication of coca from the Chapare region with significant U.S. assistance, which included a significant presence in Bolivia of U.S. DEA officials and agents, leading to the militarization of the anti-coca efforts. Under Bánzer's U.S.-supported efforts, the growers (*cocaleros*) themselves were subject to particularly harsh treatment, with punishments decided by secretive judicial processes that clearly skirted the notion of due process. Using military force and coordinated by the U.S. DEA, whose agents were clearly visible in the resulting conflict between *cocaleros* and the counternarcotics forces consisting of the DEA, UMO-PAR, and FELCN—resulting in scores of deaths among the *cocaleros*—the Bánzer regime indeed managed to achieve significant successes, reducing the roughly 110,000 acres of *coca excedentaria* to no more than around 5,000 by the year 2000.[71] It should be noted, of course, that although *Ley 1008* had been responsible for the bulk of the growth of the prison population throughout the 1990s, and the law imposed especially harsh penalties using constitutionally dubious procedures, the effects of Bánzer's crackdown were mitigated to quite a large extent by the fact that it coincided with the 1999 judicial reforms, which resulted in a very significant reduction in the amount of inmates held in pretrial detention. Thus, even though the *coca cero* effort was in full swing at the turn of the century, the years 2000 and 2001 show some of the lowest levels of incarceration in Bolivia in the past two decades.[72]

DRUG TRAFFICKING AND THE PRISON SYSTEM UNDER THE MORALES REGIME

There is an element of irony to the fact that the full effect of *Ley 1008* would not be felt in the penal system until after the departure of the president who had so vigorously pursued the goal of coca eradication. There is more irony still to the fact that the subsequent explosion in incarceration rates would not take shape fully until the presidency of Evo

Morales, a *cocalero* who rose to national prominence precisely due to his unwavering opposition to *Ley 1008* and its effects on farmers. Indeed, while a full discussion of the rise of Evo Morales to power falls beyond the scope of this chapter, it is worth noting that his electoral success was built on his ability to capitalize on the notion of *Ley 1008* as an instrument of U.S. imperialism during a moment of intense nationalistic fervor stemming from the stated intention of the Gonzalo Sánchez de Lozada regime to export recently discovered deposits of natural gas to the United States via Chile.[73] Not only was Chile popularly regarded as the country's regional archenemy due to its conquest of the Bolivian coastal province (the Litoral) in the War of the Pacific (1879-1882), but the notion of Bolivian natural gas feeding U.S. industry and power was regarded as utterly anathema to Bolivian national interests. It was during the "Gas Wars" that erupted as a result of these plans that Morales managed to position himself as the champion of the national interest, firmly opposing plans to export Bolivian natural gas to the U.S. and arguing for a change in policy with regard to coca, in effect linking the two issues as related anti-imperialist causes.[74] So successful was Morales's effort that in the span of just a few years (2003–2005), his involvement in protests over natural gas led to the fall of two presidents—Sánchez de Lozada and his replacement, Carlos Mesa Gisbert—and ultimately his own election as president in 2005.[75]

Due to the circumstances of Morales's rise to power, many expected that one of the first casualties of his ascent would be the universally hated *Ley 1008*. Indeed, Morales's rhetoric changed relatively little in the aftermath of his election in terms of his tendency to describe efforts to eradicate coca from the Bolivian landscape as an anti-cultural and imperialist effort on the part of the United States, which ignore the history of what he likes to refer to as the "sacred leaf" and have wrought nothing but misery for Bolivian farmers. As evidence of his credentials as a crusader for the rights of *cocaleros*, he expelled the DEA from the country and USAID from the Chapare region, due to its collusion with the DEA—given its role in the crop substitution programs that formed part of various strategies to eradicate coca from that region.[76]

As the data I have provided above shows, however, the Morales presidency—ongoing since 2005—has coincided with a sharp rise in the rate of incarceration, now reaching record levels and indeed exceeding the alarming rates of the mid-1990s. The reality is that in spite of the regime's rhetoric with regard to the so-called war on drugs and the role of *Ley 1008* in that effort, the law has remained in effect, including its harsh policies with regard to sentencing and its practice of parallel courts for drug offenses. Other than so far unsuccessful efforts to find new markets for licit uses of coca—including the manufacture of coca-based toothpaste and other such initiatives—and an expansion of the allowed acreage for the cultivation of coca, Bolivian policy has remained one of eradication—

though with less violent means that heretofore—and harsh persecution of offenders.

In effect, Morales has found himself in a difficult position. Notwithstanding his public defense of the "sacred leaf," the undeniable reality remains that the majority of Bolivian coca does not go to traditional uses, but rather feeds an extensive cocaine industry. A further complication has been that Bolivian *pasta base* and cocaine are not generally destined for U.S. markets, but rather supply neighboring Brazil and Argentina, important trading partners and sources of moral support for the Morales regime, where the trade in Bolivian drugs finances powerful, dangerous, and violent criminal organizations. Consequently, his public displays of contempt toward the United States and associated symbolic acts of defiance—including the expulsion of the DEA—do not alleviate pressure on his regime to actively combat drug traffickers, or indeed the growers responsible for the supply of raw materials.

Moreover, Morales has been faced with increasing public demands for safety and security, which rank among Bolivians' chief concerns.[77] There are, in effect, popular calls for his administration to be "tough on crime," resulting in the sorts of measures described earlier, whereby judges are effectively forced to incarcerate suspects without regard for evidence of guilt. Such is Bolivians' concern for safety and security that sympathy for those suspected of criminal activity is virtually absent.[78] This intolerance for criminal activity of any kind—drug dealing and abuse included—is further visible in the rather too common practice of public lynching as a means of exacting immediate justice, rather than awaiting lengthy trials and the perception of impunity they engender.[79] Herein lies part of the difficulty in resolving the problem of the excessive use of pretrial detention. On the one hand, public pressure to incarcerate those accused of criminal activities has led to a massive overpopulation of the prison system and a tremendous backlog for prosecutors, while on the other hand there is no public support to provide more funding for the judicial system, since it comprises "criminals" who do not deserve a larger share of the limited pie, while poverty remains rampant. As a result, justice is interminably delayed for both the accused and the victims of crime, leading to a perception that the judicial system cannot be trusted to mete out justice.

CONCLUSION

Contrary to the dire predictions made by U.S. officials who warned the Bolivian public against electing Evo Morales to the presidency for fear that the country would become a narco-state, Bolivia is increasingly "tough on crime" and arrest and incarceration rates for drug-related criminal activity have remained relatively constant throughout the current century. No grand amnesty for *cocaleros* has taken shape, and it remains true that drug-related crimes result in the harshest penalties, far outstripping those for homicide and other violent crime. In that sense, Bolivia is no haven for drug traffickers.

Not that it matters much what the punishment for criminal behavior is, given that only a small proportion of those held in detention have convictions of any kind: the vast majority of those who suffer the humiliations and inhumane conditions found throughout Bolivian penal institutions are being held pending trials that, due to the utterly broken state of the judicial system, are very long in coming. In the meantime, these men and women—as well as their spouses and children—are denied access to healthcare, housing, and even their most basic nutritional needs, as neither cells nor food can be taken for granted in these societies-within-society. Massive overcrowding—with rates that reach up to 1,000 percent of capacity—guarantees unsanitary conditions that result in unnecessary suffering. The DGRP, meanwhile, complains that it is unfair that it should be held accountable for the share of electricity used by the cohabiting spouses and children.

The legal structures through which this system is maintained have been shown time and again to be rotten to the core with rampant corruption. The maligned *Ley 1008*, resistance to which was largely responsible for Morales's ascent to power, has remained the law of the land in spite of the administration's anti-imperialist rhetoric. Scholars and international institutions alike have noted that this law—again the subject of much protest by members of the very government that enforces it today—deprives Bolivians of their most basic human rights and constitutional protections, enforcing punishments that exceed the constitutionally allowed maximum sentences. Indeed, *Ley 1008* has effectively abrogated the principle of assumed innocence—also a constitutional guarantee—as it virtually guarantees years of pretrial detention for anyone held on drug-related charges.

It may be so that, as Morales has so publicly proclaimed, the United States was responsible for the law and its many injustices. It is nevertheless Morales himself who is now responsible for each and every one of the excesses that flow from it under his presidency.

NOTES

1. The National Geographic Channel's "Locked Up Abroad" being one example. The Netherlands alone has two such programs: "Gevangen in het Buitenland" ("Prisoner abroad") on the SBS network and "Vreemde Tralies" ("Foreign prison bars") on the EO network.

2. Enough so that it received an official write-up in the popular "Bolivia on a Shoestring."

3. Rusty Young and Thomas McFadden, *Marching Powder: A True Story of Friendship, Cocaine, and South America's Strangest Jail* (New York: St. Martin's Griffin, 2003).

4. See Young and McFadden, *Marching Powder*.

5. Carlos Corz, "Desbaratan red de corrupción y extorsión en la que operaban dos asesores del Ministerio de Gobierno." *La Razón*, 27 November 2012. Section: Nacional.

6. See, for example, Mabel Azcui, "Palmasola muestra el precario sistema penitenciario en Bolivia." *El país*, 25 August 2013. On Jacob Ostreicher, who eventually escaped with the help of Sean Penn, see Joseph Berger, "Bolivian Jail, an Actor's Help and Now a Return to New York." *New York Times*, 16 December 2013, Section: New York/Region.

7. United States. Department of State (USDS). *Bolivia 2012 Human Rights Report.* Washington, DC, 2012: 3. Also see: Ramiro Arias, Susana Saavedra, and Claudia V. Alarcón, *Reforma Procesal Penal y Detención Preventiva en Bolivia.* La Paz: Fundación Construir, 2012: 63–64.

8. USDS, *Bolivia 2012 Human Rights Report*: 4.

9. While many sources cite Bolivia's prison capacity at 5,000, the Defensoría del Pueblo indicates that it is somewhat smaller, at 4,884. Estado Plurinacional de Bolivia. Defensoría del Pueblo, *Informe sobre el ejercicio de los derechos humanos en el estado plurinacional de Bolivia: defensoria del pueblo – 2013*, La Paz, 2013: 37.

10. As quoted in: Organization of American States. *Access to Justice and Social Inclusion: The Road Towards Strengthening Democracy in Bolivia.* Washington, D.C.: Inter-American Commissionon Human Rights, 2007: 52.

11. Roy Walmsley, *World Prison Population List* (sixth edition), London: International Centre for Prison Studies (ICPS), 2005: 3–4.

12. Bolivia. Instituto Nacional de Estadística. http://www.ine.gob.bo/indice/EstadisticaSocial.aspx?codigo=30904.

13. Defensoría del Pueblo, *Informe sobre el ejercicio de los derechos humanos*: 68–69.

14. Roy Walmsley, *World Prison Population List* (tenth edition), London: International Centre for Prison Studies (ICPS), 2013: 3–4. Bolivia. Defensoría del Pueblo. *XV informe a la asamblea legislativa plurinacional.* La Paz: Canasta de Fondos, 2013: 75–77.

15. See: OAS, *Access to Justice and Social Inclusion* and Defensoría del Pueblo, *XI informe*: 97. UNOHCHR, *Report of the United Nations High Commissioner for Human Rights on the activities of her office in the Plurinational State of Bolivia.* 2013.

16. Bolivia. Defensoría del Pueblo. *Boletín institucional* No. 5 (November 2013): 4.

17. Arias, Saavedra, and Alarcón, *Reforma procesal*: 139;

18. In part as a result of changes in the law governing pretrial detention, which decreased the legal requirements for prolonged pretrial detention. United Nations General Assembly. *Informe de la Alta Comisionada de las Naciones Unidas para los Derechos Humanos sobre las actividades de su oficina en el Estado Plurinacional de Bolivia*: 14.

19. Defensoría del Pueblo. *XV informe*: 77.

20. Bolivia. Defensoría del Pueblo, *Boletín institucional*, 5 (November 2013): 5.

21. Organization of American States. *Access to Justice and Social Inclusion: The Road towards Strengthening Democracy in Bolivia.* Washington, D.C.: Inter-American Commission on Human Rights, 2007: 55–56. *Reforma procesal*: 130n6.

22. Aya Fujimura-Fanselow and Elisabeth Wickeri, "We Are Left to Rot': Arbitrary and Excessive Pretrial Detention in Bolivia." *Fordham International Law Journal* 36 (2013): 876–877. USDS, *Bolivia 2012 Human Rights Report*: 4–5. David B. Skarbek, "Self-Governance in San Pedro Prison." *The Independent Review* 14/4 (2010): 575–578.

23. Arias, Saavedra, and Alarcón, *Reforma procesal*: 66.

24. Some place the estimate significantly higher: TNI claims a total of 3,000 children living in the Bolivian penal system. Diego Giacoman, "Drug Policy and the Prison Situation in Bolivia." In Pien Metaal and Coletta Youngers, *Systems Overload: Drug Laws and Prisons in Latin America* (Washington, DC: WOLA, 2011), 24.

25. It is interesting to note that the DGRP itself has complained that the presence of women and children along with their inmate fathers and husbands creates an undue burden on the agency, since it is left holding the bag for the electricity bill. Bolivia. Ministerio de Gobierno, *La situación de las cárceles en Bolivia.* La Paz: 2006: 52.

26. Skarbek, "Self-Governance," 577; OAS, *Access to Justice*: 56.

27. Skarbek, "Self-Governance," 576; OAS, *Access to Justice*: 55.
28. Arias, Saavedra, and Alarcón, *Reforma procesal*: 66.
29. Anonymous, "Gobierno cierra la cárcel de San Pedro de La Paz," *La Prensa* 07/15/2013. Estimates for the number of wives and children of inmates "cohabiting" in Bolivian prisons vary greatly, and are notoriously difficult indeed to pin down. At Palmasola, the DGRP estimated the number of children at 1,400 in 2007, noting that this number triples during the winter, when schools are out of session. Bolivia: Ministerio de Gobierno, *La situación de las cárceles en Bolivia*. 2006: 42. Defensoria, *Derechos humanos*, 39.
30. Elisa Medrano, "Tras violación a niña, sugieren anticipar cierre de San Pedro," *La Razón*, 21 June 2013, section: Nacional. USDS, *Bolivia 2012 Human Rights Report*: 4.
31. Elisa Medrano, "Se flexibiliza el 'cierre' de cárcel de San Pedro." *La Razón*, 04 August 2013, section: Nacional.
32. USDS, *Bolivia 2012 Human Rights Report*: 4.
33. Diego Giacoman, "Drug Policy and the Prison Situation in Bolivia." In Pien Metaal and Coletta Youngers, *Systems Overload: Drug Laws and Prisons in Latin America* (Washington, DC: WOLA, 2011), 26. Skarbek, "Self-Governance," 580–582.
34. Organization of American States. *Access to Justice and Social Inclusion*: 53.
35. Skarbek, "Self-Governance," 573–575.
36. Skarbek, "Self-Governance," 578–579.
37. Defensoría del Pueblo, *Boletín institucional*: 4.
38. Pinto Quintanilla (2004), *Las cárceles en Bolivia*, p. 54; Arias, Saavedra, and Alarcón, *Reforma procesal*: 65.
39. Skarbek, "Self-Governance," 573.
40. Arias, Saavedra, and Alarcón, *Reforma procesal*: 65–66.
41. Wilma Pérez, "Una niña muere en la cárcel de San Pedro por meningitis." *La Razón*, 9 July 2014: Section Salud.
42. Anonymous, "defensor critica estado de cárceles rurales." *La Razón* 8 September 2010. Section Nacional.
43. Bolivia: Ministerio de Gobierno, *La situación de las cárceles en Bolivia*. 2006: 28.
44. Fujimura-Fanselow and Wickeri, "We Are Left to Rot," 866. The national ombudsman noted in 2012 that Palmasola prison has a number of cases that have been pending for more than six years, while the prosecutor of La Paz admitted having pending cases dating back to 2011. Defensoría del Pueblo, *Derechos Humanos*: 37.
45. Fujimura-Fanselow and Wickeri, "We Are Left to Rot," 822.
46. Iván Gutiérrez, *La Razón*. 24 June 2013. "Sociedad."
47. Fujimura-Fanselow and Wickeri, "We Are Left to Rot," 858.
48. As quoted in Arias, Saavedra, and Alarcón, *Reforma procesal*: 222 [my translation].
49. OAS, *Access to Justice*: 27.
50. Fujimura-Fanselow and Wickeri, "We Are Left to Rot," 856.
51. Fujimura-Fanselow and Wickeri, "We Are Left to Rot," 850–852.
52. Arias, Saavedra, and Alarcón, *La Reforma Procesal*, 68.
53. Instituto Nacional de Estadísticas. http://www.ine.gob.bo/indice/EstadisticaSocial.aspx?codigo=30904, retrieved on April 4, 2014. It should be noted that the data provided by the INE are suspect in a number of ways and show some inconsistencies that call the accuracy of the data into question.
54. As cited in Arias, Saavedra, and Alarcón, *Reforma Procesal*: 137.
55. Instituto Nacional de Estadísticas. http://www.ine.gob.bo/indice/EstadisticaSocial.aspx?codigo=30904, retrieved on April 4, 2014. In addition, Giacoman notes that FELCN officials have noted that the drop in arrests for drug trafficking has been the result of improved methods in the production of *pasta base*, which require fewer laborers and the increased use of minors who are exempt from prosecution. Giacoman, "Situación de las cárceles," 25. Also: Arias, Saavedra, and Alarcón, *Reforma procesal*, 139–140.

56. Michelle Alexander, *The New Jim Crow: Mass Incarceration in the Age of Colorblindness* (New York: The New Press, 2010), 4–7.

57. Bettina Schorr, "Von nützlichen Feinden," 180.

58. Healy, "The Boom within the Crisis," 112.

59. Kathryn Ledebur, "Bolivia: Clear Consequences," in *Drugs and Democracy in Latin America: The Impact of US Policy*, ed. Coletta Youngers and Eileen Rosin (Boulder: Lynne Riener Publishers, 2005), 151–155.

60. Linda Farthing, "Social Impacts Associated with Antidrug Law 1008."

61. Steven B. Karch, *A Brief History of Cocaine* (Boca Raton: CRC Press, 2006), 11. Paul Gootenberg, *Andean Cocaine: The Making of a Global Drug* (Chapel Hill: University of North Carolina Press, 2008), 16–20.

62. Lehman, *Bolivia and the United States*, 202. Reisinger, "The Unintended Revolution," 257–259

63. Giacoman, "Drug Policy and the Prison Situation in Bolivia," 22–23.

64. Ibid. Giacoman, "Situación cárceles," 14.

65. Fujimura-Fanselowe and Wickeri, "We Are Left to Rot," 823; For a treatment of the impact of the *Ley 1008* on the sentences handed out under the still used inquisitorial system implemented by the *Códigos Bánzer*, see: Arias, Saavedra, and Alarcón, *Reforma procesal*: 14–15 and Diego Giacoman, "Drug Policy and the Prison Situation in Bolivia."

66. Farthing, "Social Impacts": 258–260; Fujimura-Fanselowe and Wickeri, "We Are Left to Rot": 825; Arias, Saavedra, and Alarcón, *Reforma Procesal*: 13–15.

67. Arias, Saavedra, and Alarcón, *La Reforma Procesal*, 68.

68. It should be noted, for example, that consumption of cocaine—while rising—remains low in Bolivia, and drug addiction has not historically been regarded as a serious social problem until recently. Santos, "Unintended Consequences" 138.

69. Farthing, "Social Impacts": 258–261.

70. Washington Estellano, "From Populism to Coca Economy," *Latin American Perspectives* 21, no. 4 (1994): 39–40. Kenneth D. Lehman, *Bolivia and the United States: A Limited Partnership* (Athens: University of Georgia Press, 1999), 199.

71. Reisinger, 'Unintended Revolution," 259–262. Schorr, "Von nützlichen Feinden," 184–185. Ledebur, "Bolivia," 154–157.

72. OAS, *Access to Justice*: 27.

73. For a full treatment of this episode in Bolivian history, see: Robert Lessmann, *Das neue Bolivien: Evo Morales und seine demokratische Revolution* (Zürich: Rotpunkt Verlag, 2010); Marten Brienen, "Interminable Revolution: Populism and Frustration in 20th Century Bolivia," *SAIS Review* 27, no. 1 (2007); James Dunkerley, "Evo Morales, the 'Two Bolivias' and the Third Bolivian Revolution," *Journal of Latin American Studies* 39, no. 1 (2007); Benjamin Kohl, "Bolivia under Morales: A Work in Progress," *Latin American Perspectives* 37 no. 3 (2010); Will Reisinger, "The Unintended Revolution: U.S Anti-Drug Policy and the Socialist Movement in Bolivia," *California Western International Law Journal* 39, no. 2 (2009): 280; Bettina Schorr, "Von nützlichen Feinden und verfehlter Politik: Der Drogenkrieg der USA in Bolivien," in *Bolivien: Staatszerfall als Kollateralschaden*, ed. Thomas Jäger (Wiesbaden: VS verlag für Sozialwissenschaften, 2009); Jeffrey R. Webber, *From Rebellion to Reform in Bolivia: Class Struggle, Indigenous Liberation, and the Politics of Evo Morales* (Chicago: Haymarket Books, 2011).

74. Pilar Domingo, "Evo Morales, the MAS, and a Revolution in the Making," in *Governance after Neoliberalism in Latin America*, ed. Jean Grugel and Pía Riggirozzi (New York: Palgrave MacMillan, 2009), 118–123.

75. Brienen, "Interminable Revolution," 21–22.

76. Reisinger, "Unintended Consequences," 280; William Marcy, *The Politics of Cocaine: How U.S. Foreign Policy Has Created a Thriving Drug Industry in Central and South America* (Chicago: Chicago Review Press, 2010), 254.

77. In fact, Bolivia ranks among the top in Latin America when it comes to the perception of insecurity: Mitchell Seligson, Amy Erica Smith, and Elizabeth E. Zechmeister, *The Political Culture of Democracy in the Americas, 2012: Towards Equality of*

Opportunity (Nashville: LAPOP, 2012), 139. This despite the fact that Bolivia remains, by far, one of the safest countries in Latin America.

78. Seligson, *The Political Culture of Democracy*, 197. Bolivians rank at the very bottom in Latin America when it comes to demands for the rule of law. That is to say that Bolivians are the most likely in Latin America to accept rule-breaking among law enforcement.

79. Defensoría del Pueblo, *XV informe*: 77–78.

TEN

Drugs and the Prison Crisis in Peru

Lucía Dammert and Manuel Dammert G.

"The degree of civilization in a society can be judged by entering its prisons."
—F. Dostoevsky

Latin America is the second most violent region in the world. The latest global report on homicides showed that ten out of the twenty most violent countries in the world are located in Latin America, especially in Central America and the Caribbean.[1] Most of the violence is directly linked to drug trafficking and other crimes related to the production, trafficking, and sale of drugs.

Peru is the single largest producer and exporter of cocaine in the world, yet its homicide rates are below world and regional averages.[2] Official data from the Peruvian National Police (PNP) shows that increasing levels of property and personal crime are not directly correlated to similar trends in homicides.[3] In fact, citizens' concerns about insecurity are less focused on organized criminal activities but rather on the increasing levels of street violence, predatory crimes, and specific property crimes.

What would be a sound explanation of such a situation? What elements of the Peruvian context explains lower levels of the use of violence despite increasing presence of illicit activities? There are no clear answers to those questions but lack of reliable data should be noted as an important factor that could be underestimating the magnitude of the problem.

Despite lower levels of violence, Peru has increasing trends in incarceration levels. Clearly, the lack of a sound governmental response to criminal issues has resulted in the enforcement of punitive populism[4] by which the prison serves as a vessel for action and effectiveness. Similar to the case of South African prisons, as analyzed by Buntman, in Peru, policies and practices of imprisonment reflect the societal structure of inequality. Almost all governments have consistently neglected the relevance of prisons; society in general does not recognize the role of prisons, and punitive populism is growing stronger.[5] These elements have helped contribute to a general crisis of the prison system in Peru, which is characterized by high levels of overcrowding, minimal infrastructure, corruption, and a complete lack of rehabilitation programs.

The crisis of the prison system is profound. Responding to this crisis requires strong and continuous political will to define and implement policies that could increase the number of prisons, improve living conditions in existing prisons, and focus on the most efficient ways to punish criminals. In the short and medium term, there is no sign that any political party or leader intends to take this crisis seriously by addressing the underlying causes of the problem.

In this grim context, the relationship between organized crime, drug trafficking, and prisons in Peru are key issues that should be researched in order to allow for better and more innovative policies. Lack of information and transparency with regard to criminal issues becomes a barrier to identifying not only the drug problem and general presence of organized criminal activities in the country but also hinders the development of solutions. Nevertheless, based on the information that is available, the present chapter is organized into four sections. The first section of the chapter analyzes the problem of crime as well as impunity by examining both official and secondary information that confirms that violence is increasing in the country and drug trafficking is playing a role in this process. The second section analyzes the Peruvian drug market, which is characterized not only in terms of its global role but also by the increasing consolidation of its internal market. The third section focuses on the Peruvian prison system, with an emphasis on the population charged with drug-related offenses. Finally, the conclusions focus on potential innovations in the arena of public policy that could help address the aforementioned problems.

THE DRUG PROBLEM

The 2013 World Drug Report named Peru as the world's largest grower of coca bush with an estimated 64,400 hectares under cultivation in 2011.[6] Furthermore, Peru is the leading producer of dried coca leaf, with the potential to produce more than 126,100 tons annually. The same source estimates that more than 90 percent of the leaves go toward the illicit production of drugs. Thus, the United Nation's figures indicate that Peru has once again ascended to reclaim its position as the leading cocaine-producing nation in the world.

Even though consumption has decreased in the United States, the drug market of Peruvian cocaine has consolidated as a result of increasing demand in the world's second leading consumer of cocaine: Brazil. In that sense, the diversification of the drug market is a new challenge for already weak institutions that cannot keep abreast of the technological innovations, diversification of strategies, and corruption schemes implemented by national and international criminal organizations.

National security is also challenged by the increasing presence of the cocaine market, since there are signals of growing involvement of remnants of the guerrilla movement Shining Path (*Sendero Luminoso*) in the drug trafficking business.[7] During the 1990s, the insurgent group had indirect links to traffickers, most by selling their services to protect traffickers from the police and armed forces. In 2014, however, there have been clear indications that remaining members of the movement have links with foreign criminals and have become the intermediaries between peasants and cartels.

The drug problem in Peru is not only an external issue. There is mounting evidence that shows that the growing drug trade is expanding within the internal market and is causing increases in violence. According to a report published by CEDRO, cocaine use has increased by more than 60 percent in just three years—from a rate of 1.5 percent of the population aged twelve to sixty-five in 2010 to 2.4 percent in 2013.[8] Over the same time period, use of crack (*pasta base*) and marijuana jumped from 2.1 percent to 2.9 percent and from 5.6 to 7.5 percent, respectively. Furthermore, the highest prevalence of drug users live in Peru's main

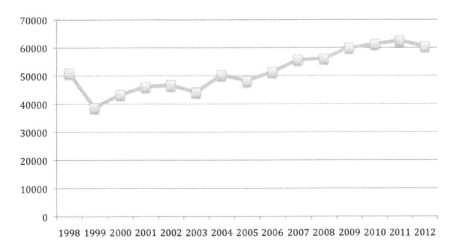

Figure 10.1. Area of Coca Cultivation, Peru (1998-2012). Source: Pasta base de cocaína. Cuatro décadas de história, actualidad y desafios (2013) UNODC

cities as cocaine and marijuana use in Lima stands at 5.1 and 8.9 percent, respectively.[9]

Increasing availability of low-cost crack and cocaine has increased the number of drug addicts committing crimes such as robberies and assaults while under the influence.[10] Another social malaise that is proliferating in Peru includes killings by *sicarios* (hired assassins), which increased by over 50 percent between 2005 and 2008. In many cases, these killings have targeted members of drug cartels from Colombia and Mexico.

THE PERUVIAN PRISON CRISIS[11]

The crisis of the Peruvian prison system is evident with the national average rate of overcrowding in prisons being 119 percent. In fact, at the end of 2013 the number of beds available nationwide in prisons was 31,010 while the number of inmates reached 67,676.[12]

Many years of limited governmental funding to the prison system have contributed to increasing levels of overcrowding. For example, the number of beds available in the year 2006 was 22,548, which failed to respond to the need to accommodate 37,445 prisoners. The unresolved issue of prison overcrowding is exacerbated by the increasing number of people being imprisoned daily. The latest numbers show that between 2006 and 2012, the number of inmates inside the prison system almost doubled, increasing from 37,445 to 61,390 inmates. During the period of 2006-2013, the number of beds increased by 37 percent while the prison population grew by 80 percent. Every day there are more inmates than spaces that are being created for them, which over the years has led to a crisis of monumental proportions.

Furthermore, there is no clear link between the increasing number of people incarcerated and crime rates in the country. The increasing use of pretrial detention for drug-related crimes can last up to fifteen days.[13] However, most of Peru's prisoners have not actually been found guilty of any wrongdoing and are awaiting trial. Figures from Peru's prison service estimated that by the end of 2013, around 59 percent of those currently in prison were awaiting trial. To further complicate the matter, the foreign inmate population is growing quickly. In the year 2013, foreigners represented 3 percent of Peru's total prison population, with half of them in pre-trial detention.

The prison population is comprised mostly of men (94 percent) younger than thirty-five years old (54 percent) of whom only have a high school education (66 percent). In most cases those being imprisoned in Peru are first timers (47 percent) who are not being separated from other inmates based on criminal records or criminological traits. In fact, as of 2014 no classification method exists that ensures that first time offenders are housed in separated areas from repeat offenders. Moreover, of the

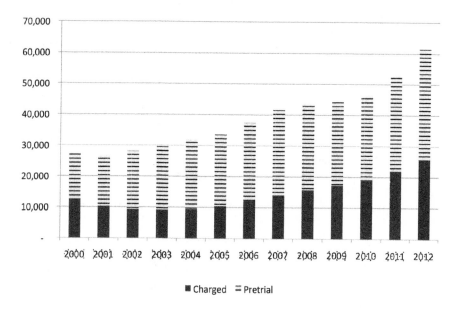

Figure 10.2. Prison Population, Peru (2000–2012). Source: INPE, 2014.

17,742 inmates that were released in 2012, around 12,000 had spent less than one year in prison. This goes against all empirical evidence that confirms that short periods of time in prison do have long-term consequences for those imprisoned as well as their families.[14] In fact research conducted in other countries shows that short-term sentences could do more harm than good, especially to nonviolent inmates.[15] If that is the situation in countries whose prison systems are adequately funded and have acceptable living conditions, clearly short sentences for nonviolent crimes will not be effective in overcrowded prisons. By the end of 2013, more than six thousand inmates in Peru were charged with crimes that carry sentences of five years or less. Also, of the number of inmates who left the prison system in the year 2012, around 68 percent (12,036 inmates) had been imprisoned for less than a year. It is worth mentioning that 5,731 people were inside the prisons for less than three months.

Punishment is a clear tactic in Peru. More than 41 percent of those sentenced were sentenced to more than ten years, most of whom have no possibility of requesting any benefits such as early release for good behavior, which would allow them to leave the prison earlier. Inmates are incarcerated mainly for three types of crimes: property crime is the leading cause of imprisonment in Peru, accounting for more than 38 percent of the prison population, followed by drug-related crimes (25 percent) and sex crimes (21 percent).

The chronic problems of overcrowding, the poor living conditions of inmates and corruption in the penitentiary system have reached a crisis point. President Humala (2011 to present) recently declared a state of emergency in the country's penal system.[16] The U.S. State Department's 2012 report on human rights in Peru[17] stated that prisoners were vulnerable to abuse by guards and other prisoners and confirmed that prisoners who lacked money to pay for basic essentials experienced much more difficult conditions than those with funds. Another report stressed that inmates had intermittent access to potable water, inadequate bathing facilities, and unhygienic kitchen facilities. Furthermore, inmates with money had access to mobile phones, illegal drugs, and meals prepared outside of the prison.

The number of people who died within the prison system in 2013 reached 193. These deaths are associated with health problems of the inmate population. In fact, 89 percent died due to health problems, with a disproportionate number of people affected by TBC (17 percent) and HIV (9.3 percent). Both illnesses require a strong health infrastructure that is not currently present in the prison system in Peru, where there is only one doctor for every 568 inmates in the country.

All available information depicts a grim picture characterized by overpopulation, substandard living conditions and the volatile mixing of violent and non-violent criminals. Contrary to common perceptions, most of the inmate population is charged with petty crimes. These inmates find themselves sharing spaces with murderers, drug traffickers, and the leaders of criminal organizations. In this sense, prisons become "universities of crime" as non-violent inmates and first time offenders are housed with hardened criminals.

PRISON AND DRUGS

One cause of the crisis in the penitentiary system is the number of inmates imprisoned for drug-related offenses. It is quite striking that in 2012 only 4 percent of the total crimes in the country were linked to the drug trade, while the prison population incarcerated for drug offenses comprises 25 percent of the total prison population in the last decade. The following figure illustrates the increasing trend of imprisoning those linked to drug offenses (see figure 10.3).

Three key factors help explain the prison crisis and the importance of drug related offenses: The adoption of stricter laws; the increased use of pretrial detention, and the increasing imprisonment of women and foreign nationals.

Criminal legislation regarding drugs can best be described as draconian. In the last two decades, legislation has resulted in increased penalties while removing and creating new types of crimes, all of which are

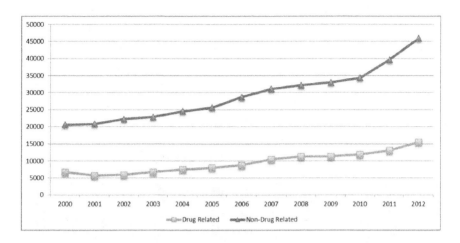

Figure 10.3. Population Imprisoned for Drug-Related Crimes, Peru (2000–2012). Source: INPE, 2014.

linked to drug trafficking. Possession of drugs for personal use continues to go unpunished, and the law does not define precise criteria for police action. This situation opens the door for police corruption and allows for the abuse of those who possess drugs for personal consumption. An example of this punitive populism is a law approved in August 2013 that included "aggravated assault," "promotion of drug trafficking," "extortion," and "illicit association" as crimes without bail or any early release alternative. At the time around, 16 percent of all inmates (10,416) were not able to receive any benefits in order to reduce their sentences, but with the new law, which was conceived for those who are already in the prison system, increased that percentage to 73 percent of all inmates (48,717). The scope of the crisis that this new juridical framework nearly created was monumental not only in terms of increasing horrible living conditions but also in terms of possible retaliations such as acts of violence from inmates that were expecting benefits[18] The rapid response of INPE's National Director changed the provisions for those already charged, but a crisis is unfolding since punitive populism is using penalties as the only tool to respond to the general fear of crime.

In the same vein, pretrial detention is widely used in the Peruvian criminal justice system. In 2013, of those who were in prison for drug trafficking and aggravated-drug trafficking, 56 percent and 48 percent, respectively, were awaiting trial. Therefore, more than 7,000 people were inside the prisons on charges that, in many cases, related more to drug consumption or small-scale trafficking operations than organized crime. Although there is no official data on recidivism, all experts interviewed stated that in most cases, prisoners make connections to criminal organizations, and risk further developing addictions, and are encouraged to

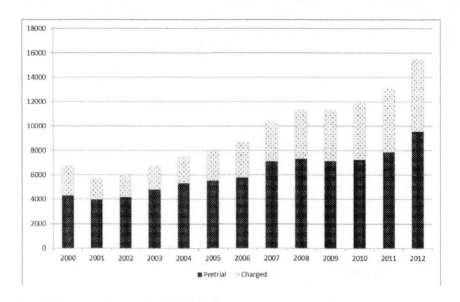

Figure 10.4.   Prison Population, Non-Drug-Related and Drug-Related, Peru (2000–2012). Source: INPE, 2014.

be involved in criminal activities. This is exemplified by the increasing instances of crimes that are planned, supervised, and sometimes even carried out from behind prison walls.[19]

Another reason for the rising number of prisoners who are incarcerated for drug-related crimes is the growing number of foreign nationals arrested in Peru—primarily for cocaine trafficking. Potential profits from the illicit trade are high, but so are the penalties for those who are caught and found guilty. This could mean six to twelve years in prison for possession with intention to traffic, or eight to fifteen years for drug production or trafficking. Peru's National Prisons Institute states that in 2013 more than 90 percent of the 1,696 foreigners in the country's prisons are either sentenced or awaiting trial for drug trafficking. In fact, 49 percent of all foreigners are in pretrial detention with little or no legal aid and family support.[20]

The participation of women in drug-related offenses is a trend that still receives little attention and even less governmental concern. Although women account for only 6 percent of the total inmate population, more than 63 percent of them are awaiting trial for drug-related offenses. Abominable living conditions, high levels of corruption, violence, and even drug trafficking in prison facilities for women affect their possible rehabilitation as well as the lives of the more than 200 children who were living inside the system at the end of 2013. Peruvian law allows incarcerated mothers to keep their children with them until they are three years old, but does nothing regarding the protection of children's basic human rights or providing the special care needed in order to allow them to develop a life separate from violence and criminal activities.

ORGANIZED CRIME AND THE PRISON CRISIS

The prison crisis also has a strong institutional component. For decades, the system was abandoned by governments that did not invest in infrastructure or policies designed to address the growing inmate population. The National Penitentiary Institute (INPE) has not undergone significant modernization, and allegations of corruption, inefficiency, and ineffectiveness of its employees are alarming. At present, the total number of prison staff officers reaches 7,000, which for a prison population of more than 67,000 signifies a ratio of one officer for every nine inmates.

Prison personnel are divided into three different areas: 59 percent are dedicated to safety, 22 percent to administration, and 19 percent to treatment. Notably, personnel dedicated to security are hired under a job regulation called "24x48" (the officer works a full day and should rest for three days), which certainly impacts the institutional performance. Thus, at any given time in the country, no more than 1,400 guards are responsible for the safety of more than 67,000 inmates. There is no doubt that this figure is inadequate for reducing insecurity behind the walls of the system.

Problems are also evident among the staff in the area of treatment. Peruvian prisons only have one doctor for every 568 inmates, which contributes to the serious health problems described in the previous section. Despite the obvious need for more medical professionals and personnel, the emphasis has been placed on ensuring lower levels of violence within the prisons and preventing prison escapes.

Ensuring security within the prisons is virtually impossible under these conditions. As previously mentioned, from 2006 to 2013, the prison population grew from 37,000 to 67,000 and the number of beds from 22,000 to 31,000, which illustrates the government's inability or lack of will to build and develop new prisons. The construction of the new projects has been particularly slow.[21] Notably, an interview with the National Director of INPE confirmed that the governmental process for the construction of a prison generally takes more than a decade, which certainly does not create incentives for the inclusion of prisons on the list of administrative priorities.

Not only have the most recent governments constructed fewer buildings, but also each one has adopted a different model of operations and have different levels of capacity. The fact that there is no clear pattern or protocol to build facilities generates multiple problems regarding safety and security measures. In that sense, each facility has its own security

Table 10.1.   Building of New Prisons in Peru, 1993–2013

Year of construction	Peruvian Departments	Beds
1993	Cajamarca, Huaraz, Pucallpa	1,238
1994	Callao, Chimbote, Huánuco, Piura	2,482
1995	Juliaca, Ayacucho	1,05
1997	Chachapoyas, Cañete, Tumbes, Huaral	1,816
2003	Arequipa	78
2008	Ancón I	972
2009	Ancón II	2,2
2011- 2013	General	4,072

Source: INPE 2014.

protocols and need specific training for guards and administrative staff. Lack of protocol is a problem that the penitentiary system faces in Peru at many different levels.

The Humala administration has emphasized the need for progress on the construction of new facilities. Projects for 2014 involve 1,912 beds that should be provided in the near future. Furthermore, future projects have planned for the creation of 3,997 new beds in 2015 and 5,463 in 2016. In that sense, during his administration, President Humala will increase the capacity of prisons by 15,444 beds by creating new infrastructure. Despite these programs, if current levels of inmates arriving to prisons each month is maintained at December 2013 levels, a total of 37,774 new inmates will be incarcerated during the Humala administration (2011-2016). As a result, the proposed building plans will not change the current deplorable conditions that most inmates experience on a regular basis. [22]

Allegations of self-government of prisons by inmates are constant and linked to prison-based criminal organizations that have been developed among inmates charged with violent crimes. The increasing presence of petty criminals, sex offenders, burglars, and small-scale traffickers may help contribute to this type of organizing within the prisons. In addition, overcrowding plays a role in the process of gang formation inside the prison system, as it can help to organize internal protection systems while facilitating access to drugs and other goods with the help of corrupt guards. In a cell that is inhabited by more than ten people with little to no space for personal activities multiple activities to ensure informal internal safety are being developed. The second stage of the development of the prison-based gangs is the planning of crime inside and outside of prisons, with the most notable being extortion and kidnapping. Prison gangs involved in extortion and kidnapping have received extensive media coverage in 2013, though very little political attention.

Prison overcrowding can lead to less careful classification, monitoring, and managing of inmates with psychological problems or who otherwise pose a threat of violence to other inmates. Various studies have shown a correlation between population density in prisons and infraction and assault rates.[23] Studies also show that overcrowded and poorly regulated prisons tend to have higher rates of rape and sexual violence.[24] Thus, prison overcrowding can cause crime both within prison walls and after inmates are released.

The Peruvian prison situation differs from the situation in other countries such as Guatemala, Brazil, and Mexico where prisons are controlled by drug traffickers and organized criminals with international links. The global pyramidal organization of drug trafficking does not have a Peruvian group in dispute over cocaine trafficking routes. Quite the contrary, there is a hierarchical organization of the drug trade that has the Peruvian groups at the base of the pyramid. Peruvians are specialized on coca plantation and some act as *burreros* (drug mules are the name given to those in charge of smuggling drugs out of Peru).

The prognosis is of great concern. Given the current conditions of the drug trade, with significant interventions in Mexico and Central America as well as the continued policies in Colombia, Peru has become a target for organized crime. This has occurred in a context of limited political interest in the prison system, low levels of investment in infrastructure, and a refusal to implement minor reforms to consolidate a public institution so that it will be prepared not only to punish criminals, but also to protect and rehabilitate them.

CHALLENGES

Peruvian prisons are in a state of increasing deterioration and crisis at all levels. The investment in infrastructure is insufficient, overcrowding is an increasing trend, and rehabilitation programs form part of public policies but lack sufficient budgetary allocations and practical implementation. Overall, the quality of life of inmates is in a state of emergency. Furthermore, alternative sentencing programs that house a significant number of offenders have not brought about clear results and face the shared problem of institutional weaknesses that exists within the prison system.

A factor that further complicates the situation is the citizens' high perception of impunity. This perception has helped consolidate the idea that the only way to solve the problems associated with crime is through the use of punishment and imprisonment. Therefore, in the last few decades, punitive populism has gained popularity at various levels of government as well as in the public sphere. Ironically, the underfunding of prisons has been one of the main consequences of the extensive use of punishment and pretrial imprisonment.

This context has seen the creation of new types of crime, increased punishment, and a proposed reduction of the age at which minors may be charged as adults. Discussions have also been held among politicians about the possible application of the death penalty for some specific crimes. At the same time, Congress has not conducted a significant analysis of the prison situation and the policies that are currently being implemented. In fact, yearly budget debates do not include the National Penitentiary Institute (INPE), as it is not seen as a relevant actor in solving this urgent matter.

The Humala administration recognizes this problem and has proposed a plan for action. Although progress is slow and there is little political will to reform the institution, it should be noted that in the last two decades the importance of INPE was only apparent when the system faced tragedies such as prison fires or scandals especially linked to corruption. The proposed program to build new infrastructure is a step in the right direction, but it is insufficient to solve the issue of overcrowding. Overcrowding will remain at current levels or even increase, as many of the new prisoners will serve extended sentences with no access to benefits such as early release.

Focusing on the criminological characteristics of the prison population, it is clear that inmates are mostly linked to crimes against property and crimes with low organizational levels. Additionally, a large group of inmates are linked to drug-related crimes, but these are mostly small-scale operators rather than large-scale drug traffickers and kingpins. It is worth noting that the strategy to combat crime has been concentrated on street crimes.

Official data also shows that many of those who enter the prison system are incarcerated for less than three years.[25] This situation is aggravated when considering the group of inmates awaiting trial, who in some cases will be released after a short stay in the prison system. The main consequence is the process of criminal contagion that involves linkages among those charged and others awaiting trial. Additionally, another negative externality is the consolidation of prison-based criminal networks.

It should be noted that unlike the prison situation faced by countries such as Brazil, Guatemala, and Mexico, the presence of organized crime inside Peruvian prisons remains weak. Prisons do not act as the main operational centers for criminal activities occurring in urban centers. However, this panorama has begun to change.

As was seen in the previous sections, the situation has slowly evolved from a prison crisis where the inmates were running much of the internal organization of prisons, toward a better strategy of internal control. Corrupt officials have helped inmates gain access to drugs, phones, and even prostitutes. However, a much more sophisticated scheme has developed. Peruvian prisons have a self-developed management system among the inmates which helps oversee internal safety while bringing protection to criminal activity on city streets. Multiple complaints of extortion have been linked to prison-based gangs in recent years. The government, however, has been incapable of adequately tackling this problem.

Faced with this situation, policies have been centered on the transfer of prisoners between prisons. But little has been done to meet the institutional challenges of the INPE that require greater investment in new staff as well as training and better administrative tools to ensure effectiveness. The corruption of officials is a problem of epidemic proportions and initiatives to deal with it have been ineffective.

Treatment programs are limited. In addition, prisons are overcrowded and lack the capacity to separate inmates based on their crimes. One area where greater emphasis should be placed includes women's prisons, which also face serious problems in terms of living conditions. Because mostly women involved in nonviolent drug-related crimes inhabit these prisons, they are ideal places to implement mechanisms and practices to help inmates receive education and job training in order for them to become productive members of society.

The signs are negative and foreshadow a future characterized by an increased presence of organized crime within the Peruvian prison system. Unfortunately, those signs are not evident to most public policy decision makers. Especially to those in Congress that although the prison crisis, continue to increase punishment for all crimes.

The solutions are not simple. They require a change in the way citizens' perceive crime and punishment, especially imprisonment. For many Peruvians, prison has lost its rehabilitative function, serving as a form of punishment that does not address the roots of the problem. The effects of confinement are not evident, and the worsening of crime, corruption and above all the criminal contagion that affects hundreds of people daily is not taken into account by a frightened citizenry.

Politics are another critical area of concern. The political use of the topic of crime, limited expertise in the criminal justice sector, the lack of prioritization of investment in prison infrastructure and the lack of a clear perspective on alternative sentences are elements of a context with many challenges.

The complexity of the problem is enormous and requires creative and appropriate responses to the crisis in the Peruvian penitentiary system. Deciding to use technology to monitor defendants under house arrest is one way. It is certainly not the solution to the problem, but it at least limits the criminal contagion and deteriorating prison conditions.

Another initiative that could be evaluated is the transfer of incarcerated foreigners to their home countries. This type of initiative has been utilized in other countries and could lead to a reduction in the rates of prison overcrowding, particularly in women's prisons.

Prisons desperately need a detailed review of the procedures utilized for the entire prison population. This would allow for the identification of people who are in prison even though they have fulfilled their sentences or who are eligible to apply for some kind of benefit but have not been informed of the possibility.

Finally, contrary to what has been done with Peru's legal architecture, it is necessary to discuss the trend to limit all possibilities to early release or conditional release for those who commit offenses. International experience shows that beyond sexual or violent crimes, the path for convicted people living in prisons are multiple. Denying alternatives to imprisonment from the beginning for various offenses does not necessarily reduce crime but could even encourage the use of violence. This is especially pertinent for those whose crimes are drug-related, whose hidden mental health problems or addictions, if treated, could lead to positive results.

If we continue to think of the prison as a remote, faraway place that is closed off from the rest of society, the situation will only continue to worsen. In Peru, the ground is fertile for more violence and deterioration within prisons since the presence of organized crime is growing and criminal justice institutions do not show any sign of concern or effective course of actions.

NOTES

1. UNODC, *Global Study on Homicide 2011*. https://www.unodc.org/unodc/en/data-and-analysis/homicide.html

2. Lucia Dammert, *Seguridad Ciudadana en Perú: las cifras del desconcierto*, (CAF, 2012).

3. The lack of reliable information in the criminal justice system in Peru is a problem that highly impacts policy design and implementation.

4. David Garland, *The Culture of Control. Crime and Social Order in Contemporary Society* (Oxford: University of Oxford Press, 2001). John Pratt, *Penal Populism* (New York: Routledge, 2007). Julian Roberts, Loretta Stalans, et al., *Penal Populism and Public Opinion* (New York: Oxford University Press, 2003).

5. Fran Buntman, "Prison and Democracy: Lessons Learned and Not Learned, from 1989–2009," *International Journal of Politics, Culture and Society* 22, no. 3 (2009): 401–418.

6. UNDOC, *World Drug Report 2013*, (United Nations Publications, 2013).

7. Phil Williams, "Insurgencies and Organised Crime," in *Drug Trafficking, Violence, and Instability*, ed. Phil Williams, Vanda Felab-Brown. (U.S. Army War College Strategic Studies Institute, 2012), 34–36.

8. CEDRO, *El problema de las drogas en Peru* (CEDRO: Lima, 2013).

9. For further information see: C. Alvarado, "Peru: Narco Trafficking Spawns Common Crimes," *Infosurhoy.com* (2013).

10. Gino Costa, "Security Challenges in Peru," *Americas Quarterly*, (2012). http://www.americasquarterly.org/node/1900

11. This section is based on information requested to the Peruvian National Prison Institute (INPE).

12. Data available by INPE.

13. Francisco Soberon http://www.druglawreform.info/en/publications/systems-overload/item/875-drug-laws-and-prisons-in-peru?pop=1&tmpl=component&print=1

14. Camille Boutron and Chloé Constant, "Gendering Transnational Criminality: The Case of Woman's Imprisonment in Peru," *Signs: Journal of Women in Culture and Society*, 39, no. 1 (2013): 177–195.

15. For further discussion about the effects of incarceration and alternative programs, see: Hilde Wermink, et al, "Comparing the Effects of Community Service and Short Term Imprisonment on Recidivism: A Matched Simples Approach," *Journal of Experimental Criminology*, 6 (2010): 325–349; M. Lipsey and F. T. Cullen, "The Effectiveness of Correctional Rehabilitation. A Review of Sistematic Reviews," *Annual Review of Law and Social Science*, 3 (2007): 297–320; F. Losel, "Offender treatment and rehabilitation: What works? In M.R. Maguire and R. Reiner (Eds.), *The Oxford Handbook of Criminology*, (Oxford: Oxford, 2012).

16. Amnesty International UK Blogs, *Peru's Prison Conditions –a state of emergency.* http://www.amnesty.org.uk/blogs/belfast-and-beyond/peru percentE2 percent80 percent99s-prison-conditions- percentE2 percent80 percent93-state-emergency

17. United States Department of State, *Peru 2012 Human Rights Report.* http://www.state.gov/documents/organization/204682.pdf

18. See El Comercio, "Noticias de Crisis Carcelaria," http://elcomercio.pe/noticias/crisis-carcelaria-221000

19. For more details see some news reports: http://peru21.pe/actualidad/extorsiones-uso-anfo-y-polvora-aumentan-lima-2166173, http://www.larepublica.pe/24-07-2011/crece-ola-de-extorsiones-en-lima, http://elcomercio.pe/mundo/actualidad/coronel-linares-creo-poder-paralelo-region-policial-lambayeque_1-noticia-1675810

20. Peru's Drug Mules, The European Magazine, http://www.theeuropean-magazine.com/sue-lloyd-roberts/7698-perus-drug-mules

21. This section is based on information requested to the Peruvian National Prison Institute (INPE).

22. For more on this subject Instituto Nacional Penitenciario: Plan Estalegico Institutional: Periodo 2012–2016.

23. Gerald G. Gaes and William J. McGuire, Prison Violence: The Contribution of Crowding Versus Other Determinants of Prison Assault Rates, 22 J. RES. CRIME & DELINQ. 41, 41 (1985); Edwin I. Megargee, The Association of Population Density, Reduced Space, and Uncomfortable Temperature with Misconduct in a Prison Community, 5 *AM. J. CMTY. PSYCHOL.* 289, 295 (1977)

24. Phil Gunby, Sexual Behavior in an Abnormal Situation, 245 JAMA 215, 215 (1981); Michael B. King, Male Rape in Institutional Settings, in Male Victims of Sexual Assault 67, 70 (Gillian C. Mezey & Michael B. King eds., 1992).

25. (INPE, 2013)

ELEVEN

Beyond Overcrowding

The Decline of the Brazilian Penitentiary System

Marcelo Rocha e Silva Zorovich

The crisis in the Brazilian penitentiary system remains a critical subject in the field of public security and criminal law. The problems with the prison system in Brazil seem endless, as prisons are overcrowded and controlled by drug traffickers and criminal organizations. This chapter highlights and examines the major tendencies and challenges of the Brazilian penitentiary system. The goal of this work is to answer several key questions: 1) what is the current state of prisons in Brazil? 2) What is the relationship between organized crime, particularly drug trafficking networks, and the penitentiary system? 3) What are the challenges that prevent policy reforms and the implementation of new strategies? To answer these questions, the chapter is organized into two parts. The first part of the chapter analyzes the main trends in Brazilian prisons and highlights the linkages between drug trafficking, organized crime, and the penitentiary system. The second part of this work examines a combination of factors, including institutional inefficiency and corruption, in order to explain the current state of the prison system. The chapter concludes by analyzing the major challenges to reforms of the penitentiary system.

Prisons in Brazil are best characterized by extreme levels of overcrowding. In addition to overcrowding, a combination of factors has contributed to the degradation of prisons over the past decades. Brazilian prisons have become living hells laden with gang activity, drug trafficking, drug abuse, corruption, rebellions, sexual assaults, and murders.[1] In addition, prison employees are unprepared and susceptible to bribes from prisoners. All of these variables have contributed to the violation of the human rights of prisoners, who are forced to live in horrific conditions.

Various cases highlight the major obstacles and challenges that the Brazilian penitentiary system faces. Perhaps one of the most famous cases of the ineffectiveness of the Brazilian prison system is the case of Carandiru, a prison located in São Paulo, one of the richest cities in Brazil. In 1992, a prison riot occurred, resulting in military intervention. The consequences of the ensuing massacre—also known as the "Massacre of Carandiru"—was the death of over 100 prisoners.[2] This bloodshed highlights the ineptitude of the staff to control the prisons and serves as an example of the grave human rights abuses that have occurred. The prison known as the Pedrinhas Complex, located in the state of Maranhão, sheds light on the characteristics of a prison located in one of the poorest states in Brazil. The prison lacks adequate resources, and, as a result, is laden with high levels of corruption, criminal activity, and violence.[3] The state of Maranhão has neglected the problem for a long time, either as a result of incompetent authorities, lack of preparedness to deal with the situation, and the lack of financial investment, representing a problem that occurs at the national level, and suggesting that prisons in Brazil do not function effectively in any Brazilian state due to overcrowding, lack of financial and human resources, corruption, and mismanagement.

AN ALARMING SCENARIO: THE BRAZILIAN PENITENTIARY SYSTEM

Since Brazil's transition from dictatorship to democracy in the 1980s, the country has undergone important political and economic transformations. However, despite Brazil's rise as a regional power, human rights violations can still be found in the penitentiary system. Described as being "medieval,[4] Brazil's prison system has frequently been condemned by human rights experts due to the animalistic like conditions in which the prisoners live."[5] In addition, prisons in Brazil have failed to effectively treat and rehabilitate offenders, and, therefore, recidivism rates remain extremely high.[6] As a consequence of the proliferation in organized crime and violence in Brazil, Brazilian society has called for increased efforts by law enforcement and the judicial system to punish criminals and increase safety in the streets. The government, however, has failed to implement effective policies, reduce criminality, and improve the prison system. As a result, prisons have become breeding grounds for organized criminal activities.[7]

Even while behind bars and allegedly being punished for their crimes, many prisoners continue to participate in illegal activities.[8] Organized criminal networks operate inside the prisons with defined hierarchies and have subcommands or cells that also operate outside the prison. Moreover, they bribe officials with money from a variety of illegal activities in order to purchase weapons, narcotics, and mobile devices. Bribes and official corruption, therefore, enable drug traffickers to communicate with people outside the penitentiary system and continue their operations while incarcerated.[9]

Paixão argues that organized crime groups operating within prisons date back to the 1970s and 1980s with the emergence of *Falange Vermelha* in Rio de Janeiro and a group known as the *Serpentes* (São Paulo).[10] By the end of the 1970s, the former Penal Institute *Cândido Mendes* (Rio de Janeiro), the penitentiary that was built to accommodate around 540 prisoners , housed over 1200 men who struggled to survive in an institution home to some of the most dangerous individuals in Brazil. The prison became known as the "Devil's Caldron" due to scenes of terror and bloodshed that occurred within the prison walls.[11] The Pedrinhas Complex[12] is a prison that is a continuation of the "Devil's Caldron," as the institution is a fertile ground[13] for organized criminal networks that operate in other areas outside the south-southeast states of Brazil.[14] That is to say that organized crime has proliferated to various parts of Brazil such as the northern and northeastern states and is no longer concentrated in the most important economic regions of the country such as São Paulo, Rio de Janeiro, Paraná, Santa Catarina, and Rio Grande do Sul.

Prisons in Brazil are best characterized by horrific living conditions[15] that perpetuate organized crime as powerful organized criminal groups participate in various illicit activities that occur inside and outside the prisons such as illegal gambling, kidnapping, money laundering, among other illicit activities. The prisons also have fomented gang membership as prisoners join gangs for protection. Prisoners have even planned robberies of homes and other locations while incarcerated.[16] Prisons, therefore, are part of a vicious circle characterized by extreme levels of criminal activity as well as high levels of violence.[17] Prisons have been completely ineffective in their ability to rehabilitate convicts and enable them to return to society and become productive citizens. Prisons have become "schools of crime," where prisoners are housed with some of the most hardened criminals. The Brazilian penitentiary system, in essence, creates a pernicious environment that makes it nearly impossible to rehabilitate prisoners.[18]

According to Judge Douglas Martins, who nationally denounced the wave of killings and abuses in the Complex of Pedrinhas, Brazil's inadequate prisons are not a problem of one government, but of many states administered by different political parties. According to him, overcrowded prisons put defendants who committed minor crimes in contact with dangerous criminals. An individual sentenced for a crime enters prison and must immediately join a criminal faction for protection. After serving their sentences, former prisoners are forced to remain in criminal organizations, such as gangs, which encourage them to commit crimes in order to pay taxes or debts that have accrued in exchange for protection.[19]

The previous discussion has provided some anecdotal evidence regarding the penitentiary system in Brazil. This next section analyzes descriptive statistics to highlight the current state of prisons in Brazil. Between 1995 and 2005, the inmate population grew from over 148,000 to 361,402, representing an increase of 143 percent in a decade. Between 2005 and 2009, the inmate population increased from 361,402 to 473,626, representing an increase of 31 percent in the span of several years. Recent data published in 2012 reveals that Brazil has 548,003 inmates, which means 287 inmates exist for every 100,000 individuals.[20]

Overcrowding is one of the most serious problems of Brazil's prisons, and a cause of many others. The state of the prison system is so precarious that in the state of Espirito Santo, containers were used as cells due to severe overcrowding. The same situation occurred in a prison in the metropolitan region of Vitoria, which had 306 inmates in a facility with an official capacity for 144 inmates. Undoubtedly, the individual rights and guarantees of prisoners have not been respected.[21] In addition, overcrowding makes prisons unmanageable as authorities are outnumbered and unable to control unruly inmates as seen in the two previously mentioned cases of Carandiru[22] and Pedrinhas as well as various other cases such as Presídio (prison) Central de Porto Alegre, in Rio Grande do Sul, Centros de Detenção Provisória of São Paulo, Cadeia Pública Vidal Pessoa, in Manaus, among other cases. Because of these conditions, prison officials are even more susceptible to corruption as a result of overcrowding and often turn to various abusive measures to control detainees as violence and acts of corruption (such as bribery) serve as mechanisms to control the often unruly prison population.

Overcrowding, therefore, has resulted in the violation of the human rights of many prisoners who are forced to live in animalistic conditions. The Brazilian Constitution guarantees that all Brazilians, including inmates, should have the right to physical and moral integrity. In other words, prisoners should not have to suffer from physical violence while paying for their crimes, seeing as human dignity is one of the basic principles of the Brazilian constitution.

Currently, Brazil has a major crisis of where to house inmates as the number of prisoners exceeds the capacity by 40 percent.[23] Brazil still has a deficit of almost 200,000 beds for prisoners,[24] reflecting the lack of infrastructure required to house inmates. Despite the existence of a national penitentiary policy,[25] the policy has not been implemented and the result has been extreme levels of chaos and deadlock in the penitentiary system. The inability of the Brazilian leadership to solve the crisis has only perpetuated this vicious cycle. Magistrates, prosecutors, prison officials, and activists have identified other critical cases where overcrowding, violence, violations of human rights, and gang activities have led to extreme levels of chaos. The list of critical cases includes: the Presídio Central of Porto Alegre (Rio Grande do Sul), the Complexo do Curado (formerly the Anibal Bruno) in Pernambuco, the Urso Branco prison in Rondônia, the Centros de Detenção Provisória in São Paulo, and the Cadeia Pública Vidal Pessoa in Manaus, Amazonas.[26]

Despite the fact that the federal government has acknowledged[27] for many years that such problems exist, it has failed to produce any significant reforms to the penitentiary system. This complex situation involves the intersection of judicial, penitentiary, and crime prevention components[28] on a daily basis as violence continuously erupts in Brazilian prisons. The President of the Federal Supreme Court (STF), Joaquim Barbosa, has criticized the Brazilian penitentiary system, which he describes as a hellish system. He declares that prisons are under the control of two main organized crime entities: the "First Command of the Capital (PCC)" and "Comando Vermelho." Barbosa confirmed that prisons in Brazil are "inadequate for a human being. He argues that the problem is not new, and 'horror' is the best word to define the Brazilian penitentiary system. . . ."[29] He also criticizes the lack of investment by the government in the prison system. Assis agrees with such criticisms and highlights the high recidivism rates, stating that prisoner revolts and escapes serve both as an answer and a warning to authorities about the inhumane living conditions of the prisoners, despite legislation designed to protect inmates. In addition to human rights violations within prisons, Assis points out the ineffectiveness of the socialization programs designed to help convicts reintegrate into society. In fact, approximately 90 percent of prisoners relapse into crime and return to prison.[30] Moreover, in the vast majority of these establishments, there is no incentive to study or participate in work programs that can provide inmates with the necessary skills to help them reintegrate into society and find steady employment. Assis concludes that "permanent support to ex-convicts may be the main solution for the problem of recidivism, for if the present situation continues, today's unaided ex-convict will keep on being tomorrow's relapsed criminal."[31] In essence, prisoners are abandoned by the state after being convicted and are permanently branded as criminals, which only increases recidivism rates.

REFORMS AND POLICY SOLUTIONS

For the renowned lawyer Miguel Reale Junior, the tragic picture of prison overcrowding and the absence of any assistance to prisoners led to the Federal Council of the Brazilian Bar Association's decision to examine the prison system and create an agency designed to monitor its operations.[32] Such efforts must analyze the situation in each state and initiate civil suits, forcing governments to improve prison conditions. This would improve the living conditions of the prisons. However, prisoners should also be allowed to work inside prisons in order to provide them with the jobs skills that will serve them if they are released into society.[33] The problem, however, has been the implementation of the national policy. The National Plan for Criminal and Penitentiary Policy[34] recommends fourteen priority measures/actions:

1. Systematize and institutionalize restorative justice;
2. The creation and implementation of a policy of social integration of former convicts;
3. Alternative options to prison;
4. The implementation of mental health programs in prisons;
5. Directed action to protect special groups;
6. Pretrial detainees;
7. Access to public defenders;
8. Strengthening of social control;
9. Combatting drug availability, trafficking, and sales;
10. Improving the overall prison structures;
11. Improving prison management;
12. Combating inefficiency;
13. Improving the efficiency of the legislative process;
14. Building a vision of criminal justice and social justice.

While this is an exhaustive list, the government has failed to implement such strategies. What prevents the Brazilian leadership from implementing many of these actions is a combination of the judicial system's inefficacy, bureaucracy, and corruption.

Barbosa discusses the political obstacles to implementing the reforms, stating that "politicians do not care about this issue because they have no political return, no voting gains."[35] The restructuring of the prison system is a key part of the policy recommendations due to the archaic structure of the prison system as well as the obsolete infrastructure, resource limitations, and endless levels of corruption. Few prisons are equipped with the proper mechanisms for implementing appropriate security measures. Such observations highlight some of the challenges and obstacles along the road to institutional reform.[36] According to Aravena, state police forces do not have the necessary investigative capacities, yet "the training of its commanders has been influenced by military conceptions that emphasize the idea of repression" and lack of prevention.[37] Soares criticizes Brazilian institutions such as the police forces, which are laden with corruption, declaring that such institutions are "inefficient at prevention and delimited repression, in investigation and in winning the indispensable confidence of the population."[38] It is time that law is translated into reality so that Brazil can implement the reforms and improve the conditions of the prisons.

Reforming the penitentiary system alone is not sufficient as other law enforcement and judicial institutions in Brazil remain extremely weak and corrupt. The police, for example, contribute to the problem of organized crime as they have inefficient management structures and do not evaluate their own performance or allow the monitoring of their actions. In many instances, the police neither plan their activities nor do they correct their errors by analyzing the results of their initiatives; instead, errors are simply ignored.[39] Queiroz claims that organized crime has increasingly been supported by material, technical, and strategic resources and has required the adaptation of the police.[40]

In addition, there is a lack of professionals prepared to deal with "high-tech" criminals inside and outside of prison walls. The United Nations Office on Drugs and Crime (UNODC) argues that " organized crime takes advantage of new technologies and benefits as a result of globalization to coordinate and lead their businesses from . . ." nearly anywhere in the world. "Transnational organized crime is a major threat to public safety and is an obstacle to social, economic and political development of societies around the world."[41] Bagley argues that "in the countries of Latin America and the Caribbean, the consequence of ignoring organized crime and its corrosive effects may well be institutional decay or democratic de-institutionalization."[42] Such comments are particularly applicable in the case of Brazil, which has experienced long-standing institutional[43] weaknesses, particularly prisons that have enabled organized criminal networks to proliferate.

Connections between organized crime such as international drug trafficking from within the prisons have increased in Brazil, fostering ideal conditions for the rapid spread of transnational organized crime. Global illicit trafficking requires a combination of strategic actions from the Brazilian government to combat organized crime, particularly within prisons.[44] As part of this concern, the Brazilian Minister of Justice, José Eduardo Cardozo, highlights that a new border control system has been developed through the integration of Federal Government bodies—the Ministry of Justice, the Ministry of Defense, and other ministries—and state governments in order to strengthen international relations with other countries.[45]

THE UN WEIGHS IN ON PRISONS IN BRAZIL

After a visit to Brazil, a delegation of the United Nations Human Rights, Office of the High Commissioner concluded that there is excessive deprivation of liberty in the country, very low use of alternatives to imprisonment, and serious disability measures for public defenders. The Working Group on Arbitrary Detention of the United Nations[46] notes that the country has one of the largest prison populations in the world and highlights the vast number of individuals awaiting trial in prisons, police stations, detention centers for immigrants, and forensic psychiatric hospitals. Among the 548,003 prisoners, nearly 40 percent were awaiting sentencing. The report states that 192,000 arrest warrants have yet to be completed. [47]

This situation in the Brazilian prisons raises questions in terms of human security, as it affects inmates, the entire administration that supervises the prisons, and the outside population due to overcrowding and frequent rebellions. Kay[48] underlines the challenges to human security, whose core elements are economic security, health security, food security, environmental security, personal and community security, and political security.[49] Hampson et al. to identify three approaches to human security: "liberty, human rights, and the rule of law as a source of security."[50] Clearly, the prison system in Brazil has not been effective in providing basic human security and ensuring the rights of the prisoners.

With particular attention to health concerns, Assis[51] argues that the overcrowding of prison cells as well as the unsanitary conditions of the Brazilian prisons creates an environment conducive to the proliferation of epidemics and contagious diseases. Various structural factors as well as poor eating habits, drug use, and hygiene of the prisoners contribute to the inmates' poor health conditions. As a result, Brazilian prisoners are infected by various dangerous diseases such as HIV.[52] The most common are respiratory diseases, such as tuberculosis and pneumonia, but there are also high transmission rates of diseases such as hepatitis and HIV. Around 20 percent of inmates have HIV as a result of various sexual activities, drug usage, and sexual assaults against inmates. There also are a high number of inmates with mental disorders, cancer, leprosy, and various disabilities.[53] Julita Lemgruber,[54] founding director of the Center for Studies on Public Security and Citizenship in Rio de Janeiro, claims that greater rationality in the allocation of alternative sanctions and engagement of the state in improving existing prisons and building new ones are key measures to solving such problems.

CONCLUSION

The Brazilian penitentiary system is inhumane and inefficient, seeing as it has failed to achieve the basic goal of any prison: to punish and rehabilitate offenders. Instead, prisons have become schools of crime as they are environments conducive to organized crime due to overpopulation and the fact that they are controlled by drug traffickers and organized criminals. An astonishing 95 percent of the inmates[55] are from a marginalized social class, poor, unemployed, and often illiterate. In many cases, individuals from this marginalized class have been driven to criminal activities as a result of the lack of social opportunities and ineffectiveness of the government to create conditions for social inclusion. It is a vicious circle and the penitentiary system in Brazil has systematically ruined the lives of thousands of Brazilians as opposed to providing them with the necessary skills to become productive members of society. Ultimately, the range of issues related to the Brazilian prison system seems endless. More money must be allocated to strengthening the institutions and combatting corruption. However, this requires political will and is not an easy task.[56] If the situation does not change many Brazilians will continue to be victims of the prison system.

NOTES

1. Estado de Sao Paulo. "Para presidente do STF, prisões brasileiras são 'um inferno.'" http://www.estadao.com.br/noticias/cidades,para-presidente-do-stf-prisoes-bras ileiras-sao-um-inferno,1124561,0.htm Accessed January 29, 2014.

2. "TJ inocenta coronel Ubiratan por massacre do Carandiru ," *Folha de S. Paulo,* 15/ 02/2006 http://www1.folha.uol.com.br/folha/cotidiano/ult95u118348.shtml Accessed August 30 2014.

3. "Maranhão: mais um detento morre após ser espancado em presídio." Conectas: Direitos Humanos. January 31, 2014.

4. Becky Branford, "Brazil's 'medieval' prisons." BBC News. http://news.bbc.co.uk/2/hi/americas/3768145.stm (accessed January 10, 2014).

5. Paul Kiernan, "U.N. Human-Rights Body Expresses Concern Over Brazil's Prisons." *The Wall Street Journal,* January 8, 2014, http://online.wsj.com/news/articles/ SB10001424052702304347904579308490612605018 (accessed January 2014).

6. Drauzio Varella. Estação Carandiru. Cia das Letras, 1999.

7. Haroldo dos Anjos, "As raízes do Crime Organizado. Florianopolis": IBRADD, 2002.

8. Carlos Alberto Marchi de Queiroz, "Crime Organizado no Brasil—Comentários à Lei No. 9034/95"—Aspectos Policiais e Judiciários, Teoria e Prática, 1998.

9. Guaracy Mingardi, "O Estado e o Crime Organizado." Tese de doutorado, Faculdade de Filosofia e Ciências Humanas, USP, São Paulo. (1998). Guarac Mingardi, "O Que É Crime Organizado: Uma Definição das Ciências Sociais." *Revista do Ilanud,* n. 8, pp. 25–27.

10. Antonio Lui Paixão, "Recuperar ou punir? Como o Estado trata o criminoso." São Paulo, Cortez, 1987.

11. Regina Campos Lima, "A Sociedade Prisional e suas facções criminosas." Londrina: Edições Humanidades, 2003.

12. *Revista Forum.* "Maranhão: mais um detento morre após ser espancado em presídio." January 31, 2014.

13. Pedrinhas Complex is similar nowadays to what Candido Mandes was in the 1970s.

14. João. Sabóia, "Desconcentração industrial no Brasil nos anos 90: um enfoque regional." Pesq. Plan. Econ., Rio de Janeiro, v. 30, n. 1, abr. 2000.

15. Drauzio Varella. Estação Carandiru. Cia das Letras, 1999.

16. Oliveira, Adriano. "As Peças e os Mecanismos do Crime Organizado em Sua Atividade Tráfico de Drogas," *Revista de Ciências Sociais,* Rio de Janeiro, Vol. 50, n. 4, 2007, 699–720.

17. Drauzio Varela. Estação Carandiru. Cia das Letras, 1999, http://www. companhiadasletras.com.br/detalhe.php?codigo=11141 , accessed September, 2014.

18. "Sistema carcerário brasileiro. A ineficiência, as mazelas e o descaso presentes nos presídios superlotados e esquecidos pelo poder público. Sande Nascimento de Arruda, *Revista Jurídica* 2013.

19. Luis Kawaguti, "As seis piores prisões do Brasil." BBC News. http://www.bbc.co.uk/portuguese/noticias/2014/01/140115_seis_prisoes_lk.shtml (accessed January 22, 2014).

20. Ministério da Justiça do Brasil. Departamento Penitenciário Nacional. Infopen. Available at http://portal.mj.gov.br/main.asp?View={D574E9CE-3C7D-437A-A5B6-22166AD2E896}&BrowserType=IE&LangID=pt-br&params=itemID%3D%7BC37B2AE9-4C68-4006-8B16-24D28407509C%7D%3B&UIPartUID=%7B2868BA3C-1C72-4347-BE11-A26F70F4CB26%7D Accessed January 20, 2014.

21. "Sistema carcerário brasileiro. A ineficiência, as mazelas e o descaso presentes nos presídios superlotados e esquecidos pelo poder público. Sande Nascimento de Arruda, *Revista Jurídica*. 2013.

22. "Brazil Carandiru jail massacre police guilty." BBC News, August 3, 2013, http://www.bbc.co.uk/news/world-latin-america-23560362 (accessed January 2014).

23. Ministério da Justiça do Brasil. Departamento Penitenciário Nacional. Infopen. Available at http://portal.mj.gov.br/main.asp?View={D574E9CE-3C7D-437A-A5B6-22166AD2E896}&BrowserType=IE&LangID=pt-br&params=itemID%3D%7BC37B2AE9-4C68-4006-8B16-24D28407509C%7D%3B&UIPartUID=percent7B2868BA3C-1C72-4347-BE11-A26F70F4CB26%7D Accessed January 20, 2014.

24. Ibid.

25. Ministério da Justiça do Brasil. Conselho Nacional de Política Criminal e Penitenciária, 04-26-2011.

26. Luis Kawaguti, "As seis piores prisões do Brasil." BBC News, January 20, 2014, http://www.bbc.co.uk/portuguese/noticias/2014/01/140115_seis_prisoes_lk.shtml (accessed January 2014).

27. "Brazil Carandiru jail massacre police guilty." BBC News.

28. "Sistema carcerário brasileiro. A ineficiência, as mazelas e o descaso presentes nos presídios superlotados e esquecidos pelo poder público. Sande Nascimento de Arruda, *Revista Jurídica*. 2013.

29. Estado de Sao Paulo. "Para presidente do STF, prisões brasileiras são 'um inferno." http://www.estadao.com.br/noticias/cidades,para-presidente-do-stf-prisoes-brasileiras-sao-um-inferno,1124561,0.htm. Accessed January 29, 2014.

30. Rafael Damaceno de Assis, "A realidade atual do sistema penitenciário brasileiro." Revista CEJ, Brasilia, Ano XI, n.o 39, p. 74–78, out-dez. 2007.

31. Ibid.

32. Miguel Reale Junior, Estado de Sao Paulo: Opinião."As masmorras consentidas," http://www.estadao.com.br/noticias/impresso,as-masmorras-consentidas,1125476,0.htm Accessed February 01, 2014.

33. Miguel Reale Junior, Estado de Sao Paulo: Opinião."As masmorras consentidas," Miguel Reale Junior. http://www.estadao.com.br/noticias/impresso,as-masmorras-consentidas,1125476,0.htm Accessed February 01, 2014.

34. Ministério da Justiça do Brasil. Conselho Nacional de Política Criminal e Penitenciária. 04-26-2011.

35. Estado de Paulo. "Para presidente do STF, prisões brasileiras são 'um inferno." http://www.estadao.com.br/noticias/cidades,para-presidente-do-stf-prisoes-brasileiras-sao-um-inferno,1124561,0.htm Accessed January 29, 2014.

36. Michael Misse, "Dossiê, crime, segurança e instituições estatais: problemas e perspectivas. Crime organizado e crime comum no Rio de Janeiro: diferenças e afinidades," *Revista Sociologia Política*, Curitiba, v. 19, n. 40, outubro 2011, 13–25.

37. Francisco R. Aravena, "Organized Crime in Latin America and The Caribbean: summary of articles," Edited by Luis Guillermo Solis Rivera. 1a ed.—San José, C.R.: Flasco, 2009.

38. Luiz E. Soares, "Public security: present and future," estudos avançados 21 (56), 2007.

39. Ibid.

40. Carlos A. Marchi de Queiroz, "Crime Organizado no Brasil—Comentários à Lei No. 9034/95"—Aspectos Policiais e Judiciários, Teoria e Prática, 1998.

41. "Prevenção ao Crime e Justiça Criminal," UNODC. http://www.unodc.org/lpo-brazil/pt/crime/index.html Accessed January 12, 2014.

42. Bruce M. Bagley, *Drug Trafficking and Organized Crime in the: Major Trends in the Twenty First Century* (Washington, D.C.: Woodrow Wilson Center International Center for Scholars, 2012).

43. Michel Misse, "Dossiê, crime, segurança e instituições estatais: problemas e perspectivas. Crime organizado e crime comum no Rio de Janeiro: diferenças e afinidades," *Revista Sociologia Política*, Curitiba, v. 19, n. 40, outubro 2011, 13–25.

44. Bureau of International Narcotics and Law Enforcement Affairs (INCRS), "International Narcotics Control Strategy Report," Volume I, Drug and Chemical Control, March 2012.

45. UNODC. http://www.unodc.org/southerncone/en/frontpage/2012/03/13-interview-jose-eduardo-cardozo.html, Accessed June 14, 2012.

46. United Nations Human Rights. Office of the High Commissioner. http://acnudh.org/en/2013/03/arbitrary-detention-un-expert-group-launches-first-information-gathering-visit-to-brazil/ Accessed January 15, 2014.

47. UNESCO Office in Brasilia. Arbitrary Detention: UN expert group launches first information-gathering visit to Brazil. http://www.unesco.org/new/en/brasilia/about-this-office/singleview/news/arbitrary_detention_un_expert_group_launches_first_information_gathering_visit_to_brazil/#.Uu0G0_ldWWY Accessed January 15, 2014.

48. Sean Kay, *Global Security in the Twenty-First Century: The Quest for Power and the Search for Peace* (Lanham, Maryland: Rowman & Littlefield, 2006), 267-370.

49. Kerr examines the concept of human security, which emerged in the mid-1990s and its main role within security studies and the policy community.

50. Laura Neack, *Elusive Security: States First, People Last* (Lanham, MD: Rowman & Littlefield, 2007), 219-224

51. Rafael Damaceno de Assis, "A realidade atual do sistema penitenciário brasileiro," *Revista CEJ*, Brasilia, Ano XI, n.o 39, out-dez. 2007, 74–78.

52. Drauzio Varella, Estação Carandiru. Cia das Letras, 1999.

53. Rafael Damaceno de Assis, "A realidade atual do sistema penitenciário brasileiro." Revista CEJ, Brasilia, Ano XI, no 39.

54. "Sistema carcerário brasileiro. A ineficiência, as mazelas e o descaso presentes nos presídios superlotados e esquecidos pelo poder público." Sande Nascimento de Arruda, *Revista Jurídica*. 2013.

55. Rafael Damaceno de Assis, "A realidade atual do sistema penitenciário brasileiro." *Revista* CEJ, Brasilia, Ano XI, n.o 39, p. 74–78, out-dez. 2007.

56. Ministério da Justiça do Brasil. Conselho Nacional de Política Criminal e Penitenciária. Pdf docuemnt. 04-26-2011.

TWELVE

The Drug-Crime-Prison Nexus

What the U. S. Experience Suggests for Argentina

Khatchik DerGhougassian and Sebastián A. Cutrona

Security concerns began to rise in Argentina by the end of the 1990s, when crime rates increased drastically reaching historical levels during the 2001-2002 economic collapse and social crisis. As official reports indicate,[1] a total of 498,290 crimes of all types were registered in 1991, whereas in 1999 the figures are almost double, accounting for a total of 1,062,241. In 2002, Argentina recorded a high of 1,340,529 crimes before the trend goes downward thereafter.[2] With the economic recovery and growth in 2003, official initiatives such as the Second Police Reform in the Province of Buenos Aires[3] and law 26.216,[4] as well as social mobilization to build awareness against crime and the use of firearms,[5] citizens' concern for security decreased in public opinion polls—although it never went away.[6] Since 2010/11, however, amidst growing economic difficulties and falling public support for the government, security concerns once again started to become a priority for Argentines. According to a 2012 study, 39.8 percent of the population mentioned insecurity as their main concern—followed by the economy and politics with 35.5 and 6.1 percent, respectively.[7] Not surprisingly, newspapers, especially those critical of the government, heavily publicized the insecurity phenomenon. Insecurity is often linked to drugs with stories typically describing adolescent and young criminals acting violently while under the influence. Newspaper headlines such as "They Live to Consume, and Can Kill,"[8] "Drugs and Crime, a Sinister Relationship,"[9] or "Paco: the Drug that is Connected to Crime and Poverty"[10] illustrate the growing hysteria fomented by Argentina's most influential newspapers.

Little doubt exists that in Argentina, as in neighboring South American countries, illicit drug consumption and related activities have dramatically increased since the beginning of the century,[11] and consequently, the drug-crime nexus is much more complex than what often oversimplified accounts suggest. Nevertheless, the argument that drug consumption leads to criminal activity has become the favorite strawman of politicians and pundits. Guillermo Montenegro, the Security Minister of Buenos Aires, for example, declared that "the level of violence in crimes is scary. In my opinion, whether you like it or not, this is related to drug use."[12] Likewise, Buenos Aires governor Daniel Scioli observed that "drugs are the origins of crime, my enemy, the opposite of life."[13] It is not surprising, therefore, that in public opinion, insecurity is often related to drugs; a report by the Catholic University in Argentina (UCA), reveals that fear of victimization has increased in households near drug distribution centers.[14] The relation between drugs and the sense of insecurity, the report indicates, is present along every socioeconomic stratum with the exception of the population living in slums. Accordingly, it is to be expected that demand for tough measures against drug-related activities, including distribution and consumption, increases[15] despite experts' warnings not to confuse insecurity with the "feeling of insecurity."[16] In other words, despite the evidence of increases in both security concerns and drug activities, the case for an inevitable drug-crime nexus, if not rationalized properly, could be nothing more than a "*sentimiento*"[17] and have consequences for sentencing and incarceration policies.

In the United Sates, tough drug laws of the 1980s and the criminalization of consumption led to a dramatic increase in the prison population. Harsher sentences, which in turn punished the most marginalized and least protected segments of society, provided arguments for conservative pundits and politicians that tough measures against drugs will increase public security. Crowded prisons once supported the argument that such harsh policies removed criminals from the streets. However, the reality is that most prisoners will return to society. Since 2000, when prisoners were released in record numbers of more than 1000 per day, leading experts have begun to question whether prisoners who are released are equipped with the necessary tools to become productive members of society.[18] Only by 2009, the U.S. prison population started to decline, a trend that has continued for three consecutive years. The economic recession and budget cuts seem to be a first explanatory factor, but experts also highlight changes in federal and state laws for minor offenses like those involving drugs, shifts in public attitudes and the diminishing support for tough-on-crime policies, diversion programs for offenders as an alternative to incarceration, and so forth.[19]

Is the past U.S. experience nexus a mirror for the current Argentine situation? What could it suggest for the Argentine context? These two questions are the starting point for this study which analyzes the complex relationship between drugs and crime by focusing on Argentina's prison system. This work also examines the driving forces behind the upsurge of Argentina's growing sense of insecurity. For that purpose, we rely on findings from a series of recent statistical studies on drugs and crime correlation to argue that the drug-crime nexus in Argentina is not linear, and we stress that both phenomena are themselves fostered by the general degradation of living conditions, a deproletarized and informalized labor market, an increasing familiarization with the use of violence, and the contradictory role of law enforcement. Our argument draws from contemporary sociological findings. In other words, our argument indicates that the drug-crime nexus is endogenous, meaning that the effect of drug use on crime can function only under some specific conditions or at least that the effects of drug consumption depend on the context under which they occur.

The discussion is organized in three main sections. The first section briefly assesses the state of the research on the relationship between drugs and criminal behavior, focusing on the most relevant theoretical accounts that have attempted to explain the different ways in which drugs affect crime. The second section describes the main features of Argentina's prison system, paying special attention to the population incarcerated for drug-related crimes. After examining the empirical findings that indicate that drugs and crime are associated, the third section discusses the social, economic, cultural, and institutional settings that may affect both drug usage and criminal behavior in Argentina. In the conclusion, we consider again the initial questions that triggered this research to highlight differences between the U.S. and Argentine cases, but also propose some reflections about lessons that the former can suggest for the latter.

UNDERSTANDING THE DRUG-CRIME CONNECTION: A CONCEPTUAL APPROACH

Theories explaining the relation between drugs and crime can be divided into five general types:[20] (i) those that suggest that drug use causes crime; (ii) those that claim that crime causes drug use; (iii) those that suggest that drugs and crime influence one another; (iv) those that acknowledge the presence of a third or common variable; and (v) those based on the idea that the so-called drug-crime nexus is either spurious or the result of a problematic set of similar causes.

The first group of theories posits that crime is more likely to develop with high rates of drug use. Research suggests that drugs affect crime in a plethora of ways. Goldstein's psychopharmacological approach,[21] for example, contends that individuals, after using illicit drugs, may become irrational, excitable, and violent. This psychophysical condition, in turn, leads the person to commit different kinds of crimes. Another variant of the drug-use-causes-crime theories states that drug users engage in economically oriented violent crimes. This economic-compulsive approach, Goldstein[22] claims, contemplates illicit activities such as robbery, burglary, or assault committed to finance the use of illicit drugs. Perhaps most notable about this perspective is the idea that addicts and drug abusers eventually become "enslaved," meaning that they turn to crime because they are unable to support the costs of their addiction by working at a regular, legitimate job.[23]

The second strand of relevant theorizing reverses the causal link by arguing that criminal behavior precedes drug use; that is, it is not addicts who turn to crime but criminals who turn to the world of illicit drugs. Long before criminals become dependent on alcohol or illicit drugs, Goose[24] suggests, those who eventually do so were already engaged in a variety of criminal activities. The use of chemical substances, referred to as "chemical recreation," for example, may lead an individual to celebrate the successful commission of a crime in much the same way as alcohol is used to celebrate holidays, birthdays, business successes, and other conventional achievements.[25]

The third body of research indicates that the relation between drugs and crime is bi-directional—that is, illicit behavior and substance abuse reinforce each other in different ways. In this respect, Huizinga et al.[26] claim that once drug use and criminal behavior are initiated, users combining several drugs (e.g., marijuana, alcohol, heroin, cocaine, and amphetamines) are less likely to change their behavior and thus stop committing crimes than users of marijuana, alcohol or nondrug users. According to Bennett and Holloway,[27] however, this approach could be seen as a restatement of the first two models, as the only difference from the first two groups of theories is that the "reciprocal model" mentions the possible co-existence of drug use and criminal behavior.

The fourth cluster of theories posits that drug use does not directly influence crime or vice versa; they are rather effects of a third or common variable such as psychological or sociological factors. Gottfredson and Hirschi,[28] for example, note that a third common variable could be the absence of self-control, meaning that it is not drug use that causes crime or vice versa but rather some psychological features of the individual that influence them. As Bennett and Holloway point out,[29] this approach suffers from a lack of clarity, as the literature that falls into this category can indeed be considered either as part of the causal or the spuriousness models.

The fifth strand of relevant theorizing is based on the idea that the causal relation between drugs and crime is either spurious or the result of a problematic set of similar causes. As Menard et al. contend,[30] this approach blends the third and fourth explanations. This view emphasizes that criminal behavior and substance abuse coexist in a complex setting of correlated variables and problematic behaviors.[31] Goldstein's systemic approach,[32] in particular, suggests that violence and crime are seen as intrinsic to the world of illicit drugs. Systemic violence is thus related to any aggressive behavior associated with the distribution and use of illicit substances. Other variants of this approach consider the role of some subcultural phenomena inherent to nightclubs,[33] youth gangs,[34] or the organization of the community[35] as the general contexts for both drug use and criminal behavior.

Not surprisingly, empirical research on the relation between drugs and crime tends to be influenced by the theories surveyed above. Research in fields such as criminology, sociology, political science, and even health sciences have found a strong correlation between drugs and crime.[36] A few experts, however, have remained skeptical about the general association between drug use and participation in crime.[37] Broadly speaking, therefore, this trend is quite consistent with the so-called drug-crime nexus hypothesis.

PRISONS, CRIME AND DRUGS IN ARGENTINA:

THE EMPIRICAL EVIDENCE FROM A CRITICAL PERSPECTIVE

Argentina's prison system is composed of the Federal Penitentiary System (SPF) and the Provincial Prison Systems (SPP), under the authority of the Ministry of Justice and Human Rights and the provincial governments, respectively. The SPF counts with six federal penitentiary complexes and twenty-eight penitentiary units, hosting approximately 16 percent of the prisoners in Argentina. The SPP, on the other hand, holds the bulk of the country's prison population that is incarcerated for non-federal crimes[38] in each of the twenty-three provinces. Buenos Aires, in particular, accounts for about 55 percent of the inmate total under the responsibility of the SPP, followed by Córdoba and Mendoza with approximately 12 and 6 percent respectively.[39]

In 2011, Argentina had 60,106 prisoners. These figures correspond to an incarceration rate of approximately 148 prisoners per 100,000 inhabitants,[40] ranking the country in the eleventh position in South America, only ahead of Bolivia and Paraguay.[41] Overall, the number of detainees in Argentina has increased progressively since the recovery of democracy in 1983 when the country's prison population was 26,483, or 80 prisoners per 100,000 inhabitants. That is to say, in thirty years of democracy, Argentina's incarceration rate increased about 64 percent (Figure 1.0). It is worth mentioning, however, that the evidence provided by *Sistema Nacional de Estadísticas sobre Ejecución de la Pena* (SNEEP) does not always account for the inmates held in police stations or other law-enforcement dependencies which, according to a document published by *Centro de Estudios Legales y Sociales* (CELS),[42] constitute around 10 percent of Argentina's total incarcerated population.

Out of the total population incarcerated, 29,025 have been sentenced while 30,725 are awaiting trial.[43] The proportion of inmates awaiting trial is even higher among young adults (72 percent), among women (61 percent), and among foreigners (61.5 percent).[44] The bulk of the detainees (41 percent) is between twenty-five and thirty-four years old, followed by prisoners between eighteen and twenty-four years old (24 percent). Women represent around 5 percent of the total population, although this number seems to be decreasing.[45] Most of the foreigners are nationals of neighboring countries and Peru (5 percent in total). Paraguayans and Bolivians, in particular, are at the top of the list with 971 and 564 inmates, respectively.[46]

The prisoners' level of education and working situation at the moment of detainment is illustrative of their socioeconomic vulnerability. According to the 2011 SNEEP report, out of the total population incarcerated in Argentina, 5 percent never attended an educational institution, 28 percent did not finish primary school, and 16 percent dropped out of secondary school. By the same token, 40 percent had been unemployed, 35 percent had been part-time workers, and 43 percent did not have any craft or profession at the moment of detainment.[47]

In terms of the crime typology, robbery and/or attempted robbery rank first with approximately 41 percent of detainees (25,062), followed by first degree murder and the violation of the psychoactive substances law with roughly 13 percent, and 11 percent respectively (Figure 2.0).[48] In the latter case, the proportion of detainees doubles among women and

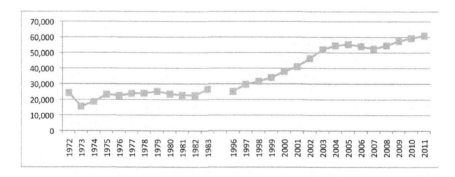

Figure 12.1.   Evolution of Argentina's Total Prison Population. Source: SNEEP Argentina 2011

foreigners and is even higher when both conditions are combined, suggesting that law-enforcement activities tend to fall upon minor actors.[49]

Violations of the psychoactive substances law (23,737) are considered federal, even though a reform in 2005, often referred as "de-federalization,"[50] paved the way for provincial governments in their fight against minor drug crimes. In this context, approximately 30 percent of the detainees (3,064) in the SPF are in prison for violating the psychoactive substances law, ranking second only after theft and/or attempted theft with about 38 percent (3,683).[51] In Buenos Aires, meanwhile, the same crime represents around 10 percent of prisoners, only outranked by robbery and attempted robbery and first degree murder.[52]

Yet the violation of the psychoactive substances law is only one way in which drugs and crime are connected. Drawing on Goldstein's tripartite model,[53] a recent statistical study conducted by the Secretary for the Prevention of Drug Addiction and the Struggle Against Narcotrafficking (SEDRONAR) and the Argentine Observatory for Drugs (OAD) has shown that in addition to the aforementioned legal connection, there is also a psychopharmacological, economic, and systemic liaison between drugs and crime in Argentina.[54]

SEDRONAR and OAD studied 73 provincial prisons. A total of 2,988 inmates, including remand and sentenced inmates,[55] were interviewed over an original sample of 3,244 cases, corresponding to an effectiveness rate of 92.1 percent. The study was performed among male and female prisoners over eighteen years old. The survey, which was voluntary and

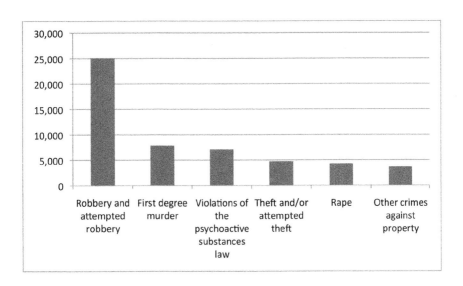

Figure 12.2. Ranking of Crimes Mentioned in Argentina. Source: SNEEP Argentina 2011

anonymous, contained 121 questions organized under several categories, including the types of criminal acts, the legal situation of the detainees, and the relation between drug use and criminal behavior.

The results indicate that 28.1 percent of the crimes in Argentina are connected with drug usage and trafficking as well as other drug-related crimes. More specifically, as inmates' reports show, the psychopharmacological link accounts for 20.6 percent of the crimes, the economic link 10.0 percent, the systemic link 4.0 percent, and the legal link 4.7 percent (Figure 3.0). The substances detected in 20.6 percent of the crimes are alcohol, tranquilizers, cocaine, and marijuana. Moreover, 39.0 percent of the interviewees declared that they committed the crime under the combined effects of alcohol and drugs. The perpetrators belong to the most vulnerable socioeconomic sectors of society and 26.2 percent of them are between eighteen and twenty-four years old. Not surprisingly, most of these crimes fall into the categories of crimes against property and crimes against life.

First, the psychopharmacological link contemplates crimes that are committed under the influence of drugs, where perpetrators declared that they would have not committed such crimes without drug use. As noted, the study indicates that 20.6 percent of the inmates committed a crime under the influence of drugs or alcohol. Specifically, the substances that were present at the moment of the crime were alcohol (72.4 percent), cocaine (28.2 percent), tranquilizers without medical prescription (27.8 percent), and marijuana (18.2 percent). Most of the illicit acts (26.2 per-

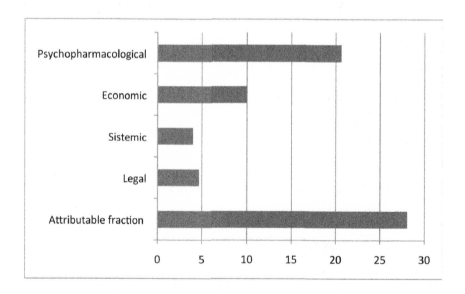

Figure 12.3.   Type of Link between Crimes and Drugs in Argentina's Prison Sentences Prisoners. Source: SENRONAR/OAD (2009)

cent) were performed by people between eighteen and twenty-four years old and the higher crime rates are found in crimes against life and crimes against property with 28.0 and 19.5 percent, respectively.

Second, the economic link considers the criminal behavior associated with the finance of drug use. According to the study, 10.0 percent of the crimes were committed in order to get money or other means to buy drugs. The highest crime rates within the economic link are found in people between eighteen and twenty-four years old, followed by young adults between thirty-five and forty-nine years old. Violations of the psychoactive substances law and crimes against life and property are at the top of the list, accounting for 44.8 and 15.3 percent of the crimes, respectively.

Third, the systemic link represents the most violent type, as it includes different kinds of violence generated by the illegality of the drug business, including score-settling, threats, and kidnappings. The study indicates that 4.0 percent of the illicit acts fall into the systemic link proposed by Goldstein. Unlike the psychopharmacological and economic link, however, the highest crime rates that fall into this category are found in people between thirty-five and forty-nine years old, although closely followed by people between eighteen and twenty-four. Likewise, violations of the psychoactive substances law account for 38.1 percent of the crimes within this typology.

Finally, the fourth link analyzed—not included in Goldstein's original tripartite model—contemplates the violations of Argentina's psychoactive substances law—that is, crimes typified by laws 23,737 and 25,256. According to the study developed by SEDRONAR and OAD, the legal link accounts for 4.7 percent of the crimes and the perpetrators are largely represented by people older than thirty-five years old. Regarding the crime typology, possession, trafficking, and commercialization of illicit drugs are first and second, with 66.7 and 48.1 percent of the crimes, respectively.

It is worth mentioning that like Argentina, Chile and Colombia have conducted statistical studies that explore the relationship between drugs and crime among their respective prison populations.[56] Thus, a Chilean report suggests that 42 percent of the crimes in that country are attributable to drugs and this figure is even higher (52 percent) when alcohol is contemplated—that is, one out of two crimes in Chile is related to drug use. These proportions are higher in the north of the country where approximately 59 percent of the crimes are connected with drugs. In Colombia, on the other hand, 32 percent of the inmates declared that they drank alcohol the same day they committed their crimes, whereas 27 percent used marijuana, 12 percent cocaine, and 11 percent *bazuco*. Marijuana, in particular, is associated with more than 40 percent of the crimes of theft and aggravated theft and drug trafficking and minor sales. By the same token, cocaine is connected with half of the cases of kidnappings for ransom, whereas *bazuco* is responsible for 60 percent of the crimes for selling drugs. In short, the so-called drug-crime nexus becomes less evident in Argentina compared to other Latin American countries such as Chile and Colombia.

THE DRUG-CRIME NEXUS: A CLOSER EXAMINATION

Although the empirical evidence presented suggests that drugs and crime in Argentina are correlated, how they interact and the context under which they occur was left largely unspecified. The goal of this final section, therefore, is to provide a more comprehensive examination of the so-called drug-crime nexus by addressing the social, economic, cultural, and institutional setting underlying these phenomena.

Most of the sociological accounts in the field suggest that the fact that drugs and crime are frequently found together does not mean that there is a causal connection. They may be found together as a consequence of other factors or they may coexist as a nexus of a specific context in which they occur. As Auyero and Berti note,[57] considering the context is crucial in order to avoid wrong interpretations and stigmatizations of violence and crime in Argentina. Exogenous factors such as the deproletarization and informalization of the labor market; a general degradation of living conditions; and the intermittent, contradictory, and highly selective role of law enforcement institutions are, together with the drug trade, crucial explanatory dimensions of the widespread violence and crime in Argentina, particularly in Buenos Aires' urban margins.

Crime and violence are not equally distributed among Argentina's urban areas. Contrary to the prevailing discourse presented by the media, Auyero and Berti[58] claim that violence and crime tend to affect the most disadvantaged sectors of society rather than the middle and upper classes. Buenos Aires' slums, in particular, have the highest rates of victimization in Argentina, as most of the homicides and serious injuries are found in high-poverty zones. The voices of the population living in the urban margins, however, are not part of Argentina's prevailing discourse about insecurity.

From this perspective, violence and crime in high-poverty zones are not the consequence of deviant individual behavior but the result of a wider context that could be referred as "structural violence," which includes the harmful interventions of the state. As Auyero and Berti point out,[59] the state perpetuates the violence it is supposed to prevent, reinforcing the Janus-faced character of the Argentine state.[60] In other words, while the police deploy tactics of shock and terror in certain areas, such as the occupation of neighborhoods with patrol cars and special squads, it also creates lawless areas where drug dealers can develop different illicit activities.

The contradictory and selective role of law-enforcement institutions is illustrated by the relationship between the police and drug dealers. According to a report developed by CELS,[61] the incarceration rate in the Federal Penitentiary System has grown almost 400 percent in the last twenty years. This trend was triggered by the growing imprisonment of petty drug dealers and consumers. Those able to afford a deal with the police, by contrast, may have a chance to avoid the legal consequences of their illicit activities. A forty-year-old *transa* (drug dealer) named Jorge testified:

> When we began trafficking in *Las Violetas* [a poor neighborhood], we had an arrangement with the police. Every weekend they come for a bribe. The police knew we were selling drugs but they did not bother us. The police freed the zone. If we do not pay them every weekend, we were in trouble and we ended up in jail. When we moved to another neighborhood, we started selling a lot of cocaine and, without knowing, we bothered the police because they had an arrangement with someone else selling drugs there. One day, a few police officers [gendarmes] wanted to know what was our problem with the police and they threatened to kill us, they were about to shoot us, but they ended up offering protection in exchange for more money.[62]

Alarcon's[63] chronicles are illuminating in this respect. The different characters' life stories presented in *Si me Querés, Quereme Transa* portrays the drug business as a world of elimination and revenge. To prosper, most of the personal accounts suggest, it is necessary to control a territory. If someone threatens that control, Alarcon claims, the answer is inevitable: he must be killed. The advice Alcira, the book's main character, received when entering the drug business illustrates this point: "this is not a joke . . . it's hard. You win some, you lose some. If it is not the police, there will be other dealers that will try to kill you . . . be suspicious of everybody."[64]

Not surprisingly, from the criminals' point of view, the police have nothing to do with the rule of law. As Kessler[65] explains, the police are perceived as another gang, one that is more powerful and better equipped. At most, the police represent a partner and protector of better organized criminal groups such as drug-trafficking organizations. The criminal's perception about the police is clear in the testimony of one interviewee:

> In the past the thief respected the police and the police respected the thief. The police did not shoot in front of people and the thief did not shoot back either. Today, without any problems, both the police and the thief shoot each other. They do not think about it . . . today everything is accepted.[66]

For amateur young criminals, however, crime is not a full-time activity. According to Kessler, they need to combine some licit economic undertakings with illegal ones, including courier services, babysitting, and cleaning services. The labor market, the author suggests, is increasingly informal. For example, the interviewees' average wage during the last three jobs was 400, 301, and 299 pesos per month. Furthermore, the duration of their jobs also decreased: the average for the first experience was twenty months, whereas for the second and third job was eleven months, respectively. The experience of one amateur criminal illustrates this trend: "[w]hat do you think I can expect? At most, I can get a job for 180 pesos for three months; then, nothing for a while; another job for 180 or 200 pesos; then nothing again, and so on."[67] The articulation between crime and work, Kessler suggests, is the result of opportunity, qualifications, success in past experiences, personal assessments of work and crime, and so forth.

In this context, violence, crime, and prison become everything but extraordinary in Argentina's high-poverty zones. That is, violence resembles a valid repertoire available to individuals and groups living in the margins.[68] The different ways "Frente Vital," Alarcon's main character in *Cuando me Muera Quiero que me Canten una Cumbia,*[69] and his rival gangs settle their differences, together with the children's drawings of shootings and young criminals presented in *La Violencia en los Márgenes*[70] suggest an increasing familiarization with the use of violence. According to Auyero,[71] however, there is no evidence indicating the presence of a "culture of violence" in Argentina, as the population still remains somehow sensitive to this problem.

Altogether, these sociological accounts are consistent with the latest report on citizen security developed by the United Nations Development Programme (UNDP).[72] According to the document, the use, supply, and trafficking of illicit drugs are not structural causes behind the ongoing upsurge in violence and crime in Latin America but rather mechanisms that may facilitate some types of criminal and violent behaviors. More specifically, the report contends that while the impact of the supply and traffic of illicit drugs on violence and crime is mediated by multiple context variables, the evidence shows that drug use is marginally connected to crime.

In short, our argument indicates that the drug-crime nexus is endogenous, meaning that the effect of drug use on crime can function only under some specific conditions or at least that the effects of drug consumption depend on the context under which they occur. Most important, the set of factors that may affect criminal behavior are predominantly present in high-poverty zones, even though the country's prevailing discourse about insecurity is monopolized by the most privileged classes in Argentina's society. Some of the factors that mediate and influence the relation between drugs and crime are the deproletarization and informalization of the labor market; a general degradation of living conditions; an increasing familiarization with the use of violence; and the intermittent, contradictory, and highly selective role of law enforcement institutions.

Despite the accumulation of empirical evidence against the so-called drug-crime nexus, this argument continues to characterize Argentina's popular debates. What explains this apparent disconnect between social science research, particularly the different sociological accounts surveyed here, and the claims of some opportunistic politicians and pundits in Argentina?

Broadly speaking, three elements are important. First, there is a political reason. The problem of drugs, framed in terms of security, is much more appealing for an electorate when the possible consequences of drug use are relatively apparent. Whereas there is widespread political support for security purposes, it may be more difficult to convince voters of the necessity of making certain policy changes to address less direct and diffuse threats such as drugs when they are defined as a health problem. Second, there is a methodological reason. If one considers Argentina's growing drug consumption, one may be tempted to find a correlation with the rise of crime. However, in doing so, we will be committing an "ecological fallacy." That is, the extrapolation of structural conditions as causes of individual behavior. Finally, there is misinformation, prejudice, and fear. Although it would be foolish to deny the harmful effects of drug use, which have been widely documented, the dangers of many illicit substances have been commonly overstated, particularly by the media. As Hart suggests, empirical evidence is frequently ignored and phenomena such as drug use and crime are often oversimplified. This trend stems, in part, from the fact that most of these accounts are focused on pathological behavior rather than on what occurs under normal conditions. In the United States, for example, 80 to 90 percent of cocaine users do not develop problems with the drug, even though their story never gets told. Moreover, half of all people with drug addictions are employed full-time and many of them are never involved in criminal behavior.[73]

CONCLUSION

The study of the relationship between drugs and crime remains problematic. Although additional research is needed, our argument indicates that the rise of violence and the increase in the incarceration rates in Argentina are not directly associated with drug usage, as the so-called drug-crime nexus suggests, but are rather mediated by other important factors, such as the deproletarization and informalization of the labor market; a general degradation of living conditions; an increasing familiarization with the use of violence; and the intermittent, contradictory, and highly selective role of law enforcement institutions.

So why do politicians, and people in general, keep focusing so much on combatting specific drug trafficking and usage as a way to solve the problems of violence and crime? As noted, security concerns are always more appealing for an electorate than problems when they are framed in terms of health; there are also methodological reasons; and the media tends to overstate the dangers of some illicit drugs, focusing on pathological behavior rather than on what occurs when people use illicit drugs under normal conditions. The confluence of these factors explains, in part, some of the main incarceration patterns underlying Argentina's penitentiary system in the last decades.

This chapter has practical and policy consequences. Most importantly, our approach calls into question the presumption that increasing the state's law-enforcement and interdiction capabilities will reduce violence. The U.S. policy since the 1980s to wage a "war" outside its borders and get tough on drugs at home by crowding prisons with minor drug offenders had social consequences. Harsh incarceration policies only partially explain the historical fall of crime levels in developed countries. Moreover, some three decades of prohibitive approaches to drugs did not fundamentally change consumption patterns and drug cycles. Overall, drugs remain a very complex issue; linking drugs to crime to create harsh incarceration policies is an even more complex issue, not to say simply a failure in its practical aspects. How, then, can we draw on the U.S. experience to analyze trends in the drug-crime-prison nexus in Argentina? We recognize that no experience in one country can suggest perfectly accurate policy consequences for another. Moreover, we can assume that while the rise of the "conservative movement"[74] during the Reagan era had an impact on American society and its levels of support for tougher policies on drugs, the democratic transition in Argentina and the centrality of the human rights issue in this transition created social awareness of the abusive potential of harsh laws. In fact, not even during the Menem administration of the Neoliberal 1990s, which included a controversial amnesty for military personnel sentenced in 1985, free-market reforms, and a "special relationship" with Washington, was there broad support for the "war on drugs" and a role for the military, as promoted, albeit carefully, by the Clinton administration. With the so-called turn-left in Argentina after the 2001–2002 economic collapse and the following decade of the Kirchner administration, engagement with Human Rights and softer stances on drugs became even stronger. In fact, the Argentine position is not too different from a general Latin American standpoint calling for Washington to recognize the failure of the "war on drugs" and alter its policies. The Latin American Commission on Drugs and Democracy, in particular, was unambiguous when it declared that "it is imperative to rectify the 'War on Drugs' strategy pursued in the region over the past thirty years."[75] Acknowledging the failure of current policies, the document suggests, "is the inescapable prerequisite for opening up the discussion about a new paradigm leading to safer, more efficient and humane drug policies."[76]

As discussed in the beginning of this chapter, it is also true that only by the end of the 2000s, Argentina became recognized as a consumer country and, more importantly, a nascent battlefield for drug trafficking, which had already deeply penetrated some state institutions in the Provinces of Santa Fé, Córdoba, and Mendoza to name a few.[77] While on the one hand denying it publicly, the Cristina Fernandez de Kirchner administration is at least discussing a minimal role of the military in providing logistical support for domestic security forces, notwithstanding the risk it runs by alienating Human Rights NGOs that have already begun to make public their growing concern.[78] A leading expert on the issue, Juan Gabriel Tokatlian, publicly expressed his concern for minority sectors advocating for the involvement of the military in the fight against drug trafficking, and argued that it would be "a bad decision" to replicate the FBI model in Argentina as the growing inclination of the Kirchner administration to approach Washington suggests.[79]

There is, at this time, no strong evidence to argue about an Argentine war on drugs on the levels seen elsewhere—such as Colombia and Mexico, and to some extent Brazil. However, if the U.S. experience suggests anything, then there is a connection between the war on drugs and tougher drug and incarceration policies. That might not be the case in Argentina; in fact, both the government and the opposition seem to be aware that getting tough on trafficking should not affect more comprehensive approaches to the social reality of increasing levels of consumption. Of course, this is easier to say than to do; especially if opportunistic politicians see electoral "rewards" in toughening their position and advocating harsher sentences. That would be unfortunate as it would build on a wrong assumption: drugs inevitably are linked to crime, and the solution, therefore, can be found in prohibitive policies including incarceration. As we have argued, if higher levels of drug consumption in Argentina are a social reality in the country, in part at least it is the consequence of growing informalization of work and the marginalization of the poor after the 2001-2002 collapse. This, however, does not underestimate the drug problem in Argentina and the inherent violence; nevertheless, the containment and even the downward trend of this violence comes from state reforms and the enforcement of its institutions to avoid creating the breeding grounds of the "narco": porous borders, uncontrolled territories, and corrupt public servants.

NOTES

1. Dirección Nacional de Política Criminal, *Informe Anual de Estadísticas Policiales 2008* (Buenos Aires: Ministerio de Justicia y Derechos Humanos, 2008). On the web at:

http://www.jus.gob.ar/media/109426/SnicARGENTINA2008.pdf. Last accessed on 02-08-2014.

2. Dirección Nacional de Política Criminal, *Informe Anual de Estadísticas Policiales 2008*.

3. León Carlos Arslanian, *Un Cambio Posible. Delito, Inseguridad y Reforma Policial en la Provincia de Buenos Aires* (Buenos Aires: EDHASA, 2008).

4. The National Plan of Voluntary Handling of Firearms ("Plan Nacional de Entrega Voluntaria de Armas de Fuego") approved on December 20, 2006. On the Web at: http://www.desarmevoluntario.gov.ar/legislacion_ley26216.html. Last accessed on 02-06-2014.

5. Khatchik Derghougassian (ed.), *Las Armas y las Víctimas, Violencia, Proliferación y Uso de Armas de Fuego en la Provincia de Buenos Aires y la Argentina*. With Diego M. Fleitas, Pablo Dreyfus, Antonio Rangel Bandeiras and Alejandra Otamendi (Buenos Aires: UdeSA, 2008).

6. Observatorio de la Deuda Social Argentina, "Inseguridad y Miedo al Delito" (Buenos Aires: Pontificia Universidad Católica Argentina, 2010. On the Web at: http://www.uca.edu.ar/uca/common/grupo68/files/Informe_Inseguridad_Miedo.pdf. Last access on: 02-09-2014.

7. Germán Lodola and Mitchell Seligson, *Political Culture of Democracy in Argentina and in the Americas, 2012: Towards Equality and Opportunity* (LAPOP, 2013). On the Web at: http://www.vanderbilt.edu/lapop/argentina/Argentina_2012_English_Report_Cover_W.pdf. Last access on 01-20-2014.

8. Hugo Marietan, "Viven para Consumir y Pueden Matar," *Perfil*, Jul. 29, 2012. On the Web at: http://www.perfil.com/ediciones/sociedad/-20127-698-0087.html. Last access on: 02-06-2014. Original in Spanish, non-official translation by authors; we translated all original quotes from Spanish to English text.

9. "Drogas y Delito, una Relación Siniestra," *La Nación*, Nov. 16, 2009. On the Web at: http://www.lanacion.com.ar/1200209-droga-y-delito-una-relacion-siniestra. Last access on: 02-06-2014.

10. "El Paco, la Droga que se Vincula al Delito y a la Pobreza," *Clarín*, Apr. 03, 2011. On the Web at: http://www.clarin.com/policiales/paco-droga-vincula-delito-pobreza_0_437956287.html . Last access on: 02-06-2014.

11. Khatchik DerGhougassian and Glen Evans, "Under (Loose) Control: Drug Trafficking in Argentina. Framing a Complex Phenomenon in Times of Paradigm Change," in Bruce M. Bagley and Jonathan D. Rosen, *Drug Trafficking, Organized Crime, and Violence in the Americas: Today* (University Press of Florida –forthcoming 2015).

12. "Montenegro: La inseguridad no es una Sensación sino una Realidad," *Infobae*, Aug. 04, 2012. On the Web at: http://www.infobae.com/2012/08/04/662857-montenegro-la-inseguridad-no-es-una-sensacion-sino-una-realidad . Last access on 02-11-2014.

13. "Scioli Volvió a Rechazar el Plan de Despenalización del Consumo de Droga," *Infobae*, Nov 24, 2008. On the Web at: http://www.infobae.com/2008/11/24/416721-scioli-volvio-rechazar-el-plan-despenalizacion-del-consumo-droga . Last access on 02-06-2014.

14. Observatorio de la Deuda Social Argentina, "El Problema de la Inseguridad en la Argentina: Factores que Influyen en la Delincuencia y Disparan el Sentimiento de Inseguridad o Miedo a ser Víctima de un Delito" (Buenos Aires: Pontificia Universidad Católica Argentina, 2011). On the Web at: http://www.uca.edu.ar/uca/common/grupo81/files/Boletin_inseguridad_2011_final_-1-.pdf. Last access on: 01-15-2014.

15. See, for example, José Pampuro, "Ley de Derribo: una Herramienta Disuasiva," *Clarín*, Sección Opinión, Nov. 11, 2013. On the Web at: http://www.clarin.com/opinion/Ley-Derribo-herramienta-disuasiva_0_1027697251.html , last access on: 02-06-2014; Julián Obiglio, "Argentina al Borde del Abismo Narco," *Infobae*, Sección Opinión, Nov. 16, 2013, on the Web at: http://opinion.infobae.com/julian-obiglio/2013/11/16/argentina-al-borde-del-abismo-narco/, last access on: 02-06-2014; and Francisco De Narváez, "El Costo Social del Narcotráfico en Argentina," *Infobae*, Sección Opinión,

Nov. 10, 2013, on the Web at: http://opinion.infobae.com/francisco-de-narvaez/2013/11/10/el-costo-social-del-narcotrafico-en-argentina/; last access on: 02-06-2014.

16. Gabriel Kessler, *El Sentimiento de Inseguridad. Sociología del Temor al Delito* (Buenos Aires: Siglo Veintiuno Editores, 2009).

17. Literally "feeling;" though the Spanish term is used pretty much in the sense of "perception," something subjective that lacks the empirical proof of its concrete reality.

18. Khatchik DerGhougassian, *Ex–Prisoners Reentry Challenge: Miami-Dade County in Perspective* (Miami: University of Miami, 2002).

19. Erica Goode, "U.S. Prison Population Decline, Reflecting New Approach to Crime," *The New York Times*, July 25, 2013. On the Web at: http://www.nytimes.com/2013/07/26/us/us-prison-populations-decline-reflecting-new-approach-to-crime.html?pagewanted=all&_r=0. Last access on: 07-26-2013.

20. See Helen White, "The Drug Use-Delinquency Connection in Adolescence," in *Drugs, Crime, and the Criminal Justice System*, edited by R. Weisheit (Cincinnati: Anderson Publishing Co., 1990); Scott Menard, Sharon Mihalic, and David Huizinga, "Drugs and Crime Revisited," *Justice Quarterly*, 18 (2) (2001); Trevor Bennett and Katy Holloway, *Understanding Drugs, Alcohol and Crime* (Maidenhead: Open University Press, 2005); Trevor Bennett and Katy Holloway, *Drug-Crime Connections* (New York: Cambridge University Press, 2007); Trevor Bennett, Katy Holloway, and David Farrington, "The Statistical Association Between Drug Misuse and Crime: a Meta-analysis," *Aggression and Violent Behavior* 13 (2008).

21. Paul Goldstein, "The Drugs/Violence Nexus: A Tripartite Conceptual Framework," *Journal of Drug Issues* v. 39 (1985).

22. Goldstein, "The Drugs/Violence Nexus."

23. Erich Goode, *Between Politics and Reason* (New York: St Martin's Press, 1997).

24. Goode, *Between Politics and Reason.*

25. Menard, Mihalic, and Huizinga, "Drugs and Crime Revisited."

26. David Huizinga, Scott Menard, and Delbert Elliott, "Delinquency and Drug Use: Temporal and Developmental Patterns," *Justice Quarterly* 6 (1989).

27. Bennett and Holloway, *Understanding Drugs, Alcohol and Crime.*

28. Michael Gottfredson and Travis Hirschi, *A General Theory of Crime* (Stanford: Stanford University Press, 1990).

29. Bennett and Holloway, *Understanding Drugs, Alcohol and Crime.*

30. Menard, Mihalic, and Huizinga, "Drugs and Crime Revisited."

31. Bennett and Holloway, *Understanding Drugs, Alcohol and Crime.*

32. Goldstein, "The Drugs/Violence Nexus."

33. Tammy Anderson *et al.*, "Exploring the Drugs-Crime Connection within the Electronic Dance Music and Hip-Hop Nightclub Scenes," Final Report to the National Institute of Justice. Newark: University of Delaware (2007). On the Web at: https://www.ncjrs.gov/pdffiles1/nij/grants/219381.pdf. Last access on: 01-11-2014.

34. Jeffrey Fagan, "Intoxication and Aggression," *Crime and Justice*, Vol. 13, Drugs and Crime (1990).

35. Helen White and D. M. Gorman, "Dynamics of the Drug–Crime Relationship, *Criminal Justice*, 1 (2000).

36. R.P Gandossy, J.R. Williams, J. Cohen J., and H.J. Harwood, *Drugs and Crime: A Survey and Analysis of the Literature* (Washington DC: Government Printing Office, 1980); David Nurco, Thomas Hanlon, and Timothy Kinlock, "Recent Research on the Relationship Between Illicit Drug Abuse and Crime," *Behavioral Sciences and the Law*, Vol.9 (1991); Alex Stevens, Mike Trace y Dave Bewley-Taylor, *Reducing Drug Related Crime: An Overview of the Global Evidence*, Report five (Oxford: Beckley Foundation, 2005); Trevor Bennett, Katy Holloway, and David Farrington, "The Statistical Association between Drug Misuse and Crime: A Meta-Analysis," *Aggression and Violent Behavior*, Vol. 13 (2008).

37. Isador Chen, Donald Gerard, Robert Lee, and Eva Rosenfeld, *The Road to H: Marcotics, Deliquency and Social Policy* (New York: Basic Books, 1965); Jan M. Chaiken

and Marcia R. Chaiken, "Drugs and Predatory Crime," in *Drugs and Crime, Crime and Justice: A Review of Research*, edited by Michael Tonry and James Q. Wilson (Chicago: University of Chicago Press, 1990); David Rasmussen and & Bruce Benson, *The Economic Anatomy of a Drug War: Criminal Justice in the Commons* (Lanham, MD: Rowman and Littlefield, 1994).

38. As we will see further in this chapter, there are some exceptions to this regulation.

39. Dirección Nacional de Política Criminal, *Informe Anual República Argentina 2011* (Buenos Aires: Ministerio de Justicia y Derechos Humanos de la Nación, 2011). On the Web at: http://www1.infojus.gov.ar/sneep. Last access on: 02-06-2014.

40. Dirección Nacional de Política Criminal, *Informe Anual República Argentina 2011*.

41. International Centre for Prison Studies. On the Web at: http://www.prisonstudies.org/info/worldbrief/wpb_stats.php?area=southam&category=wb_poprate. Last access on 02-06-2014.

42. Rodrigo Borda, Gabriela Kletzel and Denise Sapoznik, "La Situación Carcelaria: una Deuda de Nuestra Democracia" in *Derechos Humanos en Argentina*, Centro de Estudios Legales y Sociales (Buenos Aires: Siglo Veintiuno Editores S. A., 2009). On the Web at; http://www.cels.org.ar/common/documentos/carceles_ia2008.pdf. Last access on: 02-04-2014.

43. Dirección Nacional de Política Criminal, *Informe Anual República Argentina 2011*.

44. UNODC, *Evaluation and Recommendations for the Improvement of the Health Programmes, Including For The Prevention and Treatment of Drug Dependence and of HIV and AIDS, Implemented in the Establishments Under the Responsibility of the Federal Penitentiary Service in Argentina* (Vienna: UNODC, 2011). On the Web at: http://www.unodc.org/documents/lpo-brazil//Prision_Settings/UNODC_report_Argentina_Health_SPF_assessment_July_2011.pdf . Last access on: 02-05-2014.

45. UNODC, *Evaluation and Recommendations for the Improvement of the Health Programmes, Including For The Prevention and Treatment of Drug Dependence and of HIV and AIDS, Implemented in the Establishments Under the Responsibility of the Federal Penitentiary Service in Argentina*.

46. Dirección Nacional de Política Criminal, *Informe Anual República Argentina 2011*.

47. Dirección Nacional de Política Criminal, *Informe Anual República Argentina 2011*.

48. Dirección Nacional de Política Criminal, *Informe Anual República Argentina 2011*.

49. Alejandro Corda, "Encarcelamientos por Delitos con Estupefacientes en Argentina," Intercambios Asociación Civil (2010).

50. Law 26,052 was passed in July 2005.

51. Dirección Nacional de Política Criminal, *Informe Anual Servicio Penitenciario Federal 2011* (Buenos Aires: Ministerio de Justicia y Derechos Humanos de la Nación, 2011). On the Web at: http://www1.infojus.gov.ar/sneep . Last access on: 02-04-2014.

52. Dirección Nacional de Política Criminal, *Informe Anual Servicio Penitenciario Federal 2011*.

53. Goldstein, "The Drugs/Violence Nexus."

54. Observatorio Argentino de Drogas, *Estudio Nacional sobre Consumo de Sustancias Psicoactivas y su Relación con la Comisión de Delitos en Población Privada de Libertad* (Buenos Aires: SEDRONAR, 2009). On the Web at: http://www.observatorio.gov.ar/investigaciones/Informe%20Estudio%20Nacional%20en%20poblacion%20privada%20de%20libertad.pdf. Last accessed on: 02-04-2014.

55. We cannot, within the limits of this chapter, undertake the analysis of both categories of prisoners presented in the SEDRONAR/OAD study. In the rest of this section, therefore, we will only consider the relation between drugs and crime focusing on Argentina' sentenced inmates.

56. UNODC, *Consumo de Drogas en Población Privada de Libertad y la Relación entre Delito y Droga* (Vienna: UNODC, 2010). On the Web at: http://www.unodc.org/documents/peruandecuador//Publicaciones/Consumo_de_drogas.pdf. Last accessed on: 01-20-2014.

57. Javier Auyero and María Fernanda Berti, *La Violencia en los Márgenes* (Buenos Aires: Katz editores, 2013).

58. Auyero and Berti, *La Violencia en los Márgenes,* 7.

59. Auyero and Berti, *La Violencia en los Márgenes,* 139.

60. The Janus-faced character of the state refers to the contradictory role of domestic institutions in Argentina. That is, while the state ensures safety and security for individuals it also participates in the commission of crime.

61. Centro de Estudios Legales y Sociales, *Derechos Humanos en Argentina.*

62. Auyero and Berti, *La Violencia en los Márgenes,* 126–127.

63. Cristian Alarcón, *Si me Querés, Quereme Transa* (Buenos Aires: Aguilar, 2012).

64. Ibid., p. 23.

65. Gabriel Kessler, *Sociología del Delito Amateur* (Buenos Aires: Paidós, 2004).

66. Kessler, *Sociología del Delito Amateur,* 128.

67. Kessler, *Sociología del Delito Amateur,* 33–34.

68. Auyero and Berti, *La Violencia en los Márgenes,* 144.

69. Cristian Alarcón, *Cuando me Muera Quiero que me Canten una Cumbia* (Buenos Aires: Aguilar, 2012).

70. Auyero and Berti, *La Violencia en los Márgenes.*

71. Javier Auyero, "Los Sectores Populares Viven Peor que Hace 15 o 20 Años," *La Nación,* Oct. 30, 2011. On the Web at: http://www.lanacion.com.ar/1418689-los-sectores-populares-estan-peor-que-hace-15-o-20-anos. Last access on: 02-20-2014.

72. UNDP, *Seguridad Ciudadana con Rostro Humano: Diagnóstico y Propuestas para América Latina* (New York: United Nations Publications, 2013). On the Web at: http://www.undp.org/content/dam/rblac/img/IDH/IDH-AL percent20Informe percent20completo.pdf. Last access on: 02-06-2014.

73. Carl Hart, *High Price: A Neuroscientist's Journey of Self-Discovery That Challenges Everything You Know About Drugs and Society* (New York: HarperCollins Publishers, 2013).

74. Paul Krugman, *The Conscience of a Liberal* (New York: W. W. Norton & Company Ltd., 2009).

75. Latin American Commission on Drugs and Democracy, *Drugs and Democracy: Towards a Paradigm Shift* (New York: Open Society Institute, 2008), 5. On the Web at: http://www.drogasedemocracia.org/Arquivos/declaracao_ingles_site.pdf. Last access on: 02-20-2014.

76. Latin American Commission on Drugs and Democracy, *Drugs and Democracy.*

77. Gustavo Sierra, "Cómo Penetran por Salta los Grandes Carteles del Narco," *Clarín,* Nov. 24, 2013, 42–43; Daniel Gallo, "Narcotráfico. Se Vende cada vez más Cocaína Producida en el País," *La Nación,* Nov. 17, 2013, 1 and 22–25; Tomás Eliashev, "Radiografía Narco," *Veintitrés,* Jul. 18, 2013, 72-74; "¡Peligro, Policía!," *Veintitrés,* Nov. 21, 2014, 72-73.

78. Horacio Verbitsky, "Mal de Muchos," *Página/12,* Sep. 22, 2013, 16-17.

79. Juan Gabriel Tokatlian, "En la Lucha Antidroga, hay que Aprender de los Británicos," *La Nación,* Feb. 28, 2014. On the Web at: http://www.lanacion.com.ar/1668133-en-la-lucha-antidroga-hay-que-aprender-de-los-britanico Last access 02-28-2014 .

THIRTEEN

Prison Reform

An International Solution

W. Andy Knight

The history of prisons dates back a couple of centuries. Before that, the punishment for criminal behavior took various forms: penal bondage; public humiliation; isolation, banishment, or excommunication; fines; and corporal punishment, including whippings, public beheadings, and hangings. The history of prisons in the Western Hemisphere has been fraught with narratives of overcrowding, unsanitary conditions, torture, corruption, drug use, riots, high rates of recidivism, and suicide. Hence, it should not be surprising that over the years attempts have been made to reform penitentiary systems in the Americas (both in terms of operational refinements and individual improvements of conditions for inmates).

The chapters in this volume are pragmatic in the sense that they are concerned with how the existing penal system actually works in various settings. This chapter continues that pragmatism by exploring how international organizations have attempted to introduce prison reform and the rationale behind such reform efforts. In so doing, a number of important questions are asked along the way. What are the principles that ought to underpin a penal system in a liberal democracy? When is punishment justified? Should we use the justice and penal systems for revenge, retribution, deterrence, incapacitation, or rehabilitation? These are some of the questions that occupy those working within international bodies who propose prison reform.

Ian Loader notes that the "philosophical reflection on these questions is too often disconnected from analysis of how the actually existing penal system operates day-in-day-out, or of the forces that determine its size, scope, practices and effects."[1] It is terribly important therefore to find a way to connect the philosophical reflections on the principles underlying the operations of penal systems to the more concrete analysis of what ought to be done about the problems inherent in such systems, particularly in the Americas.

BASIC PRINCIPLES UNDERLYING THE OPERATIONS OF THE PENAL SYSTEM

For generations, civilizations have used enforcement as a means of keeping the peace in society and maintaining a sense of civility among populations. Removing offenders from society, through incarceration, has been one way of enforcing the norms, rules, and laws of most societies over the past couple of centuries. Prisons can be found now in almost every country in the world and according to Walmsley, there are over nine million prisoners worldwide and that number continues to grow.[2] In the U.S. alone, it is estimated that there are over two million people in the prison system. This means that there are approximately 737 prisoners per 100,000 people in the U.S. population.[3] In 1870, individuals within the American correctional system met with international colleagues in Ohio to develop principles that would guide their profession. What were these principles?

It was felt, first of all, that the incarceration of criminals was for the protection of society. However, the objective of incarceration should focus not only on punishment but also on "the moral regeneration" of the criminal. The whole idea behind corrections therefore should be to prevent and control delinquency and crime, realizing of course that society would have to assist in providing the reformed criminal with the environment in which that individual could find gainful employment and earn an honest living. Those basic principles which have since guided the American Correctional Association (ACA) are still found in the revised seven principles adopted by that organization in 2002. The revised principles are listed as 1) Humanity; 2) Justice; 3) Protection; 4) Opportunity; 5) Knowledge; 6) Competence; 7) Accountability.[4]

The first principle concerns respect for the dignity of the individual and for the rights of all people. Each individual in society has basic human rights that must be protected as well as worth and dignity that must be respected. This applies to individuals who commit crimes as well as to the victims of crimes. Thus, the purpose of corrections should be to balance the protection of the individual against excessive restrictions.

The second principle is linked to the first in the sense that to enact true justice, the justice system and correctional institutions "must demonstrate integrity, respect, dignity, fairness," and the pursuit of balanced programs of "humaneness, restoration, rehabilitation and the most appropriate sanctions" that are "consistent with public safety."[5] Therefore, major disparities in sentencing, unduly long periods of incarceration, and rigid sentencing structures are considered "unjust." Clearly, according to this principle, sanctions imposed on criminals must be commensurate with the crime committed and the criminal history of the offender. In addition, due process and impartial fact-finding should be adopted by the courts that impose the sanction. At the same time, victims of crime should be treated fairly and should "receive restitution and/or compensation whenever appropriate."[6]

The third principle suggests that the corrections system "has a duty to ensure the protection of the public, offenders under corrections supervision, correction workers, and victims and survivors of crime." People in society should have the right to be protected from any personal or psychological harm, from any loss of property, and from the abuse of power. However, those under the care of a correctional institution should also be protected from harm. This basically means that "contemporary standards for healthcare, offender classification, due process, fire and building safety, nutrition, personal well-being, and clothing and shelter must be observed" and that care should be taken to ensure that the offender is protected from the abuse of power.[7]

The fourth principle calls for the creation of opportunity for positive change or reform in the lives of the incarcerated. This principle is based on the hypothesis that "punishment without the opportunity for redemption is unjust and ineffective." Without hope that the offender can become a responsible member of the society upon leaving prison, the individual is more likely to reoffend. Thus, offenders should be given the opportunity to develop skill sets, participate in educational and vocational training, engage in religious and spiritual counseling, and engage in constructive activities that enhance their self-worth and help them reintegrate better into their communities.[8]

The continual search for new knowledge is at the heart of the fifth principle. The programming used for corrections must be based on up-to-date theoretical and applied research and bolstered by professional standards and outcome measures of performance. This knowledge would have to be shared with the general public if the public is to support reform programs within the prison system. In recognition of the importance of the knowledge principle, the ACA has called for the development of a strong relationship between local, state, national, and international agencies, professional associations, and institutions of higher learning.[9]

The sixth principle addresses the issue of professional competence. Those involved in corrections (administrators, supervisors, line employees, contract employees, and volunteers) must all be professionally competent and committed to conducting their work "in accordance with professional standards." They must understand the mission of the corrections process. They should also be provided with opportunities for professional development, additional training, and remuneration commensurate with the job requirements (protection of society and reformation of prison inmates) and their performance. [10]

The final principle is that of accountability. Correctional officers should always expect accountability with respect to the treatment and management of offenders, the selection and performance of their staff, and the interface between the offenders and the victims of crime. Indeed, "accountability is a keystone of sound corrections practice," according to the ACA. Not only must correctional officers be held accountable for their actions, so too must staff and offenders. [11]

Some scholars and observers of the penal system posit that there are at least three basic philosophic orientations of the penal system: 1) to punish individuals who run afoul of the law; 2) to repair the damaged lives of those who have been incarcerated; and 3) to minimize the harm done to offenders when they are brought into the penal system. In some respects, these three philosophic orientations have helped to guide particular reformist actions by individuals and organizations involved in prison reform.

Some suggestions for prison reform are more akin to refinement of the way prisons operate, not necessarily aiming to improve conditions for those incarcerated but rather to ensure that penitentiaries can better manage the surveillance of prisoners while operating at a reduced cost. Jeremy Bentham's conception of the Panopticon is a perfect example of this kind of suggested refinement to the operations of prisons. [12] His idea, while not operationalized at the time he suggested it, influenced the critical philosophical writings of Michel Foucault [13] and the pragmatic technological advancements that led to the development and deployment of CCTV cameras. [14]

Other prison reformist ideas have come from such individuals as John Howard, [15] Elizabeth Fry, [16] Charles Dickens, [17] Samuel Romilly, [18] Enoch Wines, Theodore Dwight, [19] and others, and have been geared toward improving conditions for prisoners, attempting to cure offenders of their criminality, providing psychological and psychiatric treatment to inmates, introducing a system of probation, ushering in educational, religious, and recreational programs for the incarcerated, and reducing the harshness of certain punishments to the prison population while focusing on the rehabilitation of certain prisoners.

In sum, it is important, when contemplating prison reform, to take into consideration not only the improvements that need to be made inside the prisons but also those that must be made within society at large.

THE STATE OF THE WORLD'S PRISONS

Prisoners and remand inmates face horrific living conditions in many local, state, and federal facilities across the globe. They are subjected to conditions that are abusive, dangerous, and degrading. Due to harsh sentencing laws, immigrant detention policies, and limited budgets and resources, prison populations have grown to the point that there is severe overcrowding in most prisons. The congested physical conditions within prisons and remand yards breach United Nations standards requiring that prisoners should be treated with the respect due to their inherent dignity and value as human beings.

Those who follow the state of prison conditions would recall the horrible incident at the National Penitentiary in Comayagua, Honduras, on February 14, 2012, when an open flame near two bunk beds ignited a fire that swept through the overcrowded prison and killed over 360 people.[20] That same year in September, *Time Magazine* reported on a prison scandal in the country of Georgia—a country which has more prisoners per capita than any other country in Europe, which eventually resulted in the defeat of President Mikheil Saakashvili at the polls. That scandal involved the torture and sodomizing of prisoners in the now infamous "Gldani Prison No.8."[21] These are just two examples of cases that demonstrate the need for prison reform to ensure that those who are incarcerated will be treated humanely in safe and secure environments.

Added to the above indignities are a slew of other legal and human rights violations that many prisoners face each and every day: lengthy trial delays, the absence of their personal physical and property security, poor and innutritious food, psychological trauma, inadequate water and toilet facilities, unsanitary conditions, insufficient sleeping facilities, little light, and poor ventilation in small spaces. Being deprived of the basic amenities of life is a human rights violation. Prisoners are generally vulnerable to various diseases, such as TB, HIV/AIDS, and STDs, and they are likely to be denied proper medical treatment in some cases. These examples demonstrate the extent to which incarcerated individuals can feel that their dignity as human beings is denigrated.

The United States has less than 5 percent of the global population and yet has 25 percent of the world's prisoners. The U.S. in fact leads the world in terms of producing prisoners.[22] As Adam Liptak puts it: "Americans are locked up for crimes—from writing bad checks to using drugs—that would rarely produce prison sentences in other countries." The spike in the rate of incarceration in the U.S. is a relatively recent phenomenon, beginning in the late 1970s.[23] Partly, this had to do with easy access to guns which produce an inordinate amount of violent crimes, like murder.[24] But it is also partly to do with the so-called war on drugs and what some authors refer to as "victimless crimes." Human Rights Watch provides an example of a small-time drug dealer who decided to reject a plea bargain of ten years for possessing fifty grams of crack cocaine with intent to deliver. Once she went to trial, the prosecutor pushed for a sentence enhancement based on prior convictions for simple drug possession. As a result, this woman was given a sentence of life without parole.[25] Federal drug offenders in the U.S. who are convicted at trial receive sentences that are on average three times longer than those who accept a plea bargain.[26]

The U.S., despite its claim of being a beacon of democracy, has some of the worse cases of inhumaneness in some of its prisons. Many prisons in that country are unsafe and overcrowded, with poor sanitation, inadequate access to clean potable drinking water, inadequate nutrition, poor medical care, and inadequate facilities for inmates with physical disabilities. There are numerous reported cases of mistreatment of prisoners by U.S. prison authorities and a failure to respect the rights of prisoners to legal redress while incarcerated.[27]

But these poor prison conditions are not limited to the U.S. The problem of prison overcrowding is so bad in Ukraine that, in at least one detention facility, inmates are forced to sleep in shifts.[28] In Eritrea, the absence of prison space has led corrections officials to place offenders in unventilated shipping containers. In Sri Lanka, it is reported that the prison system houses approximately three times its capacity. This overcrowding was most likely responsible for the violent clashes in 2012 which left twenty-seven inmates dead and hundreds injured.[29]

In most cases, overcrowding is symptomatic of deeper problems in the justice system (e.g., corrupt or poorly trained law enforcement personnel, inefficiencies in the court system, underpaid and untrained prison staff) or it is a result of the absence of proper standard operating procedures for prisons. But in most cases of overcrowding in prisons and detention centers there is a domino effect of other problems related to denigration of human beings. The Report on International Prison Conditions cites cases of: poor sanitation and physical abuse of prisoners by their guards in overcrowded Serbian prisons; degrading treatment inhumane punishment and corruption in overcrowded detention centers in Chad; unsanitary conditions and riots in the overcrowded prisons of South Sudan—where detainees are sometimes chained to a wall, fence or tree, often unsheltered from the sun; poor ventilation and sanitation in Haitian overcrowded prisons where 70 percent of detainees suffer from a lack of basic hygiene, malnutrition, poor health, and water-borne diseases; violent and deadly riots in overcrowded prisons in Lebanon and Brazil; and the outbreak of mental health problems in 62 percent of the prison population in Ethiopia.[30] The UN Office on Drugs and Crime (UNODC) considers prison overcrowding as "the most worrying emergency that the Italian penitentiary system has to deal with."[31]

Apart from the overcrowding which leads to poor prison conditions, there is a concern that in many of the world's prisons, prison officers are engaged in deliberate physical, psychological, and sexual mistreatment of inmates. This mistreatment can also involve torture as a means of extracting information or confessions from those who are detained. Political prisoners in places like Iran, Iraq, and China are especially targets of this kind of mistreatment. In North Korea, political detainees and prisoners of conscience are routinely rounded up and subjected to physical and psychological mistreatment, and sometimes death. Human Rights Watch has reported on the abuse and torture of prisoners in Syrian detention centers. Similar stories have been reported in Afghanistan, Cambodia, Pakistan, and Burma (Myanmar).[32]

Added to these indignities, prisoners in some countries are often not provided with the minimum legal protections and legal process guarantees during the pretrial phase of their detention, during the trial itself, and in the post-conviction stage. According to *America Quarterly*, throughout the Americas between 10–40 percent of the entire incarcerated population is serving time in prison without a conviction.[33] This is also happening in places like China, Cuba, Eritrea, Saudi Arabia, Uzbekistan, Vietnam, and Zimbabwe.

WHY THE PUSH FOR PRISON REFORM?

From the above section it is clear why prison reform is necessary. The rate of imprisonment seems to be increasing in most countries worldwide, exacerbating the acute problem of overcrowding in many prisons. Overcrowding leads to the deterioration of prison conditions, generates prison violence, spreads disease, and fuels human rights violations.[34] In many countries, the majority of the people held in detention are awaiting trial. A large number of detainees do not have access to legal counsel and face unfair trial procedures. In addition, in many countries a large proportion of the prison population has been sentenced for minor offenses. Harsh laws relating to drug offenses have led to the rapid growth of the prison populations.

So there are at least four reasons why prison reform should be contemplated in the Americas. The first is linked to the basic human rights argument—individuals who are incarcerated are deprived of the right to liberty. As shown above, in many cases, their human rights and dignity are being violated. Then, there is a second argument for contemplating prison reform. Incarceration has a detrimental impact not only on the prisoner but also on that individual's spouse, children, family, and community. Imprisonment generally has a disproportionate effect on poor families. It weakens the social cohesion of a family and may lead to breakdown in the family structure. There are also economic factors. When an income-generating member of the family (or the breadwinner) becomes a prisoner, the rest of the family has to adjust to a loss of income.

In addition, they will generally be subjected to additional expenses, including the cost of retaining a lawyer, the cost of food for the imprisoned individual, and the cost of transportation to visit the prisoner. When the prisoner is released, that individual is likely to suffer socioeconomic exclusion and become vulnerable to an endless cycle of poverty, marginalization, criminality, and recidivism. Moreover, there is the societal cost (both direct and indirect) associated with keeping someone in prison. The fourth reason for considering prison reform is directly related to public health concerns. Usually those who commit crimes and are incarcerated have inadequate access to healthcare to begin with. Once they are imprisoned, their health can deteriorate due to overcrowded conditions, poor nutrition, inadequate sanitary conditions, and lack of air and exercise. Prisons are "reservoirs of disease" and psychiatric disorders. Many within prison walls suffer from HIV infection, tuberculosis, hepatitis B and C, sexually transmitted diseases, skin diseases, malaria, malnutrition, diarrhea, and drug addiction. Ultimately, some inmates resort to suicide, while some others simply die.

WHAT HAS THE UN DONE ABOUT THE PROBLEM?

The United Nations has been working for quite some time to ensure that there would be guidelines for the treatment of prisoners and for the execution of criminal justice. But this effort is not without precedent. One can trace similar efforts to the Roman Empire and later to the social conduct incorporated into Islamic law. By the nineteenth century, when the establishment of prison systems in major cities became the norm, there were a series of conferences that brought together experts to consider, *inter alia*, how these prisons ought to be administered, what the alternatives to incarceration were, how best to rehabilitate prisoners, how to treat juvenile offenders, and what ought to be the terms and conditions for extradition. At one of those conferences in London in 1872, an International Prison Commission (IPC) was formed with the remit of collecting penitentiary statistics and advocating for reform of the penal system. The IPC later worked in conjunction with the League of Nations and convened three conferences between 1925 and 1935. It was at the conference in 1935 that the IPC was renamed the International Penal and Penitentiary Commission (IPPC). [35]

The IPPC, like the League of Nations, floundered with the advent of the Second World War. When the United Nations was founded in 1945, the new organization disassociated itself from the IPPC, primarily because the Commission had been misused by the Axis powers throughout World War II.

The United Nations, since its founding, has been concerned with developing alternatives to incarceration as a means of reducing the prison population and ensuring certain fundamental human rights to those who may have run afoul of the law. The basic underlying assumptions driving the UN's position on prisons are the notions that imprisonment should not be the natural form of punishment and that there are alternatives which would allow for the rehabilitation and reintegration into society of certain individuals charged with committing crimes.

The United Nations Office on Drugs and Crime (UNODC), in particular, is considered the guardian of international standards and norms in crime prevention and criminal justice. As such, it works with UN member governments to put into practice certain standards and norms for building fair and effective criminal justice systems. Some of the standards and norms directly relevant to prison conditions are used to encourage UN member governments into considering prison reform. These include: the UN's Standard Minimum Rules for the Treatment of Prisoners; the Body of Principles for the Protection of All Persons under Any Form of Detention and Imprisonment; Basic Principles for the Treatment of Prisoners; UN Standard Minimum Rules for Non-Custodial Measures (Tokyo Rules); and the UN Rules for the Treatment of Women Prisoners and Non-custodial Measures for Women Offenders (Bangkok Rules).

In addition, there are other UN instruments that are relevant to the prison system and can be invoked when calling for prison system reform. These include: the Universal Declaration of Human Rights; the International Covenant on Economic, Social, and Cultural Rights; the International Covenant on Civil and Political Rights; The Convention against Torture and Other Cruel, Inhuman, or Degrading Treatment or Punishment; Basic Principles for the Treatment of Prisoners; UN Declaration on the Protection of All Persons from Enforced Disappearance; Convention on the Elimination of All Forms of Racial Discrimination; Convention on the Elimination of All Forms of Discrimination Against Women; Code of Conduct for Law Enforcement Officials; Basic Principles on the use of Force and Firearms by Law Enforcement Officials; Safeguards guaranteeing protection of the rights of those facing the death penalty; UN Recommendations on Life Imprisonment; basic principles on the use of restorative justice programs in criminal matters; the Kampala Declaration on Prison Conditions in Africa; and the Arusha Declaration on Good Prison Practice.

The UN system, through the UNODC, has developed an integrated and multidisciplinary approach to prison reform strategy. It is a holistic approach that ensures that prison reform is not treated in isolation from broader criminal justice reform. The UNODC believes that effective prison reform is dependent on the improvement and rationalization of criminal justice policies, including crime prevention and sentencing policies, and on the care and treatment made available to vulnerable groups in the community. Thus, the reform detention centers and prisons must take into account the needs relating to the reform of the criminal justice system as a whole. This would allow for the employment of an integrated, multidisciplinary strategy to prison reform that would have a sustainable impact. This means that prison reform initiatives should be designed to encompass criminal justice institutions other than the prison service, such as the judiciary prosecution and the police service.

Such an integrated approach also takes into consideration areas that are typically not regarded as part of the "criminal justice system." These include, for example, the development of substance dependence treatment programs in the community or psychosocial counseling programs. The purpose here is to provide an alternative to incarceration and in so doing reduce the overcrowding conditions in most prisons in the Americas.

The UNODC's technical assistance to countries in the area of prison reform covers the following thematic areas: pretrial detention; prison management; alternative measures and sanctions; health; and social reintegration.

Pretrial Detention

Three issues must be taken into consideration when discussing the context of pretrial detention. First, pretrial detention is vastly overused across the world and in many developing countries the pretrial prison population is larger than the convicted prison population. This is a clear contravention of the provisions in international standards, including ICCPR, that provide for the limited use of pretrial detention, only when certain conditions are present. Second, pretrial detainees are most vulnerable to abuse during this period of the criminal justice process. This is why international human rights instruments provide for specific safeguards to protect the rights of detainees. Third, pretrial detainees should be presumed innocent until proven guilty by a court of law. Yet the conditions in pretrial detention centers are often much worse than those in prisons. This problem is compounded by the lack of resources for prisons in many developing countries, including those in the Americas. In such countries detainees may not have access to legal advice and assistance, and as such they might end up being on remand for longer periods than needed, and/or they may not receive a fair trial—further adding to the congestion of prisons.

Therefore, the UNODC has focused on improving access to justice, supporting legal and paralegal aid programs, improving information management and cooperation between courts and prisons, in order to speed up the processing of cases, as well as assisting with the development of safeguards for pretrial detainees through the introduction of independent monitoring and inspection mechanisms.[36]

Prison Management

It is important that national legislation, policies, and practices are guided by the international human rights standards developed to protect prisoners in order to ensure the proper, fair, and humane management of a prison system. As noted earlier, prison authorities have a responsibility to ensure that the treatment and supervision of prisoners falls in line with the rule of law and respect for the prisoners' human rights. It is also imperative that the period of imprisonment be used to prepare individuals for life outside prison following release. However, in many cases, national legislation and rules with respect to the management of prisons are outdated and in need of serious reform. In many countries the prison system falls under the authority of police or military institutions and managers and staff have little or no specific training in prison management. Usually, remuneration and morale are low for some of these individuals and as a result they are not interested in implementing strategies for prison reform. Information collection and management systems are also inadequate (or nonexistent) in many prison systems worldwide. This hinders the development of sound policies and strategies based on reliable, factual data. The UNODC is in a position to provide assistance for reforming national legislation, for developing training programs that would help prison managers improve their leadership skills, and for staff to apply international standards and norms in their daily practice. In other words, the UNODC can contribute to the much needed institutional capacity building of prison administrations.

Alternative Measures and Sanctions

As noted above, overcrowding is a serious concern in almost all prison systems worldwide. Punitive criminal policies, a shortage of social protection services in the community, and the absence of legal support for detainees at the pretrial level all contribute to the rapid growth in the prison population throughout many countries, including those in the Western Hemisphere. As mentioned earlier, overcrowding is the root cause of many human rights violations in prisons. This is why the UNODC has placed so much emphasis on this problem.

Overcrowding can be temporarily solved with the building of new prisons. But this is not by any means a sustainable solution. The construction of new prisons and the maintenance of these structures simply add to the government's expense and put pressure on valuable and sometimes scarce resources. What is needed instead is a "rationalization in sentencing policy, including the wider use of alternatives to prison, aiming to reduce the number of people being isolated from society for long periods."[37]

The use of noncustodial sanctions and measures also reflects a funda-mental change in the approach to crime, offenders and their place in society, changing the focus of penitentiary measures from punishment and isolation, to restorative justice and reintegration. When accompanied by adequate support for offenders, it helps some of the most vulnerable members of society to lead a life without having to relapse back into criminal activities. Thus, "the implementation of penal sanctions within the community, rather than through a process of isolation from it, offers in the long term better protection for society." A key element of the work of the UNODC in prison reform is to support the introduction and imple-mentation of noncustodial sanctions and measures. [38]

Social Reintegration

One of the principle objectives of the UN in the area of prison reform is to contribute to the successful reintegration of prisoners into society following their release. Social reintegration initiatives must start early within the criminal justice process to have maximum effect. This means diverting detainees from the criminal justice process to appropriate treat-ment programs/centers, introducing noncustodial sanctions, and intro-ducing activities and programs in prisons aimed at rehabilitating the criminals. "Interventions to support former prisoners following release from prison, continuum of care in the community for those in need, will all be more effective if the period in prison is used to prepare a prisoner for re-entry to society." This is a policy that requires close coordination between criminal justice institutions and social protection and health ser-vices in the community and probation services. The UNODC is in a posi-tion to offer key support and advice in this area, "including supporting the development of social reintegration programs in prisons and in assist-ing with the planning and implementation of continuum of care and support in the community." [39]

Healthcare

All prisoners are entitled to proper healthcare. The right to health is a principle that applies to all prisoners because they are entitled to receive the same standard of medical care that is available in the broader com-munity. However, this right is seldom realized in prisons. Prison health services are inadequate at best, and almost always severely underfunded and understaffed. In most cases, the authorities in charge of prison ad-ministration and prison health services work in complete isolation from national health authorities, including national HIV and national TB pro-grams. Specific women's health needs are rarely addressed within the confines of the prison.

The right to health includes "access to preventive, curative, reproductive, palliative and supportive healthcare" and also "access to the underlying determinants of health, which include: safe drinking water and adequate sanitation; safe food; adequate nutrition and housing; safe health and dental services; healthy working and environmental conditions; health-related education and information and gender equality."[40]

Technical assistance provided by the UNODC in this area is based on the premise that penal reform and health in prisons are interrelated, and that an integrated strategy needs to be adopted in addressing the enormous challenge of HIV/AIDS and other transmissible diseases such as tuberculosis (TB) in prison settings. Improved prison management and prison conditions are fundamental to developing a sustainable health strategy in prisons. In addition, prison health is an integral part of public health, and improving prison health is crucial for the success of public health policies.[41]

CONCLUSION

Should we in the Western Hemisphere be building our way out of overcrowding in the prison system? Or is it time for a new approach to the penal system? We need to ask ourselves whether we understand what is at stake when we as a society punish offenders. "What choices are we, as a society, expressly or implicitly making when we punish in this way or that? What does our resort to the penal system as a vehicle of social regulation say about what our society has become, or aspires to be?"[42]

It is of utmost importance that prison reform in the Americas is not regarded in isolation from broader criminal justice reform. The prison reforms discussed in this chapter cannot be properly implemented without taking into consideration broader criminal justice reform. Effective prison reform is dependent on the improvement and rationalization of criminal justice policies, including crime prevention and sentencing policies, and on the care and treatment made available to vulnerable groups in the community. Reform of the prison system should therefore always take into account the needs of the criminal justice system as a whole and employ an integrated, multidisciplinary strategy to achieve a sustainable impact. Thus, reform initiatives should encompass criminal justice institutions other than the prison system, such as the courts and law enforcement.

For the UNODC, a model prison is a prison managed on the basis of justice and humanity in which prisoners spend their time engaged in purposeful activities, such as education and vocational training, which will help them with their social reintegration following release. It is a place where vulnerable groups are not discriminated against or abused; where prison staff perform their duties professionally, in line with UN

Standards and Norms; where healthcare services meet the needs of those incarcerated and where prisoners have adequate contact with the outside world. [43]

We in the Western Hemisphere know that incarceration squanders resources and deprives society of workers who are in their prime from contributing productively to their society and the economy. Furthermore, it has tremendous negative impacts on the family members of the incarcerated and is a drain on taxes. Perhaps it is now time to step up the reform process in prisons all across the Americas and around the world.

NOTES

1. Ian Loader, "The Principles of the Penal System," in Commission on English Prisons Today, *The Principles and Limits of the Penal System: Initiating a Conversation*, found at http://www.prisoncommission.org.uk/fileadmin/howard_league/user/pdf/ Commission/HL_Commission_Seminar_1_Report.pdf , accessed March 8, 2014.

2. See R. Walmsley, *World Prison Population List*, International Centre of Studies. King's College, London (2005). According to the International Centre for Prisons, there are today approximately 10.1 million people who are imprisoned worldwide. See International Centre for Prison Studies (ICPS), found at http://www.prisonstudies.org/ info/worldbrief/wpb_stats.php?area=all&category=wb_poptotal accessed March 16, 2014.

3. BBC News, "World Prison Populations," found at http://news.bbc.co.uk/2/ shared/spl/hi/uk/06/prisons/html/nn2page1.stm , accessed on July 4, 2014.

4. See American Correctional Association website found at www.aca.org/ pastpresentfuture/principles.asp accessed March 16, 2014.

5. Ibid.

6. Ibid.

7. Ibid.

8. Ibid.

9. Ibid.

10. Ibid.

11. Ibid.

12. Jeremy Bentham, *The Panopticon Writings*, ed. Miran Bozovic (London: Verso, 1995).

13. Michel Foucault, *Discipline and Punish: The Birth of the Prison*, 2nd edition (New York: Vintage Books, 1995).

14. See www.wecusurveillance.com/cctvhistory, accessed March 13, 2014.

15. See www.howardleague.org/johnhoward/ accessed March 13, 2014.

16. See *Betsy: The Dramatic Biography of Prison Reformer Elizabeth Fry* (INorth York, ON: Monarch Books, 2006).

17. See Jan Alber and Frank Lauterbach (eds.), *Stone of Law, Bricks of Shame: Narrating Imprisonment in the Victorian Age* (Toronto: University of Toronto Press, 2009).

18. See Edward Plamer Thompson, *The Making of the English Working Class* (New York: Penguin, 2013).

19. Marilyn D. McShane and Frank P. Williams III (eds.), *Encyclopedia of American Prisons* (New York: Garland Publishing, 1996).

20. See http://honduras.uassembly.gov/pr-022112-eng.html accessed March 16, 2014.

21. Simon Schuster, "Inside the Prison That Beat a President: How Georgia's Saakashvili Lost His Election," found at http://world.time.com/2012/10/02/inside-the-prison-that-beat-a-president-how-georgias-saakashvili-lost-his-election/ accessed on March 16, 2014.

22. The US has approximately 2.3 million people behind bars today. China, which has four times the population of the US has 1.6 million people incarcerated. See the International Centre for Prison Studies, King's College, London.

23. Adam Liptak, "Inmate Count in U.S. Dwarfs other Nations," *The New York Times* (23 April 2008), found at http://www.nytimes.com/2008/04/23/us/23prison.html? pagewanted=all&_r=0 , accessed on 2 February 2014.

24. Matthew Kauffman, "States with high gun ownership have high rates of gun homicides," *The Courant*, 12 September 2013, found at http://articles.courant.com/2013-09-12/news/hc-bu-gun-homicide-study-0913-20130912_1_gun-ownership-gun-ownership-rates-study , accessed on 4 July 2014.

25. Human Rights Watch, "US: Forced Guilty Pleas in Drug Cases," December 5, 2013, found at http://www.hrw.org/news/2013/12/05/us-forced-guilty-pleas-drug-cases , accessed March 8, 2014.

26. Human Rights Watch, "US: Forced Guilty Pleas in Drug Cases," December 5, 2013, found at http://www.hrw.org/news/2013/12/05/us-forced-guilty-pleas-drug-cases , accessed March 8, 2014.

27. Vicky Palaez, "The Prison industry in the United States: Big Business or a new form of slavery?" *Global Research* (31 March 2014), found at http://www. globalresearch.ca/the-prison-industry-in-the-united-states-big-business-or-a-new-form-of-slavery/8289 , accessed on July 4, 2014.

28. See "Report on International Prison Conditions" http://www.state.gov/ documents/organization/210160.pdf , accessed on July 4, 2014.

29. The Associated Press, "Sri Lanka Opposition says 27 Prisoners died in 'Massacre,'" *The New York Times*, November 11, 2012, found at http://www.nytimes.com/ 2012/11/12/world/asia/sri-lanka-opposition-says-27-prisoners-died-in-a-massacre. html?_r=0 accessed March 16, 2014.

30. International Centre for Prison Studies (ICPS), found at http://www. prisonstudies.org/info/worldbrief/wpb_stats.php?area=all&category=wb_poptotal accessed March 16, 2014.

31. UNODC, *Strategies and Best Pracitces Against Overcrowding in Italian Correction Facilities*, November 7, 2012. http://www.unodc.org/documents/justice-and-prison-reform/EGM-Uploads/ITALY-GOV-20-En.pdf , accessed March 17, 2014.

32. International Centre for Prison Studies (ICPS), found at http://www. prisonstudies.org/info/worldbrief/wpb_stats.php?area=all&category=wb_poptotal accessed March 16, 2014.

33. Richard M. Aborn and Ashley D. Cannon, "Prisons: In Jail, but not sentenced," *Americas Quarterly*, (Winter 2013), found at http://www.americasquarterly.org/aborn-prisons accessed March 17, 2014.

34. UNODC, Central Asia, found at https://www.unodc.org/centralasia/en/news/ developing-an-effective-prison-reform.html , accessed March 9, 2014.

35. See UNODC, "International Penal and Penitentiary Commission (IPPC), found at www.unodc.org/unodc/en/crime-congress/ippc.html , accessed March 8, 2014.

36. UNODC, *Custodial and Non-Custodial Measures: Alternatives to Incarceration* (New York: United Nations, 2006), http://www.unodc.org/documents/justice-and-prison-reform/cjat_eng/3_Alternatives_Incarceration.pdf , accessed March 17, 2014.

37. UNODC, *Custodial and Non-Custodial Measures: Alternatives to Incarceration*, found at http://www.unodc.org/documents/justice-and-prison-reform/cjat_eng/3_Al ternatives_Incarceration.pdf , accessed March 17, 2014.

38. Ibid.

39. Ibid.

40. Ibid.

41. See UNODC, http://www.unodc.org/unodc/en/justice-and-prison-reform/ prison-reform-and-alternatives-to-imprisonment.html , accessed March 9, 2014.

42. These questions are also raised by Ian Loader, "The Principles of the Penal System," in Commission on English Prisons Today, *The Principles and Limits of the Penal System: Initiating a Conversation*, found at http://www.prisoncommission.org.uk/

fileadmin/howard_league/user/pdf/Commission/HL_Commission_Seminar_1_
Report.pdf , accessed March 8, 2014.

43. UNDOC, Central Asia, found at https://www.unodc.org/centralasia/en/news/
developing-an-effective-prison-reform.html, accessed March 9, 2014.

Selected Bibliography

"A World Without Prisons: Resisting Militarism, Globalized Punishment, and Empire," *Social Justice,* 31, 1/2 (2004).

Alexander, Michelle. *The New Jim Crow: Mass Incarceration in the Age of Colorblindness.* New York: The New Press, 2010.

Angela Browne, Alissa Cambier and Suzanne Agha. "Prisons Within Prisons: The Use of Segregation in the United States," Federal Sentencing Reporter, 24, No. 1, "Sentencing Within Sentencing" (October 2011).

Arslanian, León Carlos. Un Cambio Posible. Delito, Inseguridad y Reforma Policial en la Provincia de Buenos Aires. Buenos Aires: EDHASA, 2008.

Bagley, Bruce "Drug Control Policies in the United States: What Works and What? Patterns, Prevalence, and Problems of Drug Use in the United States," in *Drug Trafficking, Organized Crime, and Violence in the Americas Today,* eds, Bruce M. Bagley and Jonathan D. Rosen (forthcoming Gainesville: University Press of Florida Bagley, 2015),

Beckett, Katherine and Sassoon, Theodore. *The Politics of Injustice: Crime and Punishment in America.* Thousand Oaks, CA: Sage Publications, 2004.

Bonilla, Adrián. "Ecuador: Actor Internacional en la Guerra de las Drogas," *in La Economía Política del Narcotráfico: El Caso Ecuatoriano,* eds. Bruce Bagley, Adrián Bonilla and Alexei Páez. Quito: Flacso-Ecuador and North-South Center of University of Miami, 1991.

Braman, Donald. *Doing Time on the Outside: Incarceration and Family Life in Urban America.* Ann Arbor: University of Michigan Press, 2004.

Carpenter, Ted Galen. *Bad Neighbor Policy: Washington's Futile War on Drugs in Latin America.* New York, N.Y.: Palgrave Macmillan, 2003.

Comisión Ecumenica de Derechos Humanos. "Audiencia sobre la situación penintenciaria en Ecuador" (March 21, 2011), 1, accessed October 19, 2013, http://www.cedhu.org/index.php?option=com_content&view=article&id=40&Itemid=7.

DerGhougassian, Khatchik and Evans, Glen. "Under (Loose) Control: Drug Trafficking in Argentina. Framing a Complex Phenomenon in Times of Paradigm Change," in Bruce M. Bagley and Jonathan D. Rosen, *Drug Trafficking, Organized Crime, and Violence in the Americas: Today.* University Press of Florida –forthcoming 2015.

Davis, Angela. Are Prisons Obsolete? New York: Seven Stories Press, 2003.

Davis, Angela Y. "Masked Racism: Reflections on the Prison Industrial Complex," *Colorlines Magazine,* September 10, 1998

Dirección Nacional de Política Criminal, *Informe Anual República Argentina 2011.*

Drug Enforcement Administration, "High Ranking Guatemalan Police Officers Arrested For Conspiracy to Import Cocaine into The United States," Press Release, Washington, D.C., November 16, 2005, accessed March 9, 2014.

Dudley, Steven. "Guatemala's new Narco Map: Less Zetas, Same Chaos," *InSight-Crime,* September 16, 2013, http://www.insightcrime.org/news-analysis/guatemalas-new-narco-map-less-zetas-same-chaos.

Dunkerley, James. "Evo Morales, the 'Two Bolivias' and the Third Bolivian Revolution," *Journal of Latin American Studies* 39, no. 1 (2007);

Estellano, Washington "From Populism to Coca Economy," *Latin American Perspectives* 21, no. 4 (1994): 39–40

Foucault, Michel. *Discipline and Punish: The Birth of the Prison,* 2nd edition. New York: Vintage Books, 1995.

Foucault, Michel. *Madness and Civilization: A History of Insanity in the Age of Reason.* New York: Pantheon, 1965.

Garland, David. *The Culture of Control. Crime and Social Order in Contemporary Society.* Oxford: University of Oxford Press, 2001.

Giacoman, Diego. "Drug Policy and the Prison Situation in Bolivia." In Pien Metaal and Coletta Youngers, *Systems Overload: Drug Laws and Prisons in Latin America.* Washington, DC: WOLA, 2011.

Goldstein, Paul. "The Drugs/Violence Nexus: A Tripartite Conceptual Framework," *Journal of Drug Issues* v. 39 (1985).

Gootenberg, Paul. *Andean Cocaine: The Making of a Global Drug.* Chapel Hill: University of North Carolina Press, 2008.

Hagopian, Frances and Mainwaring, Scott (eds.) *The third wave of democratization in Latin America: advances and setbacks.* Cambridge University Press, 2005.

Human Rights Office of the Archdiocese of Guatemala. *Guatemala Never Again.* Maryknoll: Orbis Books, 1999.

Human Rights Office of the Archdiocese of Guatemala. *Guatemala Never Again.* Maryknoll: Orbis Books, 1999.

Human Rights Watch, "World Report 2013- Guatemala," accessed March 9, 2014, http://www.hrw.org/world-report/2013/country-chapters/guatemala

Isacson, Adam. "The U.S. Military in the War on Drugs," *in Drugs and Democracy in Latin America: The Impact of U.S. Policy, ed. Coletta Youngers and Eileen Rosin.* Boulder, CO: Lynne Rienner, 2005.

Jones, Van. The Green Collar Economy: How One Solution Can Fix Our Two Biggest Problems. New York: Harper One, 2008.

Ledebur, Kathryn. "Bolivia: Clear Consequences," in *Drugs and Democracy in Latin America: The Impact of US Policy,* ed. Coletta Youngers and Eileen Rosin. Boulder: Lynne Rienner Publishers, 2005.

Lehman, Kenneth D. *Bolivia and the United States: A Limited Partnership.* Athens: University of Georgia Press, 1999.

Loy, Frank and Reno, Janet. "International Narcotics Control Strategy Report (INCSR)." *The DISAM Journal,* Spring (2000): 33-44.

Marcy, William. *The Politics of Cocaine: How U.S. Foreign Policy Has Created a Thriving Drug Industry in Central and South America.* Chicago: Chicago Review Press, 2010.

Mauer, Marc. *Race to Incarcerate.* New York: The New Press, 1999.

Mauer, Marc and King, Ryan. A 25-Year Quagmire: The "War on Drugs" and Its Impact on American Society. Washington, D.C.: Sentencing Project, 2007.

Ministerio del Poder Popular para el Servicio Penitenciario, (2011). *Plan estratégico del sistema penitenciario venezolano 2011-2013.* Retrievedfromwebsite: http://www. ciudadccs.info/wpcontent/uploads/PLAN_DEL_SISTEMA_ PENITENCIARIO_230811_.pdf

Mulholland, John. "Guatemala's President: 'My country bears the scars from the war on drugs,'" *The Guardian,* January 19, 2013. http://www.theguardian.com/world/ 2013/jan/19/otto-molina-war-drugs-guatemala

Musto, David F. *American Disease: Origins of Narcotic Control* 3rd edition. Oxford: Oxford University Press, 1999.

Pérez, Wilma. "Una niña muere en la cárcel de San Pedro por meningitis." *La Razón,* 9 July 2014: Section Salud.

Phillips, Susan A. *Wallbangin: Graffiti and Gangs in L.A.*Chicago: University of Chicago Press, 1999.

Rafael, Tony. The Mexican Mafia. New York: Encounter Books, 2007.

Ribando Seelke, Clare and Finklea, Kristin M. *US-Mexican Security Cooperation: The Mérida Initiative and Beyond.* Washington, DC: Congressional Research Service, 2013.

Roth, Mitchel P. *Prisons and prison systems: a global encyclopedia.* Westport, CT: Greenwood Publishing Group, 2006.

Schlesinger, Stephen and Kinzer, Stephen. *Bitter Fruit: The Story of the American Coup in Guatemala*. Cambridge: Harvard University David Rockefeller Center for Latin American Studies, 2005.

Schmitz, David F. *The United States and Right Wing Dictatorships, 19665-1989*. Cambridge: Cambridge University Press, 2006.

Skarbek, David. "Putting the 'Con' into Constitutions: The Economics of Prison Gangs," Journal of Law, Economics, and Organization, 26/2 (2010):183–211

"The firth circle of hell," *The Economist*, 14 July 2011.

Thompson, E.P. *The Making of the English Working Class*. New York: Penguin, 2013.

"UNODC Assists Guatemala to Tackle Organized Crime," United Nations Office on Drugs andCrime, accessed March 17, 2014, https://www.unodc.org/unodc/en/frontpage/2010/March/unodc-assists-guatemala-to-fight-organized-crime.html.

UNODC, *Evaluation and Recommendations for the Improvement of the Health Programmes, Including For The Prevention and Treatment of Drug Dependence and of HIV and AIDS, Implemented in the Establishments Under the Responsibility of the Federal Penitentiary Service in Argentina* (Vienna: UNODC, 2011).

UNDOC, World Drug Report 2013, (United Nations Publications, 2013).

Ungar, Mark. "Prisons and Politics in Contemporary Latin America." *Human Rights Quarterly*. Vol 25, 4 (2003): 909–934.

U.S. Department of State. "Haiti: Bureau of Democracy, Human Rights, and Labor." U.S. Department of State. http://www.state.gov/j/drl/rls/hrrpt/2004/41764.htm (accessed October 5, 2013).

U.S. Department of the Treasury, Press Release, "Treasury Designates Sinaloa Cartel Members under the Kingpin Act," accessed March 31, 2014, 12/15/2009 http://www.treasury.gov/press-center/press-releases/Pages/tg444.aspx

Young, Rusty and McFadden, Thomas. *Marching Powder: A True Story of Friendship, Cocaine, and South America's Strangest Jail*. New York: St. Martin's Griffin, 2003.

Wacquant, Loïc. "Deadly Symbiosis: When Ghetto and Prison Meet and Mesh," *Punishment and Society*, 3/1 (2001): 95–134.

Walmsley, Roy *World Prison Population List (tenth edition)*, London: International Centre for Prison Studies (ICPS), 2013.

Watt, Peter and Zepeda, Roberto. *Drug War Mexico: Politics, Neoliberalism and Violence in the New Narcoeconomy*. London: Zed Books, 2012.

Winton, Alisa. "Young peoples' views how to tackle gang violence in post-conflict Guatemala," *Environment and Urbanization*, Vol. 16 No. 2, October 2004, http://www.crin.org/docs/QMC_Gangs_Guatemala.pdf 87.

Western, Bruce. *Punishment and Inequality*. New York: Russell Sage Foundation, 2006.

Index

About the Editors

Jonathan D. Rosen is research professor at the Universidad del Mar en Huatulco, Mexico. Dr. Rosen earned his master's in Political Science from Columbia University and received his Ph.D. in International Studies from the University of Miami. Dr. Rosen was awarded the Distinguished Fellowship at the Center for Latin American Studies at UM. He is the editor of a book series on security in the Americas in the Twenty-First Century at Lexington Books. His recent publications include: *The Losing War: Plan Colombia and Beyond* (Albany, N.Y.: SUNY Press, 2014); Jonathan Daniel Rosen. "Lecciones y resultados del Plan Colombia (2000–2012)," *Contextualizaciones Lat.* Año 6: Número 10 (enero-julio 2014); Roberto Zepeda Martínez and Jonathan D. Rosen, "Corrupción e inseguridad en México: consecuencias de una democracia imperfecta," *Revista AD UNIVERSA*, Año 4: Vol 1(Dec, 2014)

Marten W. Brienen teaches in the Department of Political Science at Oklahoma State University. Previously, he served as the director of Academic Programs in Latin American Studies at the University of Miami. In that capacity, he was responsible for advising students in the undergraduate, graduate, and dual degree programs, as well as tending to the day-to-day business of the programs. He taught at the University of Miami for the Latin American Studies Program since 2004 and has also for the Africana Studies Program since 2007. He received his bachelor's and master's degrees in Latin American History from the University of Leiden in the Netherlands, studied at the Université de Paris-Sorbonne, and received his Ph.D. in Social Sciences from the University of Amsterdam.

ABOUT THE CONTRIBUTORS

Astrid Arrarás earned her Ph.D. from Princeton University in 1998. Currently, Dr. Arrarás is a Senior Lecturer at the Department of Politics and International Relations at Florida International University. From 1999–2004, she was an Assistant Professor in the Department of Political Science at Florida International University. Previously, she has taught at Princeton University. In addition, she was a Visiting Researcher, Centro de Estudios de la Sociedad, Uruguay (CIESU), Montevideo, Uruguay, from 1989 to 1992. Her recent publications include: Astrid Arrarás and José Miguel Cruz, "Findings Report on the Strategic Culture of Hondu-

237

ras" Applied Research Center, Latin American and Caribbean Center and United States Southern Command. April 2011; "Drug Trafficking, Counter Drug Activities and the Environment in the Amazon Basin," (Co-authored with Eduardo Gamarra). *Environment and Security in the Amazon Basin*, Joseph S. Tulchin and Heather A. Golding, editors, Woodrow Wilson Center Reports on the Americas no. 4, Washington, DC: Woodrow Wilson Center for Scholars, 2002.); "Uruguay's economic and political development: 1945-2001," *The South American Handbook*, Patrick Heenan and Monique Lamontagne, editors. (London: Fitzroy Dearborn Publishers, 2002.)

Emily D. Bello-Pardo is pursuing her master's degree in Latin American and Caribbean Studies with a concentration in Political Science at Florida International University. She works as a fellow of the Drug Policy Research Program at the Latin American and Caribbean Center, where she studies the impact of marijuana legalization in Uruguay. In 2013, Bello-Pardo received her dual BAs in Political Science and International Relations from FIU, where she was a member of the Honors College, was inducted Phi Beta Kappa, graduated with honors, and attained certificates in Latin American Studies and National Security Studies. Outside of the classroom, Bello-Pardo is the Executive Director of Se Habla Venezolano Foundation, position through which she facilitated the electoral mobilization De Miami Pa' New Orleans in 2012 and 2013, when thousands of Venezuelans from four states mobilized to Louisiana to vote in the Venezuelan presidential elections.

Adrián Bonilla was the director FLACSO (Facultad Latinoamericana de Ciencias Sociales) in Quito, Ecuador from 2004 to 2012. Currently, Dr. Bonilla is the Secretary General of FLACSO. Dr. Bonilla received his Ph.D. in International Studies from the University of Miami. He is an expert in Comparative Politics in the Andean region and, more generally, security in Latin America. He is the recipient of numerous scholarships over his career. Dr. Bonilla has published five books over is career. Some of his book publications include: (*Orfeo en el infierno: Una agenda de Política exterior ecuatoriana* (2002, editor); *Las sorprendentes virtudes de lo perverso: Ecuador y Narcotráfico en los 90* (1993); *En busca del pueblo perdido: Discurso y diferenciación de la izquierda en el 60* (1991). In addition, he has published articles in Europe, the United States, Asia, and Latin America.

Nashira Chávez is a Ph.D. candidate at University of Miami. Her areas of interests include International Relations, particularly foreign policy, security and Latin America. Nashira has written on The Pacific Alliance and The War on Drugs in Ecuador post 9/11. Currently she is interested in examining Latin American responses to China's engagement in the region. Her research looks at the domestic factors influencing the bargaining power of Ecuadorian and Brazilian agreements with China in the oil sector.

Sebastián A. Cutrona is a Ph.D. Candidate in International Studies at the University of Miami and a Visiting Scholar at Universidad de San Andrés, Argentina. He holds a BA in Political Science from Universidad Nacional de La Rioja and a MA in International Relations from Centro de Estudios Avanzados (CEA), Universidad Nacional de Córdoba. Sebastián has taught at the Universidad de San Andrés, University of Miami, Universidad Nacional de Córdoba, and Universidad Nacional de La Rioja. He has held fellowships from Fulbright, Red de Macrouniversidades de América Latina, Santander Bank, the United Nations Conference on Trade and Development (UNCTAD), among others. His professional experience also includes work at UNCTAD, the World Trade Organization (WTO), and Centro de Estudios Legales y Sociales (CELS). His research interests mainly focus on Latin American politics, drug trafficking, security studies, and contentious politics.

Lucía Dammert received her Ph.D. in Political Science from the University of Leiden. She earned her master's in Urban and Regional Planning from the University of Pittsburgh. Currently, she is an Associate Professor at the Universidad de Santiago de Chile. Her recent books are: *Fear of Crime. Redefying State-Society Relations* (2012) Routledge, London. *Maras* (2012) University of Texas Press, edited with Thomas Bruneau; *Crimen e Inseguridad: Políticas, temas y problemas en las Américas Catalonia.* Santiago, 2010; *Violencia e Inseguridad Ciudadana en las Américas.* El Virrey. Lima. 2010; *Perspectivas y dilemas de la seguridad ciudadana en América Latina.* FLACSO Ecuador, 2007.

Manuel Dammert G. is a sociologist from Pontificia Universidad Católica del Perú and holds a master's degree on Antropology from FLACSO Ecuador. He is a professor of the Department of Social Science at Pontificia Universidad Católica del Perú. His research interests are urban violence, gentrification, urban segregation and social stratification.

Khatchik DerGhougassian earned his Ph.D. from the University of Miami, where he received a scholarship from the Dante B. Fascell North-South Center during his doctorate, and has a master's in Social Sciences with a specialization in International Relations from FLACSO, Argentina. His Doctoral dissertation, *Illicit Associations in the Global Political Economy: Courtesan Politics, Arms Trafficking and International Security* received the 2011 Barrett Price of the Center for Latin American Studies at the University of Miami. Currently, he is a Professor at the Universidad de San Andrés in Argentina. He specializes in International Security, the Middle East, Latin America, and the proliferation of arms throughout the world. His recent publications include: Khatchik DerGhougassian (compilador)" La Defensa en el Siglo XXI. Argentina y la Seguridad Regional" (Buenos Aires, Editorial Capital Intelectual, 2012); "The Armenian Genocide on the International Agenda: The Case for Diplomatic Engagement" Haigazian Armenological Review, vol. 32, pp. 229–260; Khatchik, Derghougassian, (compilador), "El derrumbe del negacionismo" (Buenos Aires, Planeta, 2009).

Brian Fonseca is director of Operations at Florida International University's (FIU) Applied Research Center (ARC) and has been an adjunct professor with FIU's Latin American and Caribbean Center (LACC) and the Department of Politics and International Relations since 2010. Mr. Fonseca joins ARC after serving as the Senior Research Manager for Socio-Cultural Analysis (SCA) at United States Southern Command. Mr. Fonseca has authored numerous classified and open sourced publications on a wide range of security-related topics. Mr. Fonseca has conducted extensive field research in Argentina, Chile, Colombia, Dominican Republic, El Salvador, Honduras, Panama, Peru, Uruguay, and Venezuela. Mr. Fonseca holds a master's degree in International Business and a Bachelor's degree in International Relations from Florida International University in Miami, Florida. He has attended Sichuan University in China, National Defense University in Washington, D.C., and is currently working towards his Ph.D. at the University of Miami. From 1997 to 2004, he served in the United States Marine Corps and facilitated the training of foreign military forces in both hostile theaters and during peacetime operations. Mr. Fonseca received several national awards.

Jean-Claude Garcia-Zamor earned a Ph.D. in Public Administration and a Master of Arts in Latin American History from New York University. He also holds an M.P.A. in Public Administration and a B.A. in Political Science from the University of Puerto Rico. Currently, Dr. Garcia-Zamor is a Professor of Public Administration at Florida International University. He previously taught at Howard University, the University of Texas at Austin, and the Brazilian School of Public Administration. Since 1999, he has taught and conducted research at Leipzig University in the former East Germany. He was officially designated an honorary professor at the University in June 2007. He is the author of six books, the editor of three books, and the coeditor of three other books. He is also the author of many book chapters and numerous articles that have appeared in professional journals in the United States, Canada, Puerto Rico, Brazil, Belgium, Great Britain, the Netherlands, Indian, South Korea, and Poland.

W. Andy Knight is director of the Institute of International Relations (IIR) at the University of the West Indies and Professor and former Chair of the Department of Political Science at the University of Alberta. Based at the UWI St. Augustine Campus in Trinidad from January 2013, a Barbadian by birth, Professor Knight has had a distinguished career as an academic and scholar in Canada, culminating in his heading the Department of Political Science at the University of Alberta. He serves as Advisory Board Member of the World Economic Forum's Global Agenda Council on the Welfare of Children and was a Governor of the International Development Research Centre (IDRC) from 2007 to 2012. Professor

Knight coedited the Global Governance journal from 2000 to 2005 and was Vice Chair of the Academic Council on the United Nations System (ACUNS). Dr. Knight has written and edited several books, book chapters, and journal articles on various aspects of multilateralism, global governance and peace, and United Nations reform. His recent books include: *The Routledge Handbook of the Responsibility to Protect* (with Frazer Egerton)—Routledge 2012; *Towards the Dignity of Difference?: Neither 'end of History' Nor 'clash of Civilizations'* (with Mojtaba Mahdavi)—Ashgate 2012; and *Global Politics* (with Tom Keating)—Oxford University Press 2010.

Tamara Rice Lave is associate professor at the University of Miami School of Law. She received her undergraduate degree from Haverford College, her law degree from Stanford University, and her Ph.D. from the University of California, Berkeley. After graduating from Haverford, Lave spent a year teaching at the American School of Guatemala and volunteering at Casa Alianza, an organization dedicated to helping homeless youth. While a law student, Lave worked for the Legal Aid Office at Casa Alianza under a field research grant funded by the Mellon Foundation. Some of Lave's recent scholarship includes: Lave and McCrary, Do Sexually Violent Predator Laws Violate Double Jeopardy and Substantive Due Process: An Empirical Analysis, *Brooklyn Law Review* (2013); Lave and Orenstein, Empirical Fallacies of Evidence Law: A Critical Look at the Admission of Prior Sex Crimes, *Cincinnati Law Review* (2013); Lave, Shoot to Kill: A Critical Look at Stand Your Ground Laws, *Miami Law Review* (2013); Lave, Throwing away the Key: Has the Adam Walsh Act Lowered the Threshold for Sexually Violent Predator Commitments too Far, *University of Pennsylvania Journal of Constitutional Law* (2011); Lave, Controlling Sexually Violent Predators: Continued Incarceration at what Cost (2010), and Lave, Breaking the Cycle of Despair: Street Children in Guatemala City, *Columbia Journal of Human Rights* (1995).

Pamela Pamelá holds a master's degree in Global Governance and a bachelor's degree in Political Science and International Relations, with a Certificate in Latin American and Caribbean Studies, from Florida International University. She has lived and studied abroad at Torcuato Di Tella University in Argentina and Université Catholique de l'Ouest in France, and participated in community development in impoverished communities throughout Colombia and Venezuela. Born in Venezuela, Pamela's research and publications center on transnational crime and rule of law in Latin America and the Caribbean.

Susan A. Phillips has studied gangs and the US prison system since 1990. Phillips received her Ph.D. in Anthropology in 1998 from UCLA, where she taught for four years before moving to Pitzer College. Her first book, *Wallbangin: Graffiti and Gangs in L.A.*, was published by the University of Chicago Press in 1999. Her second book, *Operation Fly Trap: Gangs, Drugs, and the Law*, was published in July 2012, also by Chicago. Phillips was named a Soros Justice Media Fellow in 2008, and received a Harry Frank Guggenheim research grant in 2005 to fund her fieldwork. Phillips is interested in theories of violence, in the relationship between gangs and the state, and in utilizing academic writing and scholarship toward criminal justice reform. She currently directs community-based research programs in Ontario, California, for Pitzer College and is a member of the Environmental Analysis field group, where she contributes curriculum on urban studies.

Christa L. Remington is a Ph.D. candidate in Public Affairs at Florida International University. In 2003, she cofounded THE Mission Haiti Inc., a nonprofit organization that focuses on education and community building in rural western Haiti, and currently serves as its project director. Since 2011, she has worked with a team of researchers under a grant from the National Institute of Health, exploring the emotional labor of aid workers after the Haitian earthquake of 2010. Her research has included fieldwork at international NGO headquarters, as well as hospitals, IDP camps, and prisons in Haiti. She has presented her research at multiple conferences on the topic of post-disaster response and recovery in Haiti, and has coauthored numerous articles on these issues.

Marcelo Rocha e Silva Zorovich has been a professor of international relations and international business at ESPM (Escola Superior de Propaganda e Marketing), in São Paulo, Brazil, since 2007. In the sixteen years prior, he worked for The Nielsen Company and Kantar Worldpanel, and led various international consulting projects for Cadbury Adams, Nestle, P and G, Unilever, Philip Morris, British American Tobacco, Johnson and Johnson, Melitta, TATA Consultancy Services, and Kraft throughout Latin America, the United States, Canada, and China. He holds degrees from the University of São Paulo (USP), ESPM, The Institut Québécois des Hautes Etudes Internationales (HEI), Université Laval, Quebec, Canada, and specialization at Graduate Institute of Geneva. He has contributed to book chapters in topics related to energy, trade and security. In early 2011, he was a visiting scholar at McGill University in Montreal. He currently is pursuing a Ph.D. in International Studies at the University of Miami.

Randy Seepersad is coordinator of the Criminology Department at the University of the West Indies, Trinidad and Tobago. Dr. Seepersad holds a Ph.D. from the University of Toronto and an M.Phil. degree from the University of Cambridge. Dr. Seepersad has a research interest in economic deprivation and crime, gang violence, youth crime and justice, and penology.

Dianne Williams holds an MBA and a PhD. She is a Certified Criminal Justice Specialist and a Certified Sentence Mitigation Specialist with the National Association of Forensic Counselors. She is a member of the Academy of Criminal Justice Sciences, American Society of Criminologists, and the Society for the Study of Social Problems. Her teaching engagements include North Carolina Agricultural & Technical State University and the University of the West Indies (St. Augustine). She specializes in Race and Crime, Media and Crime and Juvenile Justice as well as Police and Prison Reform.

Roberto Zepeda Martínez is research professor at the Institute of International Studies at the Universidad del Mar, in Huatulco, Mexico. Dr. Zepeda Martínez holds a Ph.D. in Politics from the University of Sheffield as well as a Master's in International Studies at the University of Sinaloa (UAS), focusing on North America. He has taught politics at UNAM in Mexico City and in the Department of Politics at the University of Sheffield. His most recent publications include: Zepeda, Roberto and Jonathan D. Rosen, eds., *Cooperation and Drug Policies: Trends in the Twenty-First Century* (Lanham, MD: Lexington Books, 2014); "Collateral Effects of Migration in the Americas: Security Implications," in *Reconceptualizing Security in the Americans in the Twenty-First Century*, Bruce M. Bagley, Jonathan D. Rosen and Hanna S. Kassab, eds. (Lanham, MD: Lexington Books, 2015). Peter Watt and Roberto Zepeda, *Drug War Mexico: Politics, Neoliberalism, and Violence in the New Narcoeconomy* (London, UK: Zed Books, 2012). He is a member of the National System of Researchers (SNI, level 1) in Mexico since 2014. Dr. Zepeda is also a member of the *Latin American Studies Association, LASA.* He has published nine book chapters; eighteen articles in academic journals; and five books, focused primarily on neoliberalism, migration, labor unions, and drug trafficking.